WHO'S SORRY NOW?

1962-1969 - A memoir

PJ Taylor

ORIGINAL WRITING

978-1-908024-10-7

A CIP catalogue for this book is available from the National Library.

Published by ORIGINAL WRITING LTD., Dublin, 2010.

Printed in Great Britain by MPG BOOKS GROUP,
Bodmin and Kings Lynn.

To my cousin Lar

Lar you broke my heart telling and showing me the same bloody things day after day until I hated your guts, but then I got older and wiser and realised what you gave me. It has never left me and from the bottom of my heart I thank you.

I love you cus,

PJ

ACKNOWLEDGMENTS

To Jetta, James and Harry for their warm enthusiasm and excitement too.

To Mary from Ahane with the ten little fingers, who got me through the first quarter of this book, took sick and wasn't able to finish it, thanks Mary.

P.S. She's better now.

To Doreen the blonde from the other side of Limerick who finished the rest thanks Doreen for the use of your sitting room and letting me look over your shoulder all the time, your husband Martin should get a big thank you too.

To Michael Richard Gleeson on the other side of the planet, a Carey's roader. Who really encouraged me with e-mails and overseas contacts.

To my daughter Sorcha, her husband Gary who really got behind me with great support for my first book, thanks lads.

To my son Cory, and his wife Joanne, granddaughter Lauren and my grandson Aaron who took my first book to his class in school and proudly boasted, my granddad wrote this.

And of course, my wife Moll, who stuck her forefinger under my nose and said you'd better not write anything about me in your next book and knows that I'll leave it in one ear and out the other, because I'll tell her 'its all your fault, you started the whole thing six years ago, anyway this time next year you'll be famous'.

Then there's vourneen who proof read the book under pressure, thanks vour, of course if its
wrong its all your fault!.

Sean Curtain. For his permission to use photographs from his, Down Memory Lane collection.

Jetro Stokes, for his help with the new photographs.

To the management and staff of the Patrick Punch Hotel, Punches Cross, Limerick.

To the following business communities for their great financial support my sincerely thanks.

Hong Kong Chinese Restaurant, William Street, Limerick
Tony O'Mara of O'Mara Motors, Tipperary Road, Limerick
Texas Steakhouse Restaurant, O'Connell Street, Limerick
Savin's Music, O'Connell Street, Limerick
Cormac McCarthy, Clarina, County Limerick
Shannon Furniture, Upper William Street, Limerick
Thompsons Funeral Undertakers, Thomas Street, Limerick
J.W. Harrison Jewellers, Crescent Shopping Centre, Limerick
Leavy's Shoes, O'Connell Street, Limerick
O'Sullivan's Pharmacy, Sarsfield Street, Limerick
Bé an tí, Confectioner, Little Catherine Street, Limerick
Tom Maloney, Catherine Street, Limerick
Fine Wines, Limerick
Glasstech, Tipperary Road, Limerick
Jemma's Flowers, Henry Street, Limerick
Roma Amusements, William Street, Limerick
Lakeside Hotel, Killaloe, County Limerick
Geraldine and Louise Harrison

Authors Note

I thought I'd be a man at eighteen.

I waited a long time

And when I got there, 'well !' see for yourself!.

INTRODUCTION

It took P.J six years to write 'Between the Three Bridges' it was he says, 'the best thing I ever done'. People enjoyed it so much I had letters and e-mails from all over the world with expressions of tears and laughter and left me feeling I did the right thing recording my childhood years.

P.J has the bug now and after twelve months has brought you the next episode, let him tell you what went on at 36 Claughan Court, Garryowen, Limerick. The relationship he had with his mother. The mischief his father Harry got up to when he was on the dry, his first car and how hard he worked to make the eighty pounds to buy it, how he met his wife Mary who lived just around the corner and his heart breaking account of losing his mother, if you enjoyed Between the Three Bridges, then you'll love this.

John Prendergast
of Limerick's Live 95FM

PREFACE

The house in Careys road was on the top of a hill
The one in Garryowen, at the bottom of another
It wasn't a castle, just a home, with sparkling floors and furniture
And Mam beside herself with Pop on the dry most of the time
The headaches, a thing of the past
Nan in the corner by the fire most weekends
Moaning one minute laughing the next with Pop fuelling it all the time
It was for us all the house of laughter, a magnet drawing us to
Its irresistible source MAM
But that's all going to change now, its May 1969
Pop is at it again and by June 1st I'm saying "I bet his sorry now'

'As a young girl, I used to think I'd meet and marry a tall, dark, handsome man'...............'your father was very tall'

'your father was very good to me, he didn't bother me that much'

I hate the 'F' word, I haven't used it since the spring of 1974, it was on my tongue all the time before that. I never used it in Carey's road but when I got older in Garryowen I started, not that Garryowen was any different to any other part of Limerick City, it was my age I guess!, everything was 'F' this and 'F' that, it made me feel tougher so the more I used it, the tougher I felt, and if I had a fag in my mouth well that was the bizz. Then I went working with Pop, I'd never use it in his company, if I did I'd get a box, but when himself and cousin Lar used it, it was hilarious, the more they said it the more I laughed. So in an effort to try to convey to you why l laughed so much I have substituted the 'F' word with 'Fupp', 'Fupper', and 'Fupping'. I hope you won't be offended.

P.J.

CHAPTER 1

The year is 1948, the month is July, the date is the 22nd and the sound is my mother's screams as she tries to push my big head and shoulders into Bedford Row Maternity Hospital, Limerick City. Saturday May 31st 1969 was the day she departed it. That day when it began saw a young man two months short of his 21st birthday enter the Florists at the bottom of Henry Street, owned by Mr. and Mrs. O'Connor, who are customers of Pop but with the name O'Shaughnessy over the door. I wanted to be the first to see Mam that morning. After all, it was I who brought her to the hospital the previous day. Mrs. O'Connor hands me a card after she finished sorting the different types of flowers I had selected.

'Do you want to write something on that seeing that it's your mother? Did she have the operation yet?'

'Yes' I replied, 'at seven o'clock this morning.'

'I'll say a few prayers for her.'

She hands me the flowers in paper wrapping, beautifully sorted.

'I have an envelope for your card; you haven't written anything on it yet. Take your time; I'll tend to this other customer first.'

She walks away and leaves me scratching my head wondering what I'm going to write. Sure I've never done this before. There's another card on the counter pinned to a bunch of flowers, I can just make out what it says, 'Get Well Soon.' I'll put that down. Sure when Mam opens her eyes around eleven o'clock she won't be expecting a card, even a bunch of flowers from any of us, but she'll be pleased when the other three women in the women's only ward on the second floor of St. John's Hospital ask her, 'Who brought you the lovely bunch of flowers Mrs. Taylor? She'll smile and say, 'my eldest son, Paddy. He's getting married soon.' And the four of them will talk for hours about all belonging to them, and by the time I come in to see her I'll be a walking saint.

Sr. Benson, the small nun with the thick glasses and funny walk who stitched black eyes, bandaged every swollen and cut knee and all parts of the bodies of every young boy and girl in Limerick City, who always said that I was her best customer, takes the large bunch of flowers from my hand as, I ask 'Is my mother OK?' She just says, 'yes' and asks 'Is your father with you?' I tell her no and ask is my mother awake yet? She doesn't answer and tells me to go and find him, that they want to see him. There's no urgency in her voice, nothing in her body language to convey any sort of concern that something might be wrong.

Maybe Mam was calling for him as she came out of the anaesthetic. He's been on the batter for the last week and is breaking out every year now it's getting to be a pain for us all, mostly Mam. They are not talking either. It's her second day in hospital and the eejit never even asked her did she need or want anything. Not even a kind word and boy is he going to regret it! It's twelve o'clock in the day and I'm thinking 'what's the point of going down to the Bedford Bar or Riddler's Pub by the bridge in Sarsfield Street, sure he'll be well on his way down the road of cantankerousness and won't be in the mood to listen to the message from Sr. Benson.' I'll get back to work with James on the North Circular Road. He's been with Pop and myself now ever since Cousin Lar and Pop split up a year ago. I can go back to the hospital again in the afternoon to see Mam. She will surely be awake by then.

At four o'clock I'm back in the long corridor and there she is again, Sr. Benson,only this time she looks a bit cross. There's a faster pace to her walk as she hurries down the long corridor.

'Where's your father?' she shouts.

I don't answer, because I'm shocked at her tone.

'Didn't I ask you this morning to get your father?'

I'm beginning to realise something is seriously wrong.

'Is my mother OK?' I ask.

'No, she's not' comes the short answer. 'She is loosing a lot of blood, now will you go and find your father quickly! Your sister was here earlier and has gone looking for him too.'

I'm scouring every pub around the city centre and can't find him anywhere. My heart is pounding out my ears and my mind is imagining all kinds of awful thoughts. Mam isn't going to die is she? Sure she only went in for one of those operations, the one that has the name I heard for the first time my sister Jet told me last week when she said Mam was going into St. John's to have the kind of operation Mam won't talk about, well not to her son. The operation that takes the womb out, sure no one ever died of that before did they? Surely that's a good sign isn't it? She might be sick for a while; she'll surely get better won't she? And on it goes, my brain trying to reassure me that everything will be OK. Sure she'll be back home next week, baking the two spotted dicks that will last all the following week and talk about how much she's looking forward to having the girl who lives around the corner in 12 Claughaun Court, Garryowen living with her after the wedding, that she says she can't wait for and that's only four months away. My brain has me convinced that she'll be alright and the heartbeats are normal again.

When I get back to the hospital, to the nun with the thick glasses to tell her that I can't find Pop, only to find that he's there with Jet in the corridor outside the ward, that has its door opening every few seconds and my heart seems to take an age to start beating again. Only now it's beating out the thumps rapid, because Jet looks like she's crying and when I get to them speechless, Pop puts his arm around me and pulls me close real tight. He's never done that before. And it starts the heart going, out of control. The smell of porter from his breath is real strong. He should be scuttered by now, but the shock of what's happening has brought him to his senses. And now my heart is going crazy.

Jetta looks at me and says; 'I don't think she's going to make it Pa' and Pop holds me tighter. It's seven o'clock in the afternoon. Jetta says, 'I think we should go and find James, he needs to be here if the worst happens.' We're on our way in the small green and white minivan, that's nearly new, two years old in fact. It used to have the name R.T.V. Rentals on both sides with the guy hitting the big gong that told you it was a company affiliated to the Rank Organisation. It's not difficult to find James as he is going out with a girl from Ballynanty. He's shocked and upset and asks how this could be happening. 'Sure she only went in for a simple operation, didn't she?' He crawls into the back of the van. There's a terrible silence as we drive the short distance back to St. John's Hospital, and I know we all have the same dread, even though we're not saying it. Will Mam be still with us when we walk to the ward with the long corridor?

Cousin Lar is there with his brother Harold. Harold has a car and would come to work with us when we needed an extra pair of hands. Mostly if the work was down in Killaloe and his car was needed. Pop gives James a hug just like he gave me and James, just like I was, is awkward and uncomfortable about it. It's not surprising, because we don't know how to react to this show of emotion especially from Pop. But it does send out a message, Pop must be bricking it with worry and I'm sure his brain is taking him back over the years and the guilt must be choking him. He'll never talk about it; he'll never talk about anything to anybody. I don't know if he ever talked to Mam about these things. There's a terrible sense of gloom about the corridor, the part that has Mam in it. The women who share the ward with Mam are out in the corridor in their pink and blue night-gowns with slippers to match, smoking cigarettes one after the other and making comments like, 'God, but she's such a lovely woman, and a lovely family too. That boy over there, (pointing at me) brought her in a lovely bunch of flowers this morning. When she opened her eyes at eleven o'clock, the first thing she asked was how we all were.' Jetta pulls me to one side and tells me she was with her around that time, and said Mam was awake for a few minutes that a priest anointed her, and that Mam was frightened. Jetta said she was trying to reassure her that it was standard procedure for everyone who has that kind of operation to be anointed, but that Mam fell back into unconsciousness before she could finish. And the more I hear, the more my brain that was earlier telling me all the reasons why Mam won't be going anywhere has gone the other way now, with all the reasons why she won't make it.

The poor misfortunate girl that is going to marry me and lives around the corner will want to know why I'm not around at her house, to bring her down to see Mam. I tell Jett I'm going down for her to bring her back because she'll want to be here. The five minute drive to Garryowen has my mind in an awful state and when I arrive at 12 Claughaun Court, Mary is at the door all decked up and wondering what as kept me so long. There are five houses in Claughaun Court, that have long front gardens and Mary's house is one of them. By the time I'm half way up; Mary knows there's something up. 'What's wrong?' she asks.

'Mam', I answer. 'She's loosing a lot of blood. It's looking very bad.'

Mrs. O' Mary's mother heard me and comes out, putting the sign of the cross on her forehead saying, 'Oh God keep the poor woman alive.'

I'm trying to give Mary all the reasons why Mam won't die, like sure for God's sake she's only forty nine, she goes to Mass every Sunday, wouldn't say a cross word to anyone unless they said it to her first. Why would God take her? She's needed here to look after Harry who's only coming up to his ninth birthday; he'll need a mother for another five or six years at least. The rest of us will be alright with Jetta married and two kids very close to each other and there's no fear of me and James' who's coming up to his seventeenth birthday, he'll be OK too. I'm only saying out loud what my brain was thinking before it decided that the odds were stacked against Mam making it. By the time we get to St. John's, park the van and make our way to the second floor, Mary is gone as white as a sheet. We hold hands tight as we walk the long corridor to the larger crowd that has gathered since I left forty five minutes ago. We try to read the gloomy expressions on Pop's, James and Jetta's faces, has she gone, we're thinking. The Sister with the funny walk has passed us out. She is flying down the corridor carrying two sachets of blood and opens the door of St. Teresa's ward where Mam is. It's a good sign and a bad one too, good in the sense that she's still alive but bad that she's still loosing blood. 'No change', I said, and every head shakes from side to side. I'm getting an awful sinking feeling from the faces of everyone here along with the body language that we're just hanging around waiting for Mam to go.

Jet pulls me aside and tells me she went into see her while I was gone for Mary. They'd given her nine pints of blood and that her legs and bottom are raised into the air trying to stop the blood that's pouring out of her. Its more bad news my brain doesn't want to hear. There's tea going every five minutes from the room that has the kitchen sink and all the accessories from the three women who share the ward with Mam.

It's coming up to eleven o'clock now, and if I drink anymore tea I'll burst. I'm smoking fags one after the other, my throat is on fire. I don't know what to do with my legs and hands. Then I decide to pray to God. I try to bargain with him. I promise him that if he sorts Mam out I'll go to Mass every Sunday, that I'll never say another curse again, I'll go to Communion too, I'll do the Stations of the Cross, the nine First Fridays, confession as well every week and after I've said that I'm bursting a gasket trying to think of anything else God might need from me. Something that would be worth him leaving Mam here for another few years, but I can't think of anything. And it never dawns on me that he must be listening to prayers all around the world now, just like mine, and people are still dying young and old from violence, sickness and disease.

I'll think of Mrs. Culhane's three babies who died in three of the six years we lived in Upper Carey's Road. I'll think of the pleas she made to God, of why He asked her to carry such a load as she looked at a white coffin each year. And then it dawns on me, if he didn't answer her prayers that her infant babies might have lived, then what chance have I of my prayers being heard. Cousin Harold walks down the corridor to the window that I went to, to be alone to pray that has the night skyline of Limerick, that I looked into as I talked to God. He whispers into my ear, 'It doesn't look good Paddy, she has lost a lot of blood and there's no sign of it stopping.' I turn my head away from his face. He knows I don't want to hear. 'You've got to face it Paddy, she's not going to make it.'

'She is, she is', I cry. 'She has to.'

Harold says, 'I know you don't want to her to go Paddy, but she's exhausted. There's no fight left in her.'

I don't answer because I know he's right. I can hear him talking away but my mind wants to take me to a place like the past when everything was good, when we were all happy. Harold keeps talking but my ears don't want to listen to his whispers of more reasons why Mam isn't going to make it. I'm still staring out the window and my mind just wants to take me away and give my stomach some relief from the lump that's in it, that I've been carrying around like a bag of coal, ever since the nun with the funny walk told me the bad news.

My mind is taking me back to Garryowen where Mam would be every day when we all came home to her lovely smile that we took for granted: to the fire in the winter time that kept us warm while we ate our dinner or supper, the beautiful shine on everything that could have a shine, the house that every visitor would say you could eat off the floor. The beds that were always made with snow white sheets and changed every week. We'd talk to her as she sat, by the fire, knitting away every night with one leg over the other. She's the heartbeat of the family. I can see her clearly laughing away, the day I ran around the side of our house and nearly took the back door from its hinges.

'I'm free', I'm shouting, 'I'm free from Sexton Street CBS ye can go to blazes the whole lot of ye.'

'Oh you'll regret it later on' cries Mam and off she goes again with the usual statement word for word, every time she'll say it. 'If I had my youth back again, I'd never leave school until I was twenty. I'd get a good education.' I'm behind her back miming out the words in perfect timing. Pop will be at it too when he comes home.

I'll only have another year to do up the road at John the Baptist School; the school that most young fellows around here call John the B*****d, the school that has only two class rooms and one Christian Brother called Brother Fahy. They say he won't be too hard on us because he'll only be wasting his time and energy on brains that won't be capable of learning anything. So what's the point of trying? Sure half of us will be gone by Christmas, to the shops that will be busy and the lure of money will be too good to turn down. The other teacher a tall man with glasses named Mr. Ryan who will want to teach me more songs on the accordion only I won't be around long enough to learn. He's a kind man. And I'm wondering why most of the other teachers in Sexton Street School couldn't be like these two down here.

Brother Fahy is like all Christian Brothers that have a great interest in GAA sport, football and hurling. Our first week he'll ask if any of us would like to be part of the school team, to stay on after class and I'm saying to one of the lads 'It's not going to be much of a school team with only two classes to pick from.' But I'll stay back and see if I'll be picked. I'd love to play for the school even though I'm useless. But my brain has more sense than my heart because its desire to be part of something is greater than my brain that's telling me to go home and not to be wasting my time. Brother Fahy counts the number that has stayed back from both classes and says it's a better turn out than last year. We have just enough for a full team and five substitutes. He takes us out to the concrete yard at the back of the school, picks two teams of ten and says he'll be watching while we play. I know why he's watching. We all know why he's watching. He wants to see who's good enough to be in the first fifteen and I know I haven't a ghost of a chance, even though I'm running all over the yard, trying to get the ball, but all I'm doing is getting in the way of my own team.

'Will you get out of the way for Fups sake?' says one of the lads. I'm tripping and falling all over the place, with scratched knees and elbows full of blood and when the ball does come to me, I'll try to give it a belt with my boot, I'll miss and fall on my ass to the sound of laughter from everyone except Brother Fahy who just keeps nodding his head from side to side. When we finish he tells us to go home, that tomorrow after class he'll tell us the names of the first fifteen. And I know I won't be mentioned. I know I'll be a sub, but which one, will I get first or second? If I don't at least I know I'll get the last one, number twenty, but I don't mind.

When the following day arrives I am not in the first fifteen, I'm not first or second sub either but number five. Brother Fahy says that if anybody else wants to join the school team that I'll have to go. He's sorry but the simple fact is I'm useless. Nobody else in the school wants to bother because they don't think the school has much of a chance of winning anything and when the next day comes, he'll tell us all to queue up outside the cloakroom where we hang our coats screwed to hooks under the board with numbers overhead, when the cold winter mornings come. He says there's a pile of football boots in the corner, another pile of jerseys with white shorts in the other corner and that we are to go in, in order of our number and that means I'm bloody last again. I'll have the jersey with the number twenty on the back, but I don't mind. I'll be all decked out in the school colours. I'll be representing John the Baptist's School, God help them! And I'm all excited. I'll be wearing football boots too for the very first time and hope that there the new blackthorn type, the type everyone has that are good at sport, like rugby, hurling and soccer. Dinny, Phonsie and Noelie have them too. I'll look great in them. It takes a long time for the queue to get shorter and when the lads that got changed first come out, they're throwing all the shapes like footballers make when they're out on the pitch in Croke Park, when we see them on the black and white telly at home, with the one channel.

And here I am tearing down the lane by the Good Shepherd Laundry to the public park on the Dublin road, that has only the one playing pitch behind it. I feel like Eamon Grimes who captained Sexton Street winning school team, the day he ran onto the pitch and helped us win the Harty Cup last year. I think I look like him, wearing the last jersey, the one that was left in the cloak room, that should have number 'twenty' on it but the two is gone and all that's left is a big zero on one side. It's got a big V neck that a horse's arse could fit into; my shoulders are too small for it. One side of it is down around the elbow of my right hand exposing my right nipple and ribs that are sticking out like a sore thumb. The bottom is down around my shins covering the shorts that were white once upon a time and full of skid marks. Then there's the flopping sound coming from the huge football boot when it hits the ground that must have been made around the nineteenth century and left behind by the Black and Tans. It's a size ten and I'm a size six! It wobbles all over the place every time I lift it off the ground. It was the only boot in the whole place until I found another wedged between the steel pipes that takes the hot water to the radiators in our classroom in the winter time. It must have been there for years. It's a size five and like the other was for the left leg too. The toe of it is bent backwards all the time and no amount of bending or stretching could straighten it. It has only four cogs instead of ten.

John The Baptist School with Mr. Ryan

I'm running down the lane with a wobble and a flopping sound from the big boot and the agony of a boot that's too small, and has my toes twisted into a place that they've never been before. I'm thinking somewhere down there in the Park is a gobshite with two right feet and one bigger than the other and he's supposed to be better than me! When I hobble across the Dublin Road in agony to the field in the park before I'm too late, two messenger boys' cycle past and shout 'Look at the fupping spastic.' By the time I get to the field everybody is killing themselves laughing but not Brother Fahy.

'Taylor, where the hell did you get that yoke from?'

'Sure that's all that was left Brother.'

'Well you're not playing anything in those; you'll kill yourself or somebody else.'

He tells me to go home; that he'll try and get me some proper gear from Christian Brothers CBS in Sexton Street today, when he goes back there, because that's where he sleeps every night in the big stone building where all the Christian Brothers in Limerick stay.

I'll run home the short distance to Garryowen with the wobble and the flop. I can hear people laughing out loud, pointing fingers at me as I pass, and when I come in the back door of our house, Mam laughs as she shouts, 'Jesus, Mary and holy St. Joseph will you look at the state of my son?' When I walk into the sitting room Pop is at the table eating his dinner turns around, looks me up and down and off go the shoulders. He looks down at the size ten boot from the last century, starts coughing like he always does and just manages to get the following words out before he rises to his feet trying to get his breath.

'What's that yoke on your left foot?' Nan is laughing too, she's trying real hard to see what Pop is talking about. She's got her head stretched away from her shoulders, as far as she can get it, trying to see over the table because I'm over at the other side, she wants to see what Mam and Pop are talking and laughing about. But she has to get her bones out of the chair and walk the short few steps to see what has Pop in such a state. I know the minute she sets eyes on the yoke that's on my foot, the Holy Family will be called down from heaven and there she goes calling the three out as she howls away, I think I can hear the Holy Family laughing too. It's hard not to. It takes ages before the laughter dies down and Pop makes another comment that will start us all off again, like 'How many goals did you score with that thing?' or 'How many legs did you break?' We can't laugh anymore because our tummies are too sore. He wants to know what museum did I steal them from, why am I limping on the right foot that has my toes bent back so much they've gone numb. I am telling him that Brother Fahy has promised to get me proper gear from Sexton Street school that I'm going to be playing out in the Gaelic Grounds like the big fellows on the Limerick football team. Pop wants to know what position on the field I'll be playing when I'm out there. I tell him, 'Behind the goals.' He says he never heard of that position before and asks am I sure it's football I'm playing. I don't want to tell him that I'm the very last substitute because I'm too embarrassed. I try to change the subject. Mam says, 'Turn around so I can see you.' Pop's shoulders are off again. "Zero" he shouts. I never heard Pop use the 'F' word before but I think he said it under his breath while starting to laugh. 'Fupping zero what's that supposed to be?' And we're all at it again. In the days to come Pop will come and ask me did I find out what zero meant. We'll all laugh again and again. He'll have more comments like, 'Your mother wants you to ask Brother Fahy if you can keep that thing called a boot. She wants to grow some flowers in it for the front garden.'

Brother Fahy did keep his promise with the gear and black-thorn boots that had me looking the business. I played behind the goals out in the Gaelic Grounds with the other four subs with a spare ball to keep us warm in the month of October. Our team got walloped, I never got a chance to play but it was great to be able to say I was in St. John the Baptist's School team.

Paddy Bremen who worked at the Limerick Fire Brigade at the top of Thomas Street sent word around to all the school classes that he was starting a boys club called St. Dominic's Saviour and Phonsie, Noelie and myself were at the top of the queue of a hundred outside a classroom in the back yard of our school that Sunday. There's great excitement when Paddy Bremen tells us all there'll be three soccer teams in the club. He shows us the colours, two black squares and two amber with the new smaller V neck jersey. They're fabulous! And I'm thinking if I get to go home wearing one of those outfits, I'll look the business.

Next week we'll get our photo taken for the Limerick Leader and those who came first to the meeting last week will get to wear the brand new gear that will be coming straight from the box he'll be collecting at the sports shop in O'Connell Street, and when that day came Phonsie and myself are there outside the classroom in the yard waiting for the meeting. We're there an hour before it starts, we don't know where Noelie is. We all want to be sure that we'll get to wear the new gear for the photo.

Phonsie and myself, at St.Dominic's Saviour Club.
Fourth roll back third and fourth from right

Paddy Bremen says we'll be playing our first match up at the Bomber Field in Prospect, the field that Pop told me a German plane had dropped a couple of bombs into it, because the pilot thought they were flying over London during the Second World War. Mr. Bremen says he won't have time over the next two weeks to see for himself who can and can't play soccer and that the fairest way to find out is to let those who were at the front of the queue outside the door, at the first meeting to get the chance to play in the team. I'm gone out the door like a bullet, after Paddy Bremen took my name down and said,
'You're playing outside left.'
I haven't a bloody clue where that is.

13

'You have your own football boots I presume?'

'Oh yes,' I'm nodding my head up and down lying out through my teeth.

If he finds out I have no boots he'll think I'm no good and someone else will get my place. So I better get home fast and start the begging and the pleading for the money that will get me playing, and not hanging around the sideline feeling stupid and wishing I was like the others that are real good.

It only takes me a minute or two to get from the yard in the school to our house in Garryowen. I tear in the backdoor and stand longside Pop as he slurps away from a spoon he's putting into his mouth that takes the watery drop as well. My chest is heaving in and out trying desperately to give it the air it needs.

'Pop' I ask.

He shouts, 'No!'

I take another few seconds to get more air and say, 'What are you saying no for, sure I haven't asked you anything yet?'

'Does it involve money?'

'No Pop.'

'What does it involve?'

'Boots, Pop.'

Pop is confused and asks, 'What do you mean boots?'

Now that I have air in my lungs, I'm speaking so fast my tongue is starting to get cramp. I'm telling him the whole story about Paddy Bremen, the new club, and how I got picked, and how Paddy Bremen won't let me play unless I have proper playing boots.

'So how are you going to get a pair of boots to play for this new club you've joined?'

I better be careful the way I answer. I told him I wasn't looking for money or he'll surely say,

'I thought you said you weren't looking for money.'

So I say, 'Do you know anybody who might have a pair of boots that they don't want Pop? One of your customers' young fellows, sure they might have an old pair? Sure you're always bringing stuff home like that.'

He raises his eyebrows and gives me a look, a look that says, 'Aren't you the cute whore now?'

'I'll see' he answers and that's the answer I want.

I know that Nan will chip in a bit of her pension and Mam a bit from her housekeeping money, and in a couple of days Pop will walk in the door with a shoe box from Nestor's store in O'Connell Street. Sure he knows most of them and might get a few bob off as well; it's only a matter of waiting. But it's hard to wait. I'm going to look smashing! Everything I'll have will be brand new and not hanging off me.

I'll be down at Nestor's the following day asking one of the four or five old people that work there, in my best manners, if I can try on a pair of the new blackthorn boots. The woman says how nice it is to meet a young man with good manners. She asks for my name, like I hoped she would and when I tell her she says,

'Oh you must be Harry Taylor's son.'

I'm smiling away thinking to myself that everything is going according to plan. Any minute now she's going to tell me Pop was in this morning and bought a pair just like the ones I've on me, with all the cogs in the right places, that's making the lovely sound, and has me feeling two or three inches taller as I walk up and down the old wooden floor. But she isn't saying anything at all except asking me 'Are they comfortable?'

I'm telling her, 'They are.' But I need to find out if Pop was in this morning. So I tell her my father is coming in to buy me a pair.

'Oh that's great', she says. 'I'll put these aside for him so he'll know you were in.'

Janey, I'd better tell her it's supposed to be a surprise.

'Alright' she says, 'I won't say a word.'

A week is going to be awful long as I rush home from school at lunchtime, and wait for him to come home, every day to see if there's anything on the carrier of his bike. After four days there's still no sign of my boots and I ask real casual like, 'Any luck with the pair of boots Pop?'

And out comes a sharp sounding 'No.'

I'm bursting to tell him about my excitement but I don't want to annoy him. I'll ask Mam if I can get a quiet moment and all she'll say is,

'I'm sure your father isn't forgetting your boots, don't worry.'

And now there's only four days to go before I'll be playing for the Dominic Saviour Football Club. I can't sleep with the worry of having no boots.

When the next day comes there's Pop taking a box from the carrier of his bike. It's my new blackthorn boots, I know it is. I can see him through the window as he brings the bike through the small front gate. He walks into the sitting room and throws the box at me that has lovely brown paper wrapped around it.

'See if they fit you.'

'Gee Pop, thanks.' 'Are they new?' knowing full they are.

'Gee Pop you didn't have to go and buy a new pair of black-thorn boots. Sure an ould pair would do.'

I'm lying through my teeth and he knows I'm lying.

Nan and Mam are there. And there they are a lovely pair of blackthorn boots. I think they're the ones I walked around in Monday morning. I'm all thanks to Mam and Pop and Nan because I know that they all had a part in it.

When Saturday comes, the day for the game, I have the boots wrapped in a paper bag and under my arm. I won't want to loose them on the way to Phonsie and Noelie's up in Carey's Road, so we can all go together. We leave our clothes against the wall in Cal's park, after changing into the new gear. I'm prouncing around the field throwing all the shapes like they do in Croke Park before the match starts. Mr. Bremen says I'm to be out by the line on the right hand side and when I get the ball I'm to run up to the corner flag and give it a belt as hard as I can across the goals where the centre forward will try and get to the end of it and score. So I'm up and down the field in my new blackthorn boots waiting for the ball for nearly half an hour and the new boots are tearing into my heels. I'm knackered as well and I haven't touched the ball yet. Phonsie and Noelie are in the middle and have kicked the ball a good few times. I'm trying to catch my breath and get my legs that have aches and pains to respond. I can hear Paddy Bremen roaring at me to keep up with the play, but it's very hard. I never felt this tired when we played on the green in Garryowen or up in Carey's Road against the long wall that goes down the hill under the bridge. I can't figure out why it's so hard playing here with the new boots and now that I can't run anymore the ball has decided it wants to go where I'm not able to be. It will do it four or five times before Paddy Bremen looses the cool and calls me off. I'm exhausted. He puts on a sub in my place and I'll never forget the humiliation I felt that day.

I hated the name Taylor, I hated Mam and Pop as well because they made me and I wondered why I hadn't parents that were good at footie and pass it onto me. I never want to have that feeling again. I got all excited about kicking a stupid ball around the field, ran myself into the ground for half an hour and never touched the ball, and Pop is going to want to know if I scored any goals in my new blackthorn boots. I'll have to lie and say, 'Just the one Pop.' Paddy Bremen will never pick me again; I'll go out the door at home every Saturday with the boots under my arm. I'll come home and tell Pop I scored again when all I did was stand on the side lines next to Paddy Bremen, hoping only ten players would turn up and that he might ask me to change and give me another chance, but all I'll be is a spectator cheering on Phonsie and Noelie.

1962 is coming to an end and so is my first four months at John the Baptist's School. Brother Fahy wants to know what kind of work we all want to do when we leave at the end of next June, one or two raise their hand and say they'd like to be a Guard or a Judge in court. There's a snigger after it, 'coz they know they haven't the intelligence. He says, 'So you think that's funny do you? You won't be laughing when January of 1964 comes because the only jobs you'll get is the bike with the big basket in front, that every butcher's shop and grocery store in Limerick will want to send you out to Corbally or the Ennis Road with the pound of sausages and mince meat for half of the people that live out there or you might be unfortunate enough to get a job in Spaight's, Newsom's, Boyd's, or Hassett's to bring a couple of stone in weight in a basket that will have you totally exhausted by the time you get back and find there's another one waiting to be brought to the other side of town for a builder who needs it. You'll have to bring it out in a hurry, and if you don't keep up your job will be gone to some other young fellow around the same age as yourself who left his name in the shop, and how if we last the pace it will only last two years because the shops won't want to keep you when you reach the age of sixteen because you'll be entitled to more money and they won't want to give you more money so they'll show you the door. And why did you get the job in the first place? Can any of you tell me why you got the job?' There's no answer.' It's because ye have no brains only energy; young bodies with empty heads and loads of energy. Of course you could always go down to the Tannery and walk around all day when you won't know where your feet are in the cold winter months and come home stinking of animal's insides', has any of you ever smelt the inside of a cow's stomach? Or maybe you'll just get a job down by the Milk Market at Reidy's coal yard or Ted Castle's on the Dock Road, and when you come home every day your mothers will think a black child from Africa has walked into her home looking for a shilling and will scream at what she has to wash.'

But I have my hand high in the air, trying to get his attention. 'And what's wrong with you Taylor?

I'm telling him that I've already got a job when I leave school.

'Well aren't you the lucky lad? What kind of a job would that be now?'

'Painting and decorating, Brother, another day it will be cutting wood or even building walls and roofing too.'

'And who'll be giving you this job when you leave school?'

'My father Brother, he works for himself with my older cousin Lar.'

'Very good', he'll answer and turns to the class and says, 'I don't know what in God's name the rest of ye are going to do when ye leave this place.'

He's right. I couldn't imagine myself on a messenger bike, riding around town delivering things to people's houses and they looking at me, especially the fellows I went to school with, who are still up there in Sexton Street filling their huge brains with information, I will never understand. And if they saw me on a Butcher's bike, a job only for dunces and clowns like myself who were useless at the learning, the job that has that awful stigma attached to it, that's only for the poor, but I won't have to worry about that. When I start with Pop he'll give me creative work like hanging doors and painting as well. Sure hasn't he trained me over the last two or three years when I called down after school to work evenings, the weekends and the summer holidays too. Sure don't I know everything there is to know and that means I'll be earning more money as well. I might even be able to buy a car after a few months.

CHAPTER 2

When the break for the Christmas holidays comes Phonsie and myself are down in O'Connell Street; we want to see the new shop - the one the whole of Limerick city and county are talking about. The one that's next to O'Mahony's Bookshop; The shop with the new front that has no frames to hold the doors or the windows, like every other shop in the City, just glass everywhere and with my knowledge of woodwork and how doors need hinges screwed to frames to work, and the big frame of glass that needs putty to keep it in place in heavy wood so it won't fall out and kill somebody. I'm asking myself how can those be made of glass and nothing else? How can a door swing open without the hinges? It can't be true that the entire front is wall to wall glass. I'm telling Phonsie it can't be true and when we get into O'Connell Street and make our way to the big shop that is called The Five Star Supermarket, the new way of shopping in Limerick that some people say will close the likes of Everett and Fry at the corner of O'Connell Street and Shannon Street, Lipton's and the L & N in William Street

Photograph of the Five Star Supermarket

that has men only working behind counters with the snow white linen coats and long white aprons tied around their waist. The kind of shops you can talk about the weather or what's going on, or who's going to the church tonight, and what they've died of the day or night before, while you wait for your box of groceries to be filled from shelves as high as ten feet off the ground; shelves that might have been there for the past hundred years and held food for generations of Limerick people. Others are saying the new shop will never catch on, that it will last only for a month or two, three or four at the most. There will be the other generations, the ones that like things to stay the way they are, the way they've always been, but do they know there are three or four supermarkets in Dublin and another in Cork and that there are talks of another opening in Limerick next year?

Do they know there's a queue here every day since it opened .One like Phonsie and I have to join today, just to have a good gawk around and can tell their friends they were here.

There's all kinds of talk amongst the people here in the queue, how there's food in the supermarket, people have never seen or heard before. Washing powder from America along with things you can see in the pictures they call movies, like hot-dogs and a machine that cooks chickens by the dozen, only it's not cooked anymore. It has a new word for it now, called barbequeued. How you can go in the front door, buy everything you need for all the house and family that will last a week. Others say there's talk from all the butchers in Limerick that the housewives of Limerick might desert them for the new supermarket that has the butcher and the vegetable area too with fruit from the four corners of the world, how there isn't a counter in the entire place, just pack a basket as you walk to the sound of Christmas music that no one seems to know where it comes from. With shelves everywhere, how you can wander around to your heart's content. And the talk that's all around us filling us with enthusiasm and expectations as we reach the front entrance and here they are the glass doors with no hinges, glass floor to ceiling all around, it's hard to believe. There's someone shouting inside, 'Mind the glass doors' but it's no good. People are walking in banging their chins and knees, they laugh but come through the doors with red faces, they'll hold their foreheads with the words 'Jesus I thought the shagging door was open.' Phonsie and myself are killing ourselves laughing as we stand outside the entrance and wait our turn. Everybody is laughing, half of us out here will do the very same on the way out including myself because we'll be so amazed and intrigued with what our eyes and ears are taking in.

There's bottles, and tins of food that we've never seen or heard before, that has our brains taken away to strange countries I've never heard. I'll walk through one of the four checkouts looking and listening at what's behind us, trying to take it all in and walk smack into a door that will have those waiting outside laughing their heads off, that are well down the queue at the corner of Bedford Row, and heard those of us laughing half an hour earlier and wondered what the laughing was about. I'll go home and tell Mam about it and tell her that she should go down and do her shopping there, that it's fantastic. I'll tell Pop about the glass frontage and the glass doors with no hinges and he'll tell me how he saw the lot being installed and watched the day they put them in, how the glass is over half an inch thick, and bullet proof, how they were was sunk into the ground with a massive spring that would cause the door the close slowly.

The exterior of Five Star Supermarket after it opened

I'll go back again tomorrow morning because I've just had a great idea. I'll walk in with the big mouth and hard neck that every one of the Taylor's have, male and female, sometimes it'll be a curse but today its going be a great asset. I'll ask if I can talk to the manager. I'm told 'He's upstairs in his office', and knock on his door, a voice says 'Come in' and after closing the door gently I'm told to sit down. 'And what can I do for you?' asked the tall well-dressed man as he sits into his chair. He's got a strange accent. He's looking at me, waiting for an answer.

'I'm looking for a job Sir, I'll take anything Sir, just for the Christmas holidays Sir.'

'And why are you looking for a job? Sure you're a bit young to be looking for a job aren't you?'

'My mother is dying Sir, we don't know if she'll last the week Sir, my father has no work either. He hasn't worked for the last few weeks Sir, and if I got a job Sir we might have something to eat for the Christmas Sir.' I'm lying out through my teeth and if Mam knew I was doing this there'd by hell to pay.

I'm doing my level best with the 'Sir's' and the good manners. It's bound to make an impression.

'When can you start?'

I have the words 'Straight away' out of my mouth without giving it a second thought.

'Go down stairs and ask for a Mr. O'Leary, he will get you started.'

I'm thanking him all the time. I'll say it three or four times, I think I'm over-doing it.

Mr. O'Leary gives me a white coat, five sizes too big because he says it's the only size he has. He rolls up the long sleeves several times until he has them across my wrist. The coat is touching the ground and flows along the sparkling, shiny tiles that are polished every night at 6.00 pm after the shop closes. He takes me up to one of the checkouts to a tall woman, named Miss Wall.

He says 'You're to put the groceries into these large brown bags, as Miss Wall hands them to you.' When he walks away Miss Wall turns to me and in a soft tone says that I have to put the soaps and toiletries into a separate bag. My mouth says, 'OK' but my brain hasn't a clue what toiletries are. I'm not going to ask, not in front of all those women that are in the queue of twenty waiting and another twenty in each of the other three checkouts. She's really fast with the fingers of her right hand belting away as she presses the buttons of the register and the left hand throwing everything at me faster than I can put them in the bag. She'll talk away to everyone in the queue about everything and anything.

'Wasn't that a great film in the Savoy the other night?', how she loves Stewart Granger, or it might be the dance at the Stella Ballroom last Sunday or next Sunday, because the Royal Show band will be there. Then she lets a roar at me, that causes my face to have such a rush of blood, I'll go completely red. I can feel my face on fire. She'll grunt, 'Jesus, Mary and Holy St. Joseph, didn't I tell you not to put the toiletries into the bag of food?'

She'll mutter away under her breath while taking everything out of the brown paper bag, putting the stuff she calls 'toiletries' I've never seen or heard of before. That I'm keeping a close eye on what they look like 'because I won't want to make the same mistake again.

She has me jumping out of my skin again with the Holy Family being called down from heaven. It's just like being at home with Nan and Mam. I'm putting boxes of Omo, Persil and Daz (all washing powders) in with the groceries. While she's talking to 'Jesus, Mary and Joseph', she's rubbing her forehead just like Mam does when I have to go running to the shop for the Mrs. Cullen's Headache Powders. And I'm wondering does she have the same problem. She'll be the same tomorrow, only worse, giving me hell about other things that I don't know about. She'll have me a nervous wreck waiting for the roar every few minutes.

When tomorrow comes, it will be two days to Christmas Day. The queues inside and outside will be bigger and Miss Wall won't have time to talk about the pictures down at the Savoy or dancing at the Stella because there'll be no let up of people in Limerick City and County wanting to buy whatever there is in the shop before Christmas. She's loosing the cool with me again with spits flying out of her mouth when she starts. And I'm starting to get sick and tired of it, because she is at it now for no reason at all. She says her feet and head are killing her and I'm getting it in the neck all the time now. And then I start to enjoy it, because people are starting to give me the odd few pence, sometimes it's a tanner or a shilling. And that's making her worse and the worse she gets, the more I'll get.

And with one more day to go I've made five bob since yesterday. And there she is, worse than ever. And here I am richer than ever. I'm answering her all the time, nice and loud so all the customers can hear down the queue my good manners and the saintly look. When one sees me getting a tip it encourages the others to follow suit. And there's Mam down the queue, fourth or fifth in line. She's very cross because of the way Miss Wall is going on at me. What's she doing here? Didn't she tell me the other day she'd never shop in here, that she's used to the way she's shopped all her life? Didn't she tell me the when I got home, to tell her I got the job that she'd never be seen in this shop. She'll ruin everything now that I have a good thing going, I'm making mistakes on purpose, because I'm making so much from it. She's right in front of me with a face like Nan's with the stare, the kind of face that's ready for battle. Miss Wall is at me, right in front of her. She's going to let go any minute now God help Miss Wall and God help me too 'coz I'll be out on my ear within the next few minutes.

'Excuse me', says Mam real politely

'Yes Mrs.' answers Miss Wall.

'I hope that the staff in here are real friendly.'

Mam has the basket with only three small purchases in it on the checkout.

'Oh they are indeed' answers Miss Wall.

Mam has me real curious because she should have let fly with a real mouthful by now.

'And is it to the customers' only they're friendly?' says Mam.

'Oh goodness me, no' replies Miss Wall with a big false smile on her face. 'Why do you ask?'

'Well you see, I was out there in the queue forty minutes ago, watching and listening to you give that poor young lad a mouthful in front of everyone. You were still at it twenty minutes later when I passed you on the way in and you've been at it while I've been in this queue waiting to pay for my groceries.'

Other women in the queue are nodding their heads in agreement, saying 'Oh she's right. We heard her.'

I can see what Mam is doing. She's not going to let on she's my mother at all. She's looking up at Miss Wall who is over six foot tall.

'Now listen here to me young lady, I've a good mind to go upstairs and complain you to your boss about the way you are treating this fine young man. I'll be back here again this evening and tomorrow, and if I hear you talking to that young boy, the way you were talking to him today, I'm heading straight for the office. Do I make myself clear?'

'Yes Ma'am'.

As Mam pays for the few bits she has in her basket she hands me a shilling and says, 'Here young man, buy your mother a present out of that, she deserves it for rearing such a grand young mannered lad as yourself' and gives me a wink as she heads for the door.

I'm dead chuffed with Mam the way she handled the situation.

When I arrive home that evening around 6.30 there's Mam waiting at the door with a worried look on her face. 'Have you still got a job?' she asks.

'I have', I answer. 'But they gave me a reduction in my take home pay because of what you did.'

'Oh Jesus, Mary and Holy St. Joseph', she shouts, 'What did they say to you? her hands are over her mouth, then puts one of them on her forehead.

I'm telling her no one said a word to me but I had a reduction in my take-home pay.

'How the hell did that happen then?' she asks with a confused look on her face that can't wait for an answer.

'Well' I said, 'that woman has been at me since I started work there three days ago and everyone in the queue has been giving me the odd few pence out of sympathy. I've been milking the whole situation and making mistakes on purpose so the flow of money will continue, but after you left and shut Miss Wall's mouth today, you shut the flow from all my sympathizers. I've nearly a whole pound saved for a present for you at Christmas, a present that will cost me thirty bob and the ten bob that I thought I was going to get today and tomorrow has dried up because of you.'

Her bottom lip is trembling away; I think she is going to start bawling.

I laugh and tell her that I'm only joking and how good it felt that she put the bitch I'm working with in her place. She'll wipe her nose and sniff a couple of times and say,

'No bitch is going to talk to my son like that and get away with it. Now sit down and eat your dinner.'

The next day is Christmas Eve. It's a long busy day with smoke coming out of the cash registers and mayhem in the shop with all the staff on a short fuse because of the pressure. Miss Wall forgets herself a couple of times but is quick to correct herself. When the day ends, Miss Wall complains of sore feet and tired limbs. We're all heading down to the big table in the basement, to the lady who gives us the tea every day at 10.00 for the ten minute break in the mornings and the hour at lunchtime. The table that usually has a huge kettle and twenty or thirty mugs with the different names, now has parcels with Christmas wrapping.

The manager says, 'On behalf of the company I would like to thank you all for your hard work since the shop opened and now the company would like to show their appreciation along with your wages.'

I'm thinking this is great! I'm going to get one of those boxes. I'll give it to Mam as a Christmas present. Sure, she'll be delighted. But I'll have to wait; I'll surely be last. Off he goes with the names, starting with senior staff. He'll shake their hand and thank them again while handing them one of the bigger boxes along with the wage packet. And on he goes until there's only one left and that will be mine.

Then he says, 'Last of all we have', I'm putting one leg out in front of the other and make my way across for the small parcel with the wage envelope he has in his hand. I don't even know how much I'm getting because I never asked with the excitement of getting a job in the first place, a job I thought I got because of all the lies I told and found out later they were looking for a lad anyway, and now I'm thinking wasn't it just as well Mam never let on who she was the other day. Otherwise, people, including the manager, might be thinking she was after making a miraculous recovery. I'm two steps out in front of the entire staff with my hands out for the goodies and the handshake, when the messenger boy passes me out on my right hand side. He doesn't even get a 'thank you' or a handshake from the manager and in my embarrassment standing there in the middle of the floor. I'm making a mental note of his behaviour. The poor lad's arse is hanging out of his pants. He has dirt behind his ears and when he passes me, there's a woeful smell off him.

'I'm afraid we have nothing for you young Taylor', 'You're not here long enough. The company up in Tullamore don't even know you exist.'

There is great laughter, and after that, a couple of female voices go 'Ah' and laugh. I'm out there in the middle of the floor, I want to dig a hole and bury myself in it while listening to the male sniggers and the muffled comments.

Mrs. Doyle,the tea lady who has taken a shine to me since I got here, who always has a kind word and has me telling her all about my family at the tea breaks, has her arm around my shoulder. She's asking, 'Did you get your wages at all Paddy?'

I shake my head from side to side, still wearing the white coat that's miles too big for me. It saves the cleaner cleaning the floor because it drags and gathers the dirt into it. Mrs. Doyle goes to the manager and tells him that he can't leave me home without wages.

'Oh he'll have to wait until after the Christmas holidays for that, because the company doesn't even know he works here. He's not on the books yet.'

I'm nearly in tears because my whole bloody Christmas will be ruined. I'll have no money, so I'll be able to buy nothing. Mrs. Doyle takes the manager to one side and starts to speak in a low voice. I think she's cross with him. Whatever she says seems to have worked because he puts his hand in his pocket and gives me one pound ten shillings. This brings a smile back to my face.

I take my oversized white coat off and hang it on a hook with the others and make my way up stairs to head home.

Mr. O'Leary is at the top of the stairs, takes me by the arm and asks when am I going back to school. 'He wants to know if I'd like to come back after St. Stephen's Day for a few days.' I'm nodding my head frantically because it would mean more money in the pocket after I have spent everything. He wishes me a 'Happy Christmas' and tells me to be here at nine o'clock after the two day break. I run home and give Mam half of the thirty bob wages and half of the tips that I got from the sympathetic customers.

After my tea and a wash I'm on my way to Carey's Road to Phonsie and Noelie's and into town for the pictures. Following the film, it's into the Savoy café for the plate of chips and the glass of orange. I'm telling the lads about the job I got down at the Five Star Supermarket, putting the groceries into brown paper bags. I'll show them the money that I keep in my pocket and I can tell they're mad jealous. We'll go back to Carey's Road and over to Noelie's house for the cards that I'm bloody useless at and the luck I'll never get, no matter what we play. I'll be there all night with my humour turning sour and as I make my way down the Jail Boreen that has only the one light on the pole, scared out of my mind at one o'clock in the morning, and not a penny in my pocket after all my work during the week and listening to that ol' bitch. Noelie and his mates must be laughing their heads off because of the luck deserting me. What am I talking about? Sure, it never came to me in the first place. I'll be up there again tomorrow, losing money I borrowed from Mam that I'll have to give back after the few days' work I'll get before I head back to school. I'm an awful gobshite. I keep telling myself that I'll get some of the luck Pop has, he wins something no matter what he does, but I never will, but I'll keep on believing that I will. I'll keep on losing and learn nothing. I'll turn up for work the day after 'Stephen's Day with a puss on me because I thought this was going to be the best Christmas I ever had, that turned out to be the worst. All I got for Christmas was to go to the pictures, stuff myself with chips, orange, and chocolate, now I'll have to work three or four days for nothing. It's quieter here, now the ques have gone. Miss Wall is able to manage on her own, thanks bit oh God!. On the third and last day before I go back to school Mr. O'Leary calls me downstairs.

He says he wants to have a word with me. He puts his hand on my shoulder and in a low tone says, 'There's a full time job going here if you want it.'

Straight away my mouth says 'I'll take it.'

'Slow down now' says Mr. O'Leary. 'Don't you want to find out what it is?'

'I don't care what it is' 'I'll take it'; And off my brain goes like a bullet. I'm thinking no more school, money every Friday for the weekend; money for Mam, she'll be able to buy herself something decent to wear, now that I'll be bringing home more money every week. I'll have fags too even though Mam and Pop haven't a clue I'm smoking. I can't stand still. Then one of my ears picks up those awful words, 'Messenger Boy.' Mr. O'Leary is looking at me waiting for an answer.

'I'm sorry Mr. O'Leary what was that you said?' dreading his answer, hoping I was hearing things.

'I said', 'the messenger boy was sacked this morning. You can have his job, but you must let us know today if you want it.'

My heart sinks with disappointment.

'It pays £2.10s. a week and you'll have a brand new bike,'

I'm thinking of the way they treated the messenger boy on Christmas Eve and the awful stigma that's attached to it. But my brain is telling me how good it would be to have £2.10s. a week and half of it in my pocket every Friday night and how better off Mam will be and no more school. The shock is slowly leaving my body, so I say, 'I'll take it, Sir.'

'You'll have to go and see your parents first, go on' he says, 'off you go now.'

So I'm running all the way home to Mam at three o'clock hoping she'll be there and not downtown. My brain is doing what it always does and that is giving into whatever my heart desires. I'm thinking of Dan Ryan who started working in Lipton's as a messenger boy, then got a job serving behind the counter, bought himself a new car and hired it out to people at the weekends and look at him now with his own self-drive car company! And a big garage called Bremen Motors in Thomas Street and if it's good enough for him, it's good enough for me.

It's the usual with me when I'm excited, bursting in the door and taking the heart out of Mam and trying to get the words out and my breath at the same time muffling and spluttering away until Mam tells me to sit down and get my breath.

I'm telling her everything Mr. O'Leary told me except the part about the messenger boy. I don't think I'll have a ghost of a chance if she knows about that.

'Can I take it, can I please Mam?'

'Oh, I don't know Pa', she answers.

'You're too young to be leaving school. You should be staying on educating yourself' and off she goes again with the same bloody words, how she wished she stayed on in school and so on.

But I won't stop with the pleas of 'Ah go on sure you know I'm bloody useless, you know I hate it, ah go on Mam.'

'You'll have to go and ask your father.'

I'm gone out the door, out the gate of the front garden, before I'm back again asking, 'Where's he working Ma?'

She says, 'He's down in Bedford Row, on the top floor of Stokes and McKiernan.'

I don't know where I'm getting the energy for all the running I'm doing but the thoughts of no more school and the £2.10s. I'll be getting every Friday has put plenty of diesel in my legs that take me down to Bedford Row and up the six flights of stairs shouting, 'Are you there Pop?'

Pop comes running out the door onto the landing, shouting, 'I'm up here, I'm up here. What's wrong?'

'I got a job Pop, I got a job, can I take it please?'

'Mother of Jesus' says Pop 'you're after putting the heart crossways in me! I thought your mother was in trouble.'

'Can I Pop, can I?'

He walks back into the room he had come out of, cousin Lar is there as well. They both have the snow-white overalls on. I'm still at the 'Can I Pop? Can I?'

'Can you what?' he asks

'Can I take the job?'

'What would you be doing? What kind of a job is it?'

31

Oh Janey! I hoped he wouldn't ask me that.

'It's over at the Five Star Supermarket, Pop.'

'I didn't ask you where it is, I asked you what kind of a job it is.'

'I don't know Pop, I forgot to ask. I got so excited.'

'How old are you now?' asked Pop.

'I'm nearly fifteen, Pop.'

'But, at this very moment now, you're fourteen, right?'

'I suppose so, Pop.'

'That's too young to be leaving school.'

'How old were you when you left school Poop?'

'Never you mind.'

'I remember you telling Jetta and myself that you ran out of school and never went back again. And you said you were only twelve.'

'Things were much different then', said Pop.

'How different Pop?'

'Well first I'd no mother and my father was too soft. There weren't the opportunities there then that there are today.'

'But Pop I'll be leaving school altogether in June and you know I'm useless at school.'

'That's because you're not trying hard enough', he says.

Then I bring out the trump card. A quiver in the voice, I'll talk about the cruelty there was above in Sexton Street, making it sound worse. A tear followed that and it had the desired effect. His starting to soften.

'I wish to God I never left school.'

Then Cousin Lar says, 'So do I. Sure Jesus I can't even fupping spell'. Every time I have to do an estimate I have to get the dictionary down to see how a word should be spelt or what kind of a word to use. I always have to keep a pencil in my ear to write on a piece of paper or a lump of wood when doing a bit of measuring because I can't add or subtract in my head.'

'Sure can't I learn all these things when I go working with you?'

'Well' says Lar, 'Wouldn't it be better if we were learning them from you?'

'Did you ask your mother?'

'I did Pop.'

'And what did she say?'

'She said I was to ask you.'

'Go away and I'll talk to your mother tonight,' he said.

'Ah Janey Pop, I have to let them know today. Otherwise they'll give it to someone else.'

There's silence for about two or three minutes.

'Well then you can take the job, but I can tell you …'

I'm gone out the door. I'm not waiting around for him to finish the sentence, because I know how it will end, how I'll regret it for the rest of my life, how I'll wind up like himself and Mam not being able to converse with educated people, afraid to open their mouths in case they said the wrong thing and make an idiot of themselves in front of people he worked for, how they came from colleges and universities, who sometimes used words that he hadn't a fupping clue what they were talking about. Trying to bluff his way out of a conversation, and how he'll walk away without knowing, and feeling like a right gobshite. And if he could have another chance, he'd stay at school and make something of himself and I should do the same. If Nan is home while he's saying it, she'll throw in her tuppence worth as well. Like how she started work at the age of eight, milking the cows every morning, Sundays included, how she had to be up every morning, all on her own and how she used to dream of going to school and when she did get to go, had a fifteen mile walk every day with no shoes. Jett, James and myself will be sitting on our chairs giving her the listening ear and respect with words like, 'Janey Nan that was terrible. I never knew that', even though we heard it a hundred times before. And how the last time we heard it, the walk was only ten minutes and she didn't have to milk the cows until she came home that evening and the age was twelve! But if we don't sit down with the listening ear and respect with the faces of astonishment, we'll get a box in the ear from Mam and worse still a box from Pop that will put us flying off the chair. Mam will want to have her bit too and the three of them will be like a choir coming in and out with the old tune and the same words.

By the time, I get back to the Five Star it's nearly five o'clock. Mr. O'Leary takes me down to the basement and waits for me to tell him that I'll take the job. I'm looking at his face. He's smiling until I tell him I have permission from my parents. Now it has a look that I'll never forget and if I was any good at drawing, I could do it in minutes. I can still see it clearly, that look of contempt. I have just entered into the lower classes. I might be stupid in many areas but I have enough brains to understand what that look on his face means.

'Follow me,' he says.

I'm following him upstairs to the entrance that has all the glass.

'You're to wash the terrazzo floor every morning when you come in at nine o'clock and again in the evening before you go home. You can use a squeegee that will take the dirty water away to the gutter. You're to check with Mr. Reynolds in the Fruit and Veg. Department, the butcher, and the girls at the checkout for any deliveries you have to make. If there's none, you're to wear your white coat, get a sweeping brush, and sweep the floor.'

I don't know what the hell a squeegee is but I'll ask somebody down stairs who will show me how it works. He said I can have the bike to take home with me every day, but I won't be bringing that yoke to our house. I won't want Pop or Mam to see it, not even the lads in Garryowen.

I've started my first day with a mop, water, and the squeegee I got downstairs. Mr. O'Leary is standing beside me all the time and makes me feel like a right gobshite. When I'm finished the terrazzo floor he gives me a light thump on the shoulder and says something that sounds like 'Follow me'. We're half way down the shop; he turns and asks me where the mop is.

'Outside the front Sir,'

He'll answer and say, 'Why the hell didn't you bring it with you?' and I'll answer him and say, 'Sure you never asked me Sir.'

He shakes his head from side to side and makes me feel like an idiot with the words, 'Go back, and get it.'

I'll come back with the mop and he asks me 'Where's the bucket?'

I'll say, 'It's out in the front Sir.'

He'll say, 'Why the hell didn't you bring it in with the mop? Sure, any young fellow with a brain knows you can't have a mop without a bucket.

I'm trying to tell him that he only asked me for the mop and that if he wanted the bucket, he should have asked me to bring it in. But I'd better keep my mouth shut or I'll find myself back in John the Baptist's School tomorrow.

He shows me a large cardboard stand that's being pulled away from the wall and points to the ground that has a great big dog crap on it.

'Clean that up' he grunts.

My brain is telling me again, there's going to be a lot more of this kind of work for me the lowest kind of work for the lowest kind of worker. I'm rubbing it with the mop but he won't move.

'Get a shovel' he shouts.

'Where will I get one?'

He's annoyed, 'Go down to Mrs. Giles and get one off her.'

When I come back with the shovel I put it on the ground and give the crap a good swipe and up it comes the whole lot, except there's a ring of stain still on the tiles. After putting the crap in a box, I make several more attempts at getting the ring off, but it's no use. It won't budge.

'Get the water to it,' he shouts.

I'm wondering why the hell he just keeps standing there with his dazzling white coat that doesn't have a stain of any kind on it and won't have either because by Monday he'll get another one that's as clean from the laundry. The only thing he used in here all week is his mouth and one of his hands. I'm rubbing the ring stain up and down with the mop that I keep cleaning in the bucket every few seconds.

'It won't come off Sir.'

'Ah for God's sake use a bit of elbow grease,' he shouts.
'Where will I get that Sir?'.

I'm looking at him waiting for an answer and expecting him to be annoyed with me asking where this and that is. Only this time he's going to be more annoyed. But that cross look isn't there at all. Instead, there's a kind of a smirk. He says I'm to go up to Denis in the office to get an order made out to Nestor's across the road for a gallon of elbow grease. I'll go up to Denis and repeat what Mr. O'Leary said. Denis says, I don't need an order, just tell them that Mr. O'Leary told me. He has a smirk on his face too just like Mr. O'Leary.

There's a large wooden counter that goes all the way down the long shop and into the back with only the one break in it for any of the five assistants male and female, that Pop told me never got married. They could be right cranky most of the time and he wonders why anybody would go in there for anything when all you get is abuse. I'll stand there in front of the counter and wait for one of them to come and serve me. The tall man with the white coloured hair, which should have been cut long ago, and more growing out of his ears and nostrils, says, 'Yes young man, what can I do for you?'

And with my best manners I'm telling him word for word, what Mr. O'Leary told me. The face that was grumpy and well wrinkled is even worse now. He shows me his black and yellow teeth while shouting out the words, 'Get out'.

I'm turning around to see what or who has walked in behind me and think it might be a dirty mangy dog that has wandered in from the street, because he'd only have a voice and a look like that for a dog. When I turn my head back again, waiting for the gallon of elbow grease that he hasn't even made an effort to go and get. I have the lovely smile with the innocent look. The teeth and the look are back again only worse, as he moves down to the gap in the long counter, He shouts, 'Didn't I tell you to get out?'

I'm beginning to think that maybe he's talking to me. But that couldn't be, sure what did I do?

There he is coming out of the gap down to me. I'm turning my head everywhere in an effort to find whatever it is or who-ever it is he's telling to get out, when I got a box into the ear that sends me flying out the door. The kind of a box Pop would give me. I'm going back to Mr. O'Leary with my hand over my ear, thinking Mr. O'Leary is going to give me the sack because the auld fellow is going to ring and complain me. It's just as well; I didn't give him my name, because Pop would surely give me one in the other ear.

I'm telling Mr. O'Leary, 'I got a box in the ear for nothing, I swear to God, Mr. O'Leary. I just asked him for the elbow grease. I told him you sent me over and he told me to get out. I swear to God Sir I didn't do anything. Honest Sir!'

Mr. O'Leary still has a tiny smirk on one side of his face as he asks,

'Who told you to go over there?'

'You did Sir.'

'No, I didn't.' I said, McMahon's. What the hell would Nes-tor's be doing with elbow grease?'

'But Sir,'

'Go on, get down to McMahon's.'

I'm walking out the door and around the corner into Bedford Row muttering away, calling Mr. O'Leary every rotten name I can think of. My first day at the Five Star is turning out to be a right disaster.

When I get into McMahon's there's three departments. I don't know which one to go to, to get the elbow grease. There's a man behind one of them. He has a coat just like Mr. O'Leary, only its tan in colour he has a grin on his face just like Mr. O'Leary, 'There's plenty of elbow grease over in the paint department'.

'How much do you want?' I'm asked.

'One gallon,' Sir.

The man in the paint department opens the door at the back and shouts, 'Have we any elbow grease out there?'

'... no,' comes the answer. 'We've sold the last of it. Come back next week when we'll have a delivery, or try Spaight's across the road in Henry Street. ... 'I'll walk over to Spaight's, the shop that has the money put into the wooden canisters that fly across the ceiling on wire to the office, for the girl to send it back again with the change and receipt.

'A gallon of elbow grease Sir,'

'The man behind the counter say's 'I think we only have it in pints.

'Will you be able to manage eight pints young man?'

'If we put them in a box,' 'I will Sir.'

'He's gone off to get them for me. There's people being served by other men and they're all looking and smiling. I'm thinking isn't everybody in great form except the miserable old so-and-so over in Nestor's. The man comes back and says, 'he's sorry, he says there were eight pints of elbow grease out there in the store this morning'. He asks the other assistants if they sold pints of elbow grease to anyone. They shout back the word 'No,' laugh and carry on serving their customers who'll laugh as well.

I'll go up to Boyd's. They'll surely have some. Boyd's haven't any either and send me down to Hassett's. Hassetts haven't any and tell me to try Newsome's. They said they never kept it and sent me over to O'Malley's in Catherine Street, who said I should try Daly's in William Street. It's four o'clock now and Mr. O'Leary will be wondering where the blazes I am and will give me the sack. But I'm telling him that I tried every shop in town and there wasn't a drop of elbow grease to be got in Limerick. He said, 'It's OK' that while I was out somebody else got it off. It will be another twelve months before I realise what elbow grease is. Mr. O'Leary says that it will be another few days before people are back in the supermarket buying the weekly groceries again, as everyone will be broke after Christmas and that I should be downstairs in the vegetable department helping Mr. Reynolds.

He's not a tall man or a small one either, but he's still bigger than I am. He's got a big bundle of curly black hair that always hangs over his eyes like a bunch of grapes. He'll keep putting his fingers through it to keep it back, but it only comes down again when he talks because every time he opens his mouth his head is hopping all over the place. He has a very posh accent and addresses every female customer as madam no matter what part of Limerick they're from. Over the coming days, I'll see him helping to educate the Limerick housewives name the fruits and veg they've never seen or heard of before. It won't be long before he has a crowd around him asking 'What are they Mr. Reynolds? Where do they come from?' He'll have a green yoke in one hand and a red one in the other saying, 'Now, Madams these are called green and red peppers'. There'll be whispers in the background saying 'A green and red what'? A voice will ask, 'What would you be doing with one of those yokes? Can you eat them like an apple or a pear?'

'Well you could try Madam, they don't taste very nice. They are not a fruit even though they may look like one. They are a vegetable. You can slice them; throw them into the pot with meat to make a whole new taste for the tongue to experience'.

A voice will come from the back; 'Jesus, if I was to give those to my fellow, he'd say I was trying to poison him.'

Another will ask what those big long green things over there are. Mr. Reynolds will pick a big fat one up in his hand that has a bend on top of it, hold it high in the air for everyone to see, then say 'this lady's is a cucumber' and most of the women are having a right laugh.

Others walk away in disgust, shaking their heads. It will last the bones of an hour while he tells them what countries they come from, and places they never heard of before, just like myself.

He addresses me the same way every time, saying 'Now my good man' before he asks me to do something. I'm wondering does he know I'm the messenger boy, but sure, he must. Won't he be asking me to take deliveries all over Limerick very soon? He has an assistant called Mike Nolan who dresses like a Teddy boy with the black or blue suede shoes. He has jet-black hair that he's always combing back, just like Elvis, but looks more like Roy Orbison because of the thick black glasses he wears. He'll be downstairs every day throwing the half dozen apples, pears, oranges, tomatoes, and spuds into clear plastic bags and putting a price on them. He'll always sing the latest pop songs that will drown out the bloody awful Christmas songs that we loved before Christmas but can't stand the sound of anymore. He's a good four years older than me and is decent to me from the first day I started; with advice like who to keep away from, like Mr. Fitzmaurice, the sour ol' grump who parked his arse and desk up near the boiler to keep himself warm in the awful weather we're sure to get any day now. He's the fellow with all the coloured magic markers and makes the signs that are set up upstairs everywhere with the latest special offers. He says I'm to keep away from him, as he'll have me running out to his house in Rathbane every day with a few cigarettes or a bob or two for his wife. He won't even look at you while he's asking or say thank you when you come back with the cold hands and soaking wet. I'm not to expect a tip because he's as tight as a duck's arse and that, he's so mean he wakes up every night to see if he lost any sleep.

After that, there's Joe Rae and his girl who works at the checkouts. They'll be getting married soon. I'll be singing to him every time he passes. Joe, Rae, me, fá, so, law, tea, dough. He gives me thump on the shoulder and tells me to shut up or I'll be sorry. But Mike Nolan says that I'm not to worry, that Joe is a decent ol' skin. Then there's good looking, who keeps the shelves packed every day. God love this poor misfortune but everything he has on his face is out of proportion. It's so bad I can't say it reminds me of anything in the animal kingdom. His head is a bit like my own, too big with one ear bigger than the other. His hair has no waves or curls, and goes in every direction, like a sod of grass with all kinds of things growing out of it. He's got holes like volcanoes on the skin of his face and teeth that shoot out over his bottom lip. When he opens his mouth, I think he has gravel in his throat. He never laughs and I'm not surprised, because if I had a face like that I wouldn't be laughing either. I wouldn't be applying for a job in here either. Come to think of it, how come he got a job in here when others who applied for it didn't and I'm wondering what they looked like.

Mike and myself with Mike still wearing the Roy Orbison black glasses and curly hair outside the site were the Five Star used to be in O'Connell Street

Then there's the bully, the big fellow who dresses like Mr. O'Leary and wants to lick his arse every day, with 'Ye Mr. O'Leary', and 'No, Mr. O'Leary, 'What did you say Mr. O'Leary?' Everybody hates him because he's a snitch and Mike says I'm going to hate him too because he'll boss me around, shout at me, and give me a thump. I know it's because I'm the messenger boy. I'll take it for the first few days. After that, I'm telling him what to do with himself because I'm not taking any orders from that arse-licker. He's got me in a headlock real tight and won't let me go. 'Say you're sorry for telling me to fupp off, and I'll let you go'. Mr. Reynolds tells him to leave me go but he won't. Then I go limp, like I passed out.

'Now look what you've done,' says Mr. Reynolds.'

I can hear Mr. Reynolds telling him he's in right trouble now.

'Go up and get Mr. O'Leary, Mike', says Mr. Reynolds.

'Ah for goodness sake, Mr. Reynolds he's only pretending.' says the bully.

But I know by the sound of his voice that he's worried.

When Mr. O'Leary arrives, Mrs. Doyle is kneeling on the floor by my side, sprinkling some water on my face. Then she rubs a damp cloth around my neck and I can hear good looking's voice as well. The girls from the checkout have arrived right behind Mr. O'Leary. I'm not coming around until that bastard gets a right good telling off in front of all the staff that has gathered around me.

'What happened here?' shouts Mr. O'Leary. 'What's Taylor doing on the floor?'

Mr. Reynolds tells him everything with the words, 'I told him to leave him alone'.

'I think we should get a Doctor,' says Mrs. Doyle.

Mr. O'Leary says to Mike to go upstairs to the office and tell Dennis to phone for an ambulance, and be quick about it. I'm listening for the sound of Mike tearing up the stairs, this is working out much better than I thought. I can hear the bully starting to cry, telling Mr. O'Leary that he's sorry.

'Oh you'll be sorry all right boyo. You better hope and pray that he's going to be alright because if he's not, you won't be coming back here tomorrow.'

By this time, I decide to put into action the drama training I got in St. Joseph's Boy Scouts and the Christmas plays and put this ejit out of his misery. I start by moving a leg a small bit, then a light groan, then place my hand on my throat while making a difficult to breathe sound that will be followed by a very course cough. I open my eyes for a minute and say with a husky voice, 'Where am I?' and it's going down great. There's all kinds of heads looking down at me asking different questions like, 'Is he alright?' 'Are you alright Paddy? God love you but you're very pale.' 'Does he need a drink of water?' Now I have a look of total confusion as I ask what happened. I hear Mr. Reynolds telling the bully that he's very lucky that I'm starting to come around. The ambulance men have arrived and they want to take me out to the Regional Hospital on a stretcher. That's where I forget about the acting and make a miraculous recovery.

The following morning at nine o'clock, I'm out washing the terrazzo floor as I've been doing for the last week and a half. A man with a briefcase stops and asks me how old I am. He looks like a detective the way he's dressed.

'Well young man, are you going to tell me how old you are?'

I'm stunned, why does he want to know my age? I had done nothing wrong. But I stutter out the words, 'f-f- fifteen Sir.'

'Are you going to the one day?'

'The what Sir.'?

The one day, have you ever heard of the oneday young man?

'The one day what Sir?'

'The one day a week'

'What's that Sir?'

'It's a school,' he shouts.

Oh Jesus no I'm thinking, I'm going back to school again.

'What's the manager's name young man?'

I tell him it's Mr. O'Brien and he'll get him upstairs at the back of the supermarket.

Mr. O'Leary is out wanting to know who I was talking to and what did he want?

'He's after sacking me Sir, he says I have to go back to school,' but before I can say another word, the man with the briefcase is back telling Mr. O'Leary that his name is Tadhg Small and that he works for the Government and that from next week, I have to go to the oneday a week school up in Cecil Street. I never heard of a school up in Cecil Street before. Mr. O'Leary says that I'm not sacked and that I only have to go to school one day a week and that will be on Wednesday and that it won't affect my half-day on the Thursday. I'm thinking I don't want to be at school five minutes, never mind a day.

When my first day arrives. I'm up in Cecil Street. At a building right beside the Royal Cinema. There are messenger boys from all over Limerick and a rough looking bunch too. When the teacher comes in, he's roaring like an elephant cursing and swearing. He's Mr. Mulcahy from St. Joseph's Boy Scouts Committee. I've never seen him like this before. He's like all the other committee members, kind and helpful. This place is nothing like Sexton St.

Tadhg Small with violin

School or John the Baptist's either. He has to shout three or four times before all the boys shut up. They're sneering behind his back. The classroom is huge with several large wooden benches with huge iron vices on both sides. There are saws, hammers, mallets, wood-chisels of all shapes and sizes locked away in a large glass cabinet against the wall. Another wall has wood all the way to the ceiling stacked by the wall and it just dawned on me I'm not going to be doing the stuff I hated at the Christian Brothers Schools. I'm going to be doing woodwork just like they do in the Tech School above in O'Connell Avenue. Boy am I going to love this!

I'll be the first in every Wednesday morning waiting for the doors to open. Mr. Mulcahy will be thumping and pucking everyone except myself. Sometimes he'll put his head in his hands and I can hear him asking God what he ever did to deserve this job. My third Wednesday is the one that will have Mr. Mulcahy showing all the other lads my work. He shouts at them and asks them why they can't produce work like this?

'Look at how neat and tidy it is. When this man comes here every Wednesday he comes to learn, not like you lot who don't want to learn anything'.

I'm top of the class every Wednesday and there's none of my teachers or mates from my old class to see it.

I'm thinking of the time Brother Kenny brought the brains from Class A who had an answer to every question like a parrot and getting everyone right, just to show the rest of us what a bunch of ejits we were. I'm thinking of the look on his face, that smug look with a sneer for which we all hated him and now I don't want to come here anymore. I never thought I would be top of the class at anything. These fellows in here won't like me now, not that they were fond of me anyway; with the kind of clothes I'm wearing ever since the day Mam saw me on the messenger bike heading up William Street. and made me wear good clothes, because she bought me a pair of boots, an overcoat, a new shirt and tie because she says she doesn't want her son's arse hanging out of his pants, freezing to death in the winter. There's new gloves too, expensive ones, leather with fur on the inside. She paid for them out of the twenty-five bob I give her every week. I want to give her more money because she won't be able to buy herself something nice in Todd's or Roche's Stores. I won't get the breastbones or eye bones anymore either every Thursday because she says I'm working now. I'm bringing money into the house and I should be eating better. The afternoons in the 'one day' are bloody awful for lots of reasons. Most of the messenger boys take the evening off even though they could loose their jobs. There are only four or five in the dreary classroom. With the awful dreary Johnny Gobbler who wants to teach the few of us the imposssible Irish language.

The one day a week school in Upper Cecil Street

The bike with the basket in the front that has my arse in an awful state from the saddle and muscles in my legs where I never thought I had muscles before is now trying to cope with the snow and frost people say they've never seen before. It's the third week of January 1963. There are trucks on the main roads of the city with Corporation workers on the back throwing salt that will stop the trucks and cars skidding all over the place. But I'll be up around the railway station, where I am every morning; looking for the two boxes of frozen chickens that will come on the train from Tullamore for the Five Star Supermarket. They've a new van to deliver the bigger boxes of groceries. Dick the driver says that 'It's a bloody disgrace asking a poor young lad like myself to go to the station in weather like this, when there's an empty van outside the front of the shop every morning'. I'll walk with the bike at my side, falling on my arse several times. Other times I'll be under the bike. The CIE workers will put the parcels into the big square basket because I could never lift one of them myself, I can hear them saying, 'How the hell is he going to get that lot down to O'Connell Street on his own in this weather?' I'm asking myself the same question. I'll fall three or four times every day, my fingers frozen even though they have the fur inside the gloves. People will come over to my assistance every time I fall. They'll say, 'I have a mind to go down to that fupping Five Star Supermarket and give the manager a piece of my mind'. I'll have to say to them again and again, 'Please don't Sir, I'll loose my job'. I'll think of the lads down at John the Baptist School nice and warm next to the big roasting radiators and wish I was there.

After the end of the second week of the awful weather, Mr. O'Leary says that the manager is looking for me. Mr. O'Brien says that I'm getting the sack because I'm delaying too long with the chickens that they've nearly thawed out by the time I arrive at the shop. My hands and legs are delighted but my pocket isn't! I'll come home from the Five Star Supermarket and tell Mam and Pop what happened. Mam looks at the ceiling and says, 'Jesus, Mary and Holy St. Joseph thank you'. She'll look at me with a smile and say, 'Pa, how did you stick it so long?' Pop starts cursing and says he's going down to that bastard of a manager in the morning and give him a dig. Over the next few days I'm standing at the window looking out at the awful weather and thanking God my hands and feet are so close to the fire.

Mam will be begging me to go back down to Brother Fahy and see if he will take me back for the rest of the year. Nan will be egging her on all the time, with words like, 'he's too young to be working'. I wish to God she'd shut up, because if she's not going on at me, she's moaning and groaning about something else, especially the pains she says she has. She's been here two weeks waiting for word to come from the hospital to go in and have the operation. She must have had a hundred operations in her lifetime. I'm wondering is there any of her insides left at all? It's my second day at home looking out at the awful weather and I can't take anymore of the mood that Nan is in over the pains she says she has. She sleeps with Jet in the double bed that's pushed against the wall in the room that's next to the toilet at the back of our house.

River Shannon frozen over

Jetta has a job at the Limerick Leader. She'll come to the table every morning for breakfast with her eyes hanging out of her head because Nan will be in and out of the bed four or five times a night to use the toilet. Jet says it takes Nan five minutes to get out of bed and another ten to get back into it and how the whole process of taking off a half a dozen clothes and putting them on again, accompanied by the 'awful moans that don't sound like moans at all' has her going crazy and very cranky at work.

*Me on a old messenger bike, who knows it could have been the
one I had at the Five Star*

When Pop comes home, the laughter that's always here when
the two of them get together is dead and gone. If Pop says something funny, Nan might start to laugh and then realise she's giving the game away and starts calling on Jesus, Mary and Joseph
to give her some help from the terrible pain in her stomach. It's
hardest of all on Mam who has to wait on her hand and foot,
twenty four hours a day and will ask me, now that I have nothing to do, to keep an eye on her while she goes into town.

'Sure can't I do the shopping for you Mam? It'll give me
something to do.'

Mam will give me the money and the shopping bag and a list of things she needs. I'm gone out the door out of earshot of Nan's mouth and what's coming out of it, in the good clothes Mam got me to keep me warm.

We'll wait every day for Pop at lunch and supper time to tell us that the Regional Hospital rang Maureen Fay at the Bedford Bar for Nan to go in and have her operation. And if word does come, Maureen will have to ring Madden's Pub in Cappamore to give word to Uncle Peter to bring Nan to the hospital in his big truck. Mam won't ask the neighbour, Mrs. Jones across the road, to use the phone she had installed six months ago because her hall has been turned into a public phone booth. Since word got around the whole of Garryowen about the lovely cream coloured phone she only had to wait three years for, and is now in the hands of every neighbour who has a son or daughter in England, Australia or America that wants to book a call with the operator for a certain time the following day. Now, Mrs. Jones, who's husband has a great job and needs the phone for his work, and has her neighbours in the best of comforts with carpets and central heating for all who stand in her hall talking for ages to a loved one on the other side of the world while smoking their brains out in the lovely warmth, and not having to stand in an awful draughty phone box at the top of Garryowen with two or three panes of broken glass. If Mrs. Jones gets a break from the ringing of the door bell, the phone will be ringing with a call from England or somewhere else asking her would she mind giving a message to a family not too far away. Mrs. Jones has to put her coat on, with an umbrella if it is raining and try a half dozen homes before she finds the right one. Then give the terrible bad news - they'll want to ring back. Mrs. Jones says, 'Sure you can use my phone'. Now Mrs. Jones has a bawling female with a dozen family members in her hall that she has to make tea for. Everyone will want their turn to speak to the relative on the other side of the planet. After the bereaved neighbours have gone home, Mrs. Jones has an ashtray full of half-smoked fag ends, teacups, saucers and a bigger phone bill because, in their grief, no one thought of asking Mrs. Jones how much they owed her. Mrs. Jones is getting rightly cheesed off! She has to have the phone because of her husband's job. He's on call all the time. Now she has the phone that takes the money, just like the one at the top of the hill so that she won't have to ask her neighbours for money when they forget to give it to her to pay a bill that arrives every month and is three or four times what it should have been. And now she has no problem at all letting people use the phone as long as they pay for it. But the people in her hall that have to talk to their relatives haven't enough money for the call and are asking Mrs. Jones would she mind giving them a loan of 2/6 or even 5 bob so they can finish the call. That they will send one of the kids back with it as soon as they go home, but half of them won't and Mrs. Jones is worse off than ever.

CHAPTER 3

Pop is six years off the drink and it's hard to remember the days when he came home looking for an argument with anyone that gave him the time. The headaches that Mam used to get are few and far between now and the only time she has to worry is when Cork might be playing in the Munster Final out in the Gaelic Grounds. It will bring with it Uncle Eddie O'Callaghan, who is married to Mam's sister in Cork and is another bloody alcoholic according to everybody who knows him. He'll always call to Garryowen drunk out of his skull before a ball is pucked for a free feed so he can spend more money on liquor. Nan says that she can't stand the sight of him because he's a sly ol' git. And full of old shite and wonders what her daughter ever saw in him. And isn't it grand that he's living in Cork that she doesn't have to see his slimy ol' face. Mam doesn't want him in the house either because he won't leave Pop alone with the invites to go to the Bedford so Pop can buy him a few pints and start another week or two with Pop on the tear!

And I cant wait for the Munster Final because I'm old enough now to be down in the Bedford, washing glasses behind the bar and earning two pounds for the day, listening to drunks begging me to fill them a pint. I'll try and tell them that I wouldn't know the first thing about it and that I'm not allowed, but they'll keep on asking. Mrs. Fay says that I'm not to be looking at them, that I'm to keep my head down and work away. But it's no use, they'll reach over and tap me on the head and when I look at them, their faces will have a look of starvation, like they're going to die any minute if they don't get a drink.

Pop has the house done a second time since Aunt Eileen and Uncle Dave came home from America. The concrete shed at the side of the house where the coal is kept for the fire that heats the water and keeps the smell that Mam calls BO away from our armpits and other places, also has the tools that Pop uses every night when he comes home to keep him occupied and away from the drink. Mam makes the tea every half hour admiring whatever it is he's doing. He'll be cursing and swearing about a tool he'd had in his hand only the other night, and send me out to the shed looking for it. I'll be out there making all the sounds and noises like I'm turning the whole place upside down, looking for a hand tool that I know is not there, because I went to the Pawn Shop in Parnell Street with it yesterday. I couldn't believe how easy it was to get 2/6 for it. I'll be there again next week with his saw, hammer, vice grips and the week after with his screwdrivers, wood planes until I have the whole lot pawned because I need the money for fags. He'll buy more tools put a new lock and bolt on the door and hang the key on a shelf over the cooker in the kitchen and mutter away about how they never had keys in his day when you could leave a door open anywhere or anytime because people were so honest! And when he catches the fupper who's stealing his tools he'll break his fupping neck. And that he doesn't care whose son it is.

But I won't heed the warning because I'm addicted to stealing and how easy it is. I need the fags I'll buy every day. Now I'm going to have to figure out how I'll get the new tool to the Pawn Office for the two or five bob I'll get every week. The first week I'll take the new saw still in the cardboard cover. I'll have it under my coat and down the seat of my pants and walk with the hands in my pockets and whistle while I walk, kicking the odd stone on my way to the pawn shop because Jett, James or even a neighbour might see me and give the game away. It would cause Pop to give me a thumping like I've never had before. I'll leave the door with the lock hanging loose like someone forgot to close it after they came in to get a bucket of coal for the fire. When I come home with five bob in my pocket and the guilty conscience with the cool walk and innocent face, I'll say, 'Someone left the shed door open and I think your new saw is gone Pop'. He'll walk out the back door in a hurry fupping away under his breath; come back ten minutes later after pulling the whole shed apart, shouting his head off at everyone, including Mam, about closing the bloody door of the shed after they being in there. Mam is telling him to calm down, that it's only a saw and can't he get another one tomorrow. Pop says he's going to put a stop to all the stealing once and for all. None of us know what he's talking about, until the next day when he arrives home with three buckets and another new saw. He tells me I'm to fill each bucket to the top with coal and that I'm to give him the keys of the shed that he can keep in his pocket every day. That means my supply of goods for the two pawn shops has dried up and it's just as well the job at the Five Star came when it did. Otherwise I might have had to go back to the bus station and the rubbish pile for fag ends with lipstick on them.

It's been a week since I got the sack and there's no sign of the phone call we're all waiting for. Nan says she just can't stand the waiting anymore and says she going to tell the Doctor to take whatever it is he wants to cut out of her without any anaesthetic. What difference would it make to be in pain on an operating table for a few hours against the pain she's been having over the last three weeks? I know Pop, Jetta, and James are thinking the same about the pain as myself that we have to listen to every day and night with Jetta exhausted for the want of a good night's sleep. I can't take it any longer with the longing for the fags and no money to satisfy the awful craving and looking out the window at the terrible weather and a weekend gone with nothing to do, I'm asking Pop when I can go working with himself and Lar. He says' they haven't enough work for three at the moment but it shouldn't be too long before I'll be needed. I'll go down town every day looking for a job with more lies about Mam dying and Pop having no work. Someone asked me for my name and when I said 'Taylor' they asked 'Are you anything to Harry Taylor the painter?' I stutter out the words, 'He's my uncle' and get out of there as fast as I can. It seems my father is known everywhere. After three days I wind up in Thomas Street at the Bremen Motors and get a job cleaning cars for Dan Ryan.

I'm looking at him inside in his office talking on the phone and he's looking great in his black suit, collar and tie. I'm thinking how he started out as a messenger boy and look at him now. And I'm saying to myself, I'll be like him some day. But right now I have cars to clean and I'll only be getting thirty bob a week a whole pound less than I got at the Five Star and that means Mam will be down ten bob every week when I take the wage home for the first time. There's another young fellow here with blonde hair called Paddy. We become good friends and like Mike Nolan down at the Five Star he'll fill me in on the do's and don'ts.

Site of the old Bremen Motors in Thomas Street.

He says the main car cleaner here is Jimmy. I'm to be careful of him because he has ulcers in his stomach that give him a bad temper, especially after he's eaten jam tarts that his doctor told him to keep well away from at the tea break in the morning. Then he tells me that he's Dan Ryan's half-brother. I have the look on my face, with the comment, 'Oh yeah, right', like I know what he's talking about. I'll wait till I go home that evening to ask Mam and Pop what a half-brother is. Nan butts in with the answer, 'A half-brother is a step-brother'. Now I'm totally confused and ask 'What's a step-brother?' Pop says a step brother is when you have the same father but a different mother. And now I'm more confused than ever. I'm saying,

'How can you have a different mother? Sure your mother is your mother, how can you have a different mother?'

Nan starts laughing, then moaning with the 'Jesus, Mary and holy St. Joseph, did you hear that, how can you have a different mother?'

Then Pop says, 'You can't have a different mother but you can have another mother'.

Then Nan shouts, 'Oh Jesus Harry will you stop'. She's killing herself laughing while holding her side. Oh 'Jesus, Mary and holy St. Joseph, Harry you'll have me dead before I get to the hospital', and on she goes repeating what Pop said. 'Jesus, you can't have a different mother but you can have another mother'.

'Don't mind them Pa,' says Mam, and explains what it means.

After she finishes she'll ask me, 'Do you understand?'

I'll say 'I do', but I'm not sure.

Dan Ryan walks around the garage every day in his black suit with the hands behind his back, making us all nervous. Then he'll take his right hand from behind his back and shake all his fingers violently up and down like he burned them on something. That will be accompanied by a blowing of the lips that has the sound of Cotter's horse's arse when it was parked outside our front door at one o'clock every day in Upper Carey's Road. I'm looking around at everyone to see if they've stopped working or maybe they're staring at him like I am. But they aren't. So I'm asking Pat and the half-brother Jim, 'What was that all about?'

'Oh you'll see a lot of that everyday, it's a nervous disposition.'

They're right. He's at it every twenty minutes. Sometimes he'll do it three or four times and I'm hoping he didn't get that awful ailment from his days on the messenger bike in the cold weather, and if he did, I'm goosed.

After another few days walking around the garage and having a good look to see if he's anywhere to be seen before I do the mimicking. Later that evening, Paddy's at it, tomorrow the half brother will be at it too along with half the other lads working here and I'm only there a week and I'm doing it every five minutes I'll turn around and find Mr. Ryan right behind me. He says, 'Do you like working here young man?'

'I do Sir,' I answer with a big red face and thoughts of being at home again listening to Nan's moans, who's still waiting for a bed out in the Regional Hospital because that's where I think I'll be going any minute. 'If I catch you doing that again, you'll be fired. Do I make myself clear?'

'Yes Sir', I answer and it's great to find that I still have a job.

The Yanks that come home to find their roots or visit their relatives will come to our garage to hire a car and when they bring it back a week or two later there's bound to be some spare cash under or down between the seats. I'll always make sure that I get the cars that the Yanks have had for a week or two. I'll pull the seats asunder looking for a coin or two and if it's a Thursday, I'll be gasping for a fag and I might find just enough for the price of one that I can buy in any shop in town, that will take the awful longing that I'll go through every hour.

I'll be given the keys to a car, like a Mini or a Volkswagen that's outside O'Mara's the Pig Factory, and hear the awful screams of the pigs hanging upside down by their rear legs and slowly go one by one to the man with the knife who will stick it in their throats and rip them open. They'll wriggle all over the place with blood gushing from their throats and while I'm listening to them I'll look for the coins first. Then I'll stick the key in the ignition and try to remember the instructions Paddy gave me when I asked him 'What's the first thing I should do before I start the engine?'

Paddy says that I'm to make sure the car is out of gear. I'll ask him what does out of gear mean.

He shows me and goes over it all a good few times. And here I am with my heart in my mouth and my eyes closed as I turn the key and give the accelerator pedal a rev or two and it sounds great. I'll do it another few times before I take my left foot off the clutch and find that the car is moving. I'll do the same again tomorrow, the day after, and by the end of the week, I'm able to get the car to move a few feet forward and back again.

I'm still at the shaking of my hand and the blasting of my lips, but only when I'm absolutely sure that Dan Ryan is not around. Nan is gone to hospital now, and is due her operation. She will come home a week later and tell us how she lay on the hospital table fully awake while the surgeon cut and took away whatever it was that was giving her the awful pain. And we're all wondering has she anything left in there at all with all the cuts and scars she must have from all the years she's been in and out of the place.

I'm four weeks at the Bremen Motors now. It's Thursday and my tongue is hanging out for a fag. Paddy hasn't any and neither has Jim, the half-brother with the ulcers. Each of us are a bit on the cranky side. There's a party of four from the States outside on the footpath waiting for a car to be cleaned. Paddy, Jim and myself are told to get it ready fast. 'I'll do the back seat', I'm shouting. Hop in and start to take it apart.

Jim shouts, 'What are you taking the seat apart for? We don't need to do that'.

But I ignore him and root away with my hands looking for the coins that might be there, for the one fag, that will take the longing away.

Jimmy shouts, 'Stop looking for money for fups sake, we haven't the time'.

I'll keep rooting away, not taking a bit of notice but I'm about to find out the kind of temper Jimmy with the ulcers has especially when the ulcers are erupting along with him having no fags. He grabs me by the neck of the jacket I'm wearing and pulls me out of the back seat. I fall backwards on my pole and I don't remember anything after that until I wind up looking at a very familiar face.

It's the nun with the thick glasses and the funny walk and I'm wondering what the hell is she doing down here at Bremen Motors. She has one finger in front of my eyes, asking me how many do I see. I answer and say 'one Sister' and ask her what she's doing down here in the garage. She asks me not to speak and tells me I'm back in my favourite place in 'John's Hospital, that I got a bang on the back of my head at work. She asks if I'm feeling sick and if I'm not now, I might be later. And I can throw up into a basin that she's left beside me. I'm trying to figure out how the hell I wound up here again but I can't remember no matter how hard I try. I manage to sit up on the trolley and at the same time try to figure out what the hell happened. A nurse comes and says that she's going to wash the blood off my neck and hair. That really frightens the blazes out of me. I can feel a pain at the back of my pole. I can hear a voice outside the door saying, 'Can I see him nurse please?' It's the voice of Jimmy with the ulcers. What's he doing here? The nurse asks who he is, he says that it was an accident, how it was all his fault and he wants to say he's sorry. The nurse says he can stay but only for five minutes and that I have to stay overnight for observation. I'm totally baffled.

Jimmy comes in and Paddy is with him. They're both as white as sheets. I have the big smile on my face asking them what the hell happened. Jimmy looks at Paddy and Paddy looks back at Jimmy, while Jimmy says he's sorry. I'm asking Jimmy what is he sorry about. Jimmy says that he lost the rag because his ulcers were killing him. On top of that he hasn't had a smoke all day, how the car needed to be ready for the Yanks at the door and that he'd be very grateful if I didn't say anything to his half-brother Mr. Ryan because if Dan found out he'd surely get the sack. I'm telling the two of them that I can't remember a bloody thing. And would they mind going down the road to No. 36 Claughaun Court to tell my mother that I'm in hospital again and that I'll be home tomorrow.

The nurse with the thick glasses and the funny walk says that she'll have to give me a few stitches, otherwise the bleeding won't stop. I'm saying, 'My skull must be like a road map from all the scars and stitches you given me down through the years'. While she's putting the stitches in with the stinging pain I'm feeling the top of my pole, I can't stop thinking of the reception Jimmy with the ulcers is going to get when my mother asks him what happened, and how it happened. While I'm thinking about it, I can hear Mam's voice outside asking a nurse where her son is and can she see him now.

There she is, with a face like an undertaker's, the same face that she always brings with her every time she came here with me, I'm laughing and looking at her saying, 'Mam will you stop looking at me as if I'm going to drop dead any minute. I'll be fine'. She's fussing away with a parcel that she has in her hand. She has a clean pair of pyjamas belonging to Pop along with clean underpants. 'Put them on you straight away and don't make a holy show of me.' She looks at me again and says with a bottom lip that won't stop trembling, 'A bang on the head is very dangerous you know. People have been known to fall asleep after a bang on the head and never wake up again'. The smile that was on my face trying to assure Mam is gone out the door and now I am the one looking for reassurance. I'm saying 'I bet none of them were sitting up talking away like I am'. 'Oh indeed they were, they went back to work and were found dead several hours later and that's why I'm worried about you.' She asks me if I have a headache. I tell her 'I haven't' but have I? She has me worried. I ask her does it matter where you have the headache and she wants to know what I mean. I said I have a pain in the back of my pole where I got the fall. She says that that's normal and asks have I got a pain over my eyes like, an ordinary headache. 'No Mam I haven't got one of those.'

'Are you feeling sick?'

'No Mam.'

'Tell the nurse if you feel sick, do you hear me now?'

'Yes Mam.'

Then she starts muttering under her breath about the bastard that pulled me out of the car. I'm asking her what she said to him. 'I made him and that other yoke with him wait 'til I got your things together and told him to drive me up here and gave them a mouthful when I got out of the car, I told him he'd better not put a hand on you again.' Mam says that she'll be back again in the morning and warns me again with her finger in front of my nose to be sure and tell the nurse about my head if I'm feeling sick. I can't go to sleep that night because I'm afraid I'll never wake up again. When the morning comes it is such a relief to find myself alive and well and told I could go back to work by the nun with the funny glasses who wonders how long it will be before I'll be back here again for more stitches.

Mr. Ryan wants to know how I could be so stupid as to fall out of a car backwards and hop my pole off the ground. I can see Jimmy with the ulcers, standing behind his back giving me the wink as well as having his forefinger over his mouth telling me not to give the game away. I'm telling Mr. Ryan that I don't know what happened. 'Sure I fell unconscious and wound up at St. John's Hospital Sir, I can't recall a thing at all Sir.' Mr. Ryan walks away shaking the right hand up and down blowing out through his lips saying, 'I don't know but it's very strange indeed, very, very strange'.

Mr. Hogan, our next door neighbour, is a bread-man and works for the Imperial Bakery in Sarsfield Street. He says there's a job going up the road from where I'm working at the top of Thomas Street, in another place called The Standard Garage, that they are looking for a petrol pump attendant and the pay is one pound twelve shillings and six pence a week and I'm gone up there like a bullet from a gun, looking for the name Mr. Hogan gave me, a fellow by the name of Jack Moore; who will have a snow white coat because if I get it, it will be two and six pence more every week. Mr. Hogan warns me by saying that four young lads have lost their jobs because money was missing every week and that, if I get it, I'd better be very careful. Why should I be worried? I wouldn't dream of stealing money from my employer. That would be terrible wouldn't it? I mean I might steal Pop's tools and pawn them but I wouldn't do it to an employer.

Mr. Moore, or Jack as everyone calls him, says I can have the job but I better give Dan Ryan two days notice. Jimmy with the ulcers and Paddy says they'll miss me when I'm gone because no one can mimic Dan like me. I'll miss them too after the first few days I when all I'll have to do is serve petrol eight hours a day and walk around with my hands in my pockets and look out across the road through the big window at Paddy Bremen outside the fire station with his mates, smoking fags and talking about everything and nothing while they walk up and down outside the fire station and wait for a call to take an ambulance to a car crash or whatever. Or it could be the fire engine that has all its brass and paint work gleaming because they'll get tired of the walking and the talking, and polish the living daylights out of everything.

Standard Garage

When my first day arrives, Jack tells me my job is very simple. 'Most of your sales will be accounts,' and he shows me a list on the wall of regular customers who will call daily or weekly. If they're not on the list they have to pay cash. There's a desk very similar to the one I had in school. It has two legs and is screwed against the wall. All of the top lifts up and inside there is a small box with loose change, a one pound note, and a ten shilling note as well. 'That's your float,' he says and here we go again. I'm asking myself what the hell is a float. The only float I know is what I use when I go fishing. He'll tell me about the other four young lads who only lasted a week because they were stealing money from the float. Now I know what a float is. I'm swearing on the graves of all that belong to me that I would never in a million years take a half penny from anyone and that he needn't be worried because I come from a good background and a regular Confraternity member too. Jack says 'it's great to hear I go to the Confraternity regularly', how he would trust another member of the Confraternity, that he's a life long member as well and that he never misses Mass and Holy Communion every morning.

I don't know it yet, but I'll be robbing this place blind every day for the next six months and think I'll never get caught. When the end of the day comes everybody here will be slapping me on the back saying, 'Well done.' They'll be asking me my name while shaking my hand that will be full of grease and oil from all the hands that work here fixing the cars and trucks. I'll be the most popular fellow here for months. The two gorgeous women that work upstairs in the office will want to find out what happened. I don't think I'll ever be so popular again in all my life. Jack says he has to take the readings from the two pumps every morning before a drop of petrol is sold and again in the evening just before I go home at 6.00 pm. He shows me a long brass measuring rod that has to be put into the ground, just outside the front door, where he says there are two large tanks which store all the petrol. I'm on my own now, its 9.30 and I'm nervous. Then it starts the first of the four Limerick Dairy trucks that deliver milk all over Limerick city arrive. I can see by the body language of the driver that he's in a hurry.

'Another new pump attendant', he shouts. 'I wonder how long you'll last.'

I'm looking for the tank that takes the petrol and I don't know where it is.

'Over here', he shouts. 'It's right under your nose. I always park the truck near the pump where the tank is.

'How much will I put in Sir?'

He starts roaring laughing and shouts into the cab of his truck to a young fellow about my age. 'Did you hear that? He called me Sir. Jesus! Nobody ever called me Sir before. My name is Johnny, what's yours?

'Paddy' I answer. He tells me to fill it up, that all the trucks have to be filled up every morning and when I've finished I'll ask him to wait and sign the docket. I'm looking at the clock on the face of the pump to see how much petrol he got and before I can write anything down he says, 'Give me that and I'll sign it. You can fill it in after I'm gone. I have more deliveries to do and the sooner I'm gone, the sooner I'll be finished. I hope you'll be here tomorrow because the last four guys that were here before you only lasted a few days.' I was bad enough before he said that, now I'm a bloody bag of nerves and I'm trying to figure out how could anybody lose their job on the first few days. And why would they steal on the first or second day?

It's only minutes before another milk truck arrives. He's in a hurry too and has similar comments about how long I'll last here. After another ten minutes, the other two have arrived and gone, I'm checking everything to make sure I got it right, like the four dockets, do they have today's date, are they signed and now I'm looking out the big window terrified that I mightn't be here tomorrow.

An hour passes and not another soul wants petrol from the two pumps outside the door. I'm in the show-room that has two new cars for sale, behind the large glass window, looking into Thomas Street. I've the hands in my pockets going over everything Jack told me. I don't want to be told I've no job once six o'clock comes. There's another building next door called The National Garage. It has two petrol pumps as well. The young fellow in there seems to be much busier than me. I'm a bit more relaxed now.

There's a young guy heading up Thomas Street on a messenger bike wearing a brown shop assistant's coat. As he gets nearer I can just make out the name of the shop he works for that's written on his bike, J & G Boyd, William Street, Limerick.

Looking at him, my mind has gone back to January and the cold weather my body had to endure working for that ol' bastard O'Leary in the Five Star. I'm thinking about the two pounds ten shillings a week I got and how good the weekends were. And if I got a decent, understanding supervisor I could still be there. But life is getting better now. The messenger boy's bike seems to be heading in my direction; maybe he has a parcel for the garage. He makes his way past the pumps and into the entrance that's almost one hundred feet long before it widens out on both sides that has the car spaces for all the mechanics who work here. When he passes my door that has glass in the top portion, I can see that he doesn't have a delivery, so I assume he's here to collect something. He leans the bicycle against the wall that's opposite my door, looks over at me and immediately turns away. I was just about to flick my head sideways and say, 'How's it going?' but I won't bother my arse now. He puts his hands into the large pockets of the brown coat he's wearing and walks up and down whistling away, like he's waiting for something.

At that precise moment I can hear Jack shouting my name. When I look up to his office that's at the end of the showroom and a good eighty feet away, he's calling me up with his hand. When I get to him he says, 'Mr. O'Connell the owner, told me to be sure and tell you about so-and-so who's not to get anymore petrol on his account unless he pays'. And I'm to go down to my desk and scratch his name off the list. When I arrive back at my desk, there, standing against it, is the messenger boy with his hands still in his pockets. My first reaction is that he must be looking for a parcel or message, then I'm a bit suspicious.

I'm not a suspicious person by nature; in fact I'll always think the best of everyone, that is until the proof is overwhelming. I haven't even thought of the other guys who lost their jobs over the last four weeks, that is until I see my desk top which has a hook and eye type latch for a lock and the latch is resting on the hook. That's not the way I left it. Without saying a word, I open the top up and the float that was there this morning is gone. I turn to the messenger boy and say very strongly, 'OK out with it.'

He says, 'Out with what?'

I'm speaking stronger - nearly shouting 'the fupping' money that was here, out with it now!'

'I haven't any money, I swear to God. Search me!' he says with a big so-called innocent head on him.

'OK', I answer and start to put my hands in his pocket.

He pulls away and says, 'ok, ok I'll give it back,' putting his hands into one of the pockets and giving me back the money.

After placing the money back in the tray that's inside my desk. I check it out to make sure its all there.

'Please don't tell anyone, please, I'll never do it again, honest to God, I promise.'

I tell him to fupp off and never come back again.

He's gone, banging the door behind him, hops on his bike and off he goes down Thomas Street like a rocket.

I've barely enough time to think about it, when a strange voice shouts down at me, 'What the fupp was that all about?' The voice has knocked me out of the shock and trance I was in and now I have a confused look on my face. I don't answer.

'Do you hear me talking to you?'

'I'm sorry, what did you say?'

You heard me, 'What did that little fupper want?'

'Oh, he ah, he was looking for a parcel.'

I know I don't have the look on my face that convinces him that I'm telling the truth. He raises his voice and says, 'Did you catch that fupper stealing?'

'No'.

'Listen here now,' comes the voice, only this time he's eyeball-ing me with his finger under my nose, 'four grand young lads just like yourself, decent, well-brought up lads from good homes lost their jobs because everybody including myself thought they were stealing. But it was that little fupper all the time. Do you realise you'd be gone tonight too?'

It hits me like a ton of bricks. He's right. What was I think-ing of? Now Jack is longside the mechanic and wants to know what's going on. So I have to tell them every detail. Jack is shak-ing me by the hand while tapping my shoulder. The mechanic shakes my hand too and tells me that his name is George and he's sorry for giving out to me but if he hadn't given out to me the little fupper from Boyd's would have got away scot-free. Jack says that he's going up to see Mr. O'Connell the boss to tell him the news.

It's not long before every mechanic in the place is down at my desk wanting to know everything. I'll be blue in the face going over it with everyone. I never knew there were so many working here. Some who work near the front door say they used to see him coming in every day and leave his bike against the wall and stand around with the hands in the pockets of the brown coat and never gave it a second thought and that he might have been responsible for the missing money every week. I can hear Jack's voice coming down the stairs, from the office that's not too far away. There's a mad scatter of bodies that were gathered all around me, making me the centre of attention and me loving every minute of it. Jack's voice is getting closer and when I turn around, the man who Jack said he was going to see has his hand out while saying, 'Congratulations young man, well done.' It must be Mr. O'Connell.

He speaks very posh and is dressed in a manner that would turn your head. His skin is like that of a man from a sunny climate, hair that's black and shiny. His shirt is red and the tie too, while his suit is light grey and black shining shoes. There's a white handkerchief hanging out of the top pocket of his jacket and a pink carnation on the lapel. My nose can't help but take the strong smell of whatever it is he's thrown on his face. He's shaking my hand up and down several times with a huge grin that shows his brilliant white teeth. 'Jack has been telling me all about you, how you caught that little scoundrel from Boyd's in William Street. He wants to know how I knew it was that blighter. My brain is telling me to make the most of this situation and it's also reminding me of one of Pop's great sayings that opportunity only knocks once.

So I start telling him when the messenger boy who cycled into the entrance and left his bicycle against the wall, and just stood there doing nothing I became suspicious. Then Jack called me over to his office so, I kept an eye on him. While I'm repeating the rest of the story, Mr. O'Connell keeps looking over at Jack nodding his head in an approving way. When I'm finished Mr. O'Connell says, 'Well now Paddy you know that your awareness and good work will bring back the very good reputation that those grand lads had when they came here to work'. He looks at Jack and says, 'We're going to have to write to them and their families apologise and tell them that if they need a reference for another job we'll be glad to give it'. Mr. O'Connell shakes my hand again, turns to Jack and says, 'I'd say we have a good one here Jack, he's only here a couple of hours and look what's happened'. Mr. O'Connell thanks me again and walks away, saying that they'll have to contact the Guards. I'm thinking if it hadn't been for George the mechanic, Mr. O'Connell would be pointing at the door telling me to get lost and asking 'Is there any honest young fellow left in Limerick at all?'

The two girls who work in the office upstairs are with me now. They say they heard what happened but that they'd prefer to hear it from the horse's mouth. I've got two good busted women, smelling gorgeous listening to my every word and there's words coming out of my mouth that I haven't told anyone else. Talk about exaggeration! I can't believe I'm saying things and the more they gasp and put their hands over their mouths the bigger the lies I'll tell. I can't help it, I turning myself into Superman and they're buying the whole lot! After another one and a half hours, two Guards are in Jack's office. He'll bring them down to me; I'll have to tell the whole story again. But I don't care; I'm loving every minute of it. I told a different version to so many people, I can't remember the truth. It takes the Guards about two hours to get out of me what really happened; and I'm knackered. When I go home that evening I'm at it again, with the lies and the exaggeration. I don't think that I've spoken so much in all my life before.

When my second day at the Standard Garage comes the four milk trucks will arrive and be gone again in no time at all; the drivers scribbling their signatures on the docket any old way, as long as they can get away fast. There will be another hour before my next customer arrives in a car that's built like a tank. He looks at me and asks with a smile, 'When did you start?' and wants to know how long I'll be here before I'm gone like the others that were here before me. I'm telling him about the events of the morning and I'm off again with the lies and the exaggeration only this time I gave the messenger boy two digs, kicked him out the door and followed him half way down Thomas Street as he cycled out of my reach. Your man is amazed and throws in the odd expression in between like, 'No way!' or 'Go on outta that!' 'Fair dues to you', 'You should have given him a kick up the arse as well'.

I'm asking him what kind of a car this is and where can I find the petrol tank. He says it's a Borgward and it has two tanks. Now I want to know why a car would have two petrol tanks when all the others would only have one. He's gesturing with his hand, like he's got a pint glass in it, while putting it to his mouth. It's because the engine has a terrible thirst and if it didn't have the second tank it would be no time at all before the tank would be sucking air and says the Jaguar car needs two petrol tanks as well. He'll open both caps with a key and I don't think I've ever seen that in a car before either. 'Fill them up, the two of them please,' and when I finish there's nearly thirty gallons gone. He says he's a regular customer, twice a week in fact and unlike the four drivers coming in the morning, he'll take his time signing the docket making sure everything is right before he drives away.

It's nearly 12.00 the following day there's a woman outside the two glass doors that allows me to see if a car or a truck arrives outside looking for juice. I don't know if I'm imagining it or not. But she's got a white handkerchief over her nose and I think she's crying. She knocks on the glass and when I open the one that's closest to my desk and say, 'Yes, Misses. Do you need some petrol?' She shakes her head from side to side, blows her nose and asks if I was the one who caught her son stealing money yesterday. I nod my head and say, 'Yes Misses'. She wants to know if I would consider giving her son a second chance and promises that he will never do it again. She's got one hand on my arm, with the snotty handkerchief and the other is putting the sign of the cross on her forehead, chest and shoulders. I'm looking at this poor woman who's well dressed and I'm thinking this could be my mother, pleading on my behalf if I got into trouble and now I'm wishing I never caught the so and so at all. But before I can say another word, Jack has arrived and wants to know what's going on.

I'm telling him that this is the messenger boy's mother and she wants me to drop the charges. Jack puts one hand on her shoulder and says it's nothing to do with me 'it's out of our hands.' He tells her about the other lads who all lost their jobs all because of her son. 'The guards were here and took a statement yesterday,' and he's very sorry he can't do anything for her. We'll watch the poor woman leave while listening to Jack fupping and blinding asking what does the woman take him for at all? That little fupper needs to be taught a lesson once and for all. And he's going to make sure he gets that lesson.

But I won't be right for the rest of the day. I can't get that woman out of my mind. I'll tell Mam when I go home how I feel responsible. Mam says, 'Now look Pa, how can it be your fault? Do you not see that he would go on doing that until he was caught and if it wasn't for you another few lads along with yourself would loose their jobs?' She's right, but it's still hard. I'll sit in front of the black and white television all night and won't be able to concentrate on anything. I'll take it into bed with me later that night. I'll toss and turn in my sleep and when I wake up the next morning the awful feeling is gone.

Jack is at my desk cursing and swearing because he says the figures from the two pumps don't make up with the sales from yesterday along with the readings from the brass rod that's put into the ground every morning. I don't know what he's talking about. All I've done for the past two days is put petrol into cars and trucks then, made sure that the small bit of paper records it all. I'm doing it the way he told me to do it but he's fupping like a trooper and hopping the biro off the wall shouting, Jesus, Mary and Holy St. Joseph, I've only just come from receiving Holy Communion and you're putting the stain of sin on my soul. It will be the same every day, morning and evening when I sink the brass rod into the tank in the ground and give him the readings from the two pumps.

I'll stand longside him as he rants away blaming me for every sin he's committed in his entire life. I'll ask him over and over again, how can it be my fault, sure all I'm doing is what I was told and doing it right. But he tells me to shut up because he can't concentrate. Then he's real nice to me between the morning and the evening. I'll spend every day of the first week behind the big glass window with my hands in my pockets looking out through it waiting for a car that might need some juice. I have too much idle time on my hands and the small part of my brain that separates from the biggest part that hardly ever works at all and kept me stupid all my days in school, is working overtime and wondering if it can find another job that will keep me, my brain and hands occupied and not make the eight hours feel like twenty.

And here it comes, a great idea to make some extra money every day and if it works I could make more money than my wages. At this point, the good rearing I got from Mam and Pop should be screaming at me to stop, to forget it and not go any further with this idea. But this idea is fullproof. I can't be caught. I'll be stealing everyday. I'll be as bad as the messenger boy from Boyd's but he was stupid and bound to be caught at some stage. The little voice in my head that was put there by Mam has gone mute; my heart is ticking faster with excitement. I'll walk home that evening, going over the plan again and again, it's perfect. I'll stay awake for hours into the early morning with my hands behind my head looking up at the dark ceiling while Jimmy sleeps away longside me and it just gets more exciting. I could make five bob a day every day and if anyone says anything, I can simply say that it was a mistake. Now I'm thinking what I could spend it on. I won't be able to give Mam any of it. It's an awful pity because I'd love to see her wearing something new every week. I can't give her any of it because I have to hand her the pay packet every week with the full amount written on the outside. And a voice in my head is telling me that Mam wouldn't want anything to do with money that's stolen.

When the morning comes, Jack is fupping and blinding, I'm not taking a bit of notice of his antics because I'm waiting for the first of the milk trucks to come so I can put my plan into action. When it does, the driver does his usual routine of scribbling his signature on the docket without bothering to look at the pump to see how much the tank has taken. Each pump has a face like a clock on both sides and for the last week each of the four trucks will take anything from six to eight gallons every day. The first truck has just taken over six and a half gallons and the clock on the pump reads 6:35 but I write down 7:35 which means there'll be a gallon over and above. Now all I have to do is wait for a cash sale today and with petrol costing five bob a gallon I'll be able to take the first five bob sale into my pocket and its not long before the other three trucks are in and gone. By the time 12.00 pm comes there's a cash sale for ten shillings and five bob of it is in my pocket and life couldn't be better. I'll do the same again tomorrow and make sure it's a different truck. Jack is at it again that evening cursing and swearing. And I'm on my way home with the first of many five bobs.

Petrol pump that was used at the time

After the first week, I'm getting greedy and its ten bob a day. I have so much money I don't know what to do with it. After two months Mam wants to bring me down to Dr. Crowe at the city dispensary to find out why it is I'm not eating my dinner anymore. She says I'm putting on too much weight. I can't tell her it's because I'm around the corner at Keane's Bakery every hour for the apple tarts and the cream buns, then over to the Roma Café for the bag of chips, and two battered sausages at 1.00 pm that I'll eat while I walk home for the dinner that I won't be able to eat. Dr. Crowe will scratch his head and wonder how it's possible for someone to put on weight and not eat. I'll have a fag in my hand every five minutes with a bottle of Fanta belching and farting from all the gas and the thoughts of looking for another job is gone from my head because I am now stealing two pounds ten shillings a week and only taking home one pound twelve and six. And life couldn't be better.

The man with the Borgward car and the two petrol tanks whose name is Mr. Wallace and comes every Tuesday and Thursday is here again. I'll do the usual routine of putting the handle of the pump in the first tank after he unlocks it and goes to the other side of the car to do the same with the other one. We'll talk away or he might ask me questions like he does every time he comes here. He always wants to know how things are since I caught the messenger boy stealing, what my father's name is, what does he do, where do I live and another dozen things. I think he's very nice. The back seat of his car has layers of eggs in their cardboard holders stacked on top of one another. I'll ask him one day why the back seat of his car has so many eggs every time he comes here. He says that he owns a chicken farm outside the road and brings the eggs to the shops every day.

I'm leaning against the car keeping my ear to the sound of the pipe as it takes the constant flow of petrol into the tank. I'll always know by the sound when it's nearly full. It's taking a lot longer today and Mr. Wallace who takes an interest in me every week is about to lose the rag any minute. I'm shaken out of my concentration when Mr. Wallace shouts 'Stop.' Then he shouts, 'Jesus, Mary and Holy St. Joseph', when I look at Mr. Wallace to try and see what's wrong, he's pointing at the hands of the clock, the small hand is at four and the big hand is at three. 'Where the Fupp is all the petrol going? That's the 3rd time around on the clock. You're after putting thirty six gallons into it. There's no way one tank will take that much'. We're looking at the ground and its bone dry. So is underneath the car where the boot is. We're scratching our heads as to where all the petrol is gone. I'm telling him that judging from the sound of the tank when I was filling it, there was a lot more to go in. Then he lifts up the door of the boot and says, 'Mother of Jesus look at what you're after doing'. When I walk around and look into his boot, there's eggs, dozens of them swimming around in petrol. My mouth is wide open looking at the eggs, wondering why the hell is the petrol in the boot when its supposed to be in the tank.

'You're going to have to pay for all that petrol and the eggs too young man; do you hear me talking to you?'

'Yes Sir, Mr. Wallace Sir.'

He's pacing to and fro behind the car giving out about the shops that will be waiting for their eggs and he'll be only able to give them half of what they'll want. We're staring into the boot, looking at all the eggs just floating and I'm wondering how the hell it is all my fault.

'Go up and get Mr. O'Connell right away and don't bring me out that fupper Jack Moore. You're to get me Mr. O'Connell, do you hear me now?'

'Yes Mr. Wallace.'

As I'm wondering into get Jack I'm thinking this is God's way of getting me back for stealing the ten bob every day. I'm going to get the sack for nothing, just like the other lads, and they were innocent too. I'm going to loose my job. How am I going to pay for thirty eight gallons of petrol at five bob a gallon if I've no job? And what about the bloody eggs? I don't know how many there are floating around in his boot and how much there going to cost me.

I'll have to tell Jack first. He'll want to know why I'm going upstairs when I'm supposed to be keeping an eye on the pumps, to see if anyone needs petrol. I'm stuttering out the words to Jack and he's in a right state, he says he can't understand a word I'm saying; to hurry up because he hasn't got all day. When I do get it out, he hops his biro off the desk and shouts, 'Jesus, Mary and Holy St. Joseph how the Fupp did you manage to do that? As if I hadn't enough to deal with today, with two other customers who came in saying they weren't happy with the work that was done to their cars. I'll have to listen to them again when they come back and now you tell me that you're after filling the boot of one of our best customer's car with fupping petrol. What the

Fupp did I do to deserve this? I wish to Fupp I never got out of fupping bed this morning'.

He's walking out to talk to Mr. Wallace and I have to tell him how he doesn't want to see him that he specifically asked for Mr. O'Connell. Jack turns full circle, mutters under his breath cursing and swearing while he climbs the stairs to get Mr. O'Connell. He's not muttering now because he's beside Mr. O'Connell as he comes down the stairs. Mr. O'Connell looks at me and says, 'Now Pat, Jack tells me you filled Mr. Wallace's boot with petrol, is that right?'

'Yes Sir, Mr. O'Connell Sir. And I'm very sorry, Mr. O'Connell Sir. I just did what I always do every time he comes here Mr. O'Connell Sir.'

'Calm down now Pat, let's see how this happened.'

I don't know whether I'm hearing things or not but Mr. O'Connell hasn't said a cross word to me. He's heading out to Mr. Wallace with Jack longside him.

'Good morning Mr. Wallace, now what seems to be the problem?'

'Look for yourself Mr. O'Connell' and moves towards the boot Mr. O'Connell looks in. He seems to be taking no notice of Mr. Wallace's rants of 'I'm not paying for that petrol and somebody better reimburse me for all those eggs that are no good to anybody'.

Jack and Mr. O'Connell are pointing to one side of the boot and talking to each other in low voices. As they lift their heads from the boot, Mr. O'Connell says,

'Tell me Mr. Wallace do you carry eggs in your boot all the time?'

Mr. Wallace says that he doesn't normally, but he had to do it today because he had other things to bring in the car.

'And what way did you stack them Mr. Wallace?'

'On top of one another in three stacks.'

'And how high would the stacks be Mr. Wallace?'

'Oh very high, as high as I can get them.'

Mr. O'Connell is pointing over to the same spot himself and Jack were looking at only seconds ago.

'Can you see the rubber pipe that goes in to the tank below is not connected to the spout Mr. Wallace?'

Mr. Wallace sticks his head into the corner, Mr. O'Connell is pointing at. 'Have you any idea how that happened at all Mr. Wallace?'

There's silence. Mr. Wallace looks at Mr. O'Connell and says, 'All I want to know is who is going to pay for the petrol and the eggs because I'm not.'

'Now look here', answers Mr. O'Connell, 'it's quite obvious how it happened. You obviously turned a corner too fast and your three stacks of eggs leaned against the rubber pipe and dislodged it.'

'Oh I don't know', says Mr. Wallace.

Mr. O'Connell interrupts. 'Mr. Wallace did you know that rubber pipe was not connected properly to the inlet?'

The Borgward car

Mr. Wallace has a problem; if he says he did Mr. O'Connell will surely say, 'then why didn't you tell young Pat first or fix it before you let him fill your boot with petrol?' So Mr. Wallace says, no, he didn't. Mr. O'Connell says 'Then how the bloody hell did you expect this young man who is as honest as the day is long to know? Now let me make myself very clear. You are going to pay for this petrol the whole lot and if you don't my Solicitor will be in touch with you. Now good day!'

And there I am thanking my lucky stars I still have a job. I'll still have the ten bob I steal every day. Five minutes later my conscience is giving me an awful time because Mr. O'Connell thinks and said that I'm an honest young lad. I don't want to steal the ten bob anymore. But when tomorrow comes, the temptation is too strong. I'll be telling my conscience to shut up and mind its own bloody business while I'm off around the corner to Keane's Bakery for the apple tarts and the cigarettes again, and everything is back to normal.

Tony Cronin is a thin, cross miserable ol' get. He's one of the mechanics here and doesn't like me. I don't know why. I don't like him either. I think he's got gravel in his throat because he makes a terrible racket when he talks. He caught me sitting behind the wheel of a car in the car wash. I was putting it into first gear and driving it a few yards forward and then turning into reverse, just like I did below at the Bremen's Motors. He caught me and told Jack. Now I'm in trouble. Jack says that if I'm caught doing that again, I'll get the sack. But I'll get that bastard! I'll spend the next three days standing behind the large glass window with the hands in my pocket pacing across wondering how I'll get him and the answer is just across in the toilet that's for the ladies only who work in the office upstairs, and the two lads in their white coats who work behind the counter upstairs and sell spare parts, Jack and myself can use it too. Everybody else that has dirt on their hands or clothes has to go to the one at the back that has a black towel on the wall to clean all the grease and dirt from the constant flow of hands in their dark blue overalls that come here every day. I saw it once and I wondered how anybody could put their bare arse onto a lav that has years of skid marks everywhere and Monday morning's porter spatter stains all over it. But I won't give the idea enough thought. It's no sooner in my head than I have it executed with the pencil that's always on my desk.

There it is in big letters, his name all over the walls that are spotlessly clean that will get him into trouble and all I have to do is wait. After two weeks. I have forgotten all about it. Mr. O'Connell comes down to me with the usual 'Good morning Pat, how are you this morning?'

I'll tell him in my best manner that 'I'm fine thank you Sir.'

'He'll say good man, good man' like he always does.

'I want to ask you a question Pat. But before I ask you I want to reassure you that if you tell the truth I will simply walk away and there will be no more about it. Do you understand?'

I can feel the blood rushing to my face. I know it's giving me the guilty look. I've been found out. He knows about the ten bob I've been stealing every day. It's going on so long now, I must have stolen a bloody fortune. The Guards will be here any minute and Mam will be here tomorrow asking Mr. O'Connell to give me another chance. That's after Pop will have kicked the living day lights out of me. I'm telling Mr. O'Connell I understand and just about to say I'm sorry for stealing all the money when he asks me did I write Tony Cronin's name on the wall of the toilet across the way.

I don't believe it! It's not about the money. He doesn't know. The blood is gone from my face and now I have a confused look that also has a look of relief on it. Then I have a look of 'who me? Are you serious?' I'm crossing my fingers over my heart as I say the words that are in my head. I know I'm doing a great job with the look and the gestures.

'Now look Pat all you have to do is say, 'Yes Mr. O'Connell, it was me,' and I won't say another word I promise you. Think about it', he says. 'Now did you write Tony Cronin's name on the wall of the toilet?'

Now my brain that was never any bloody good to me in school or when I was with Dinny, Phonsie and Noelie or any other time, should be telling me to own up while the going was good. But that was if my brain was working properly. So when I go with the expressions of horror that Mr. O'Connell would even think of suspecting me. After all I was the one who caught the messenger boy stealing after only two hours on the job. I've got my eyes open as far as I can get them, I'm on my toes with my hands outstretched like I'm a walking saint and every time I use the word 'me' my hands are touching my heart. I'm doing a great job but Mr. O'Connell isn't falling for it.

'OK Pat,' he says, 'would you mind writing down Tony Cronin on this piece of paper so please?'

I'm shocked, I never saw this coming and it's all because my bloody brains are useless to me. If I had thought about it properly I'd have owned up. I manage to stutter out the words, 'Of c-c- of course Mr. O'Connell,' and my bloody useless brains are telling me what I know already. I'm goosed. I'm holding the piece of paper while trying my damnedest not to write the way I normally write but it's not the style of writing that's going to hang me but the spelling.

And there it is in big red capital letters, my first experience of what Mam and Pop were telling me that I'd regret the day I left school because Mr. O'Connell says, 'follow me,' Pat and I am right behind him knowing I've done it. I've hanged myself. I don't know how. Mr. O'Connell turns on the light in the toilet because it doesn't have a window.

I'm looking at the pencil writing of Tony Cronin; 'Now look Pat, do you see how the writing on the wall is exactly the same as what you have written on this piece of paper'. I'm looking at the wall, then the piece of paper. I'll do it four or five times and can't see what he's talking about. My heart is jumping all over the place. Mr. O'Connell says, 'Pat isn't it obvious? Both writings are the same'. I look at it again another three or four times and I feel like a right gob-shite 'because I still can't see how they are the same. He's starting to get a bit annoyed with me now, and he says, 'Ah for goodness sake Pat, stop acting the fool'. It only makes me feel ten times worse. 'Look at the letter 'n' in your writing on the wall.' I'm looking but still can't see what he's trying to tell me. Now he's really cross. He points at the letter 'n' in Tony, 'Then look at the two 'n's' in Cronin, the first one is an Irish n and the second one is an English 'n' and you've done the very same on the piece of paper'. Now I can see it and off Mr. O'Connell goes with 'I'm disgusted with you Pat, I gave you every chance. I promised if you'd admit it I wouldn't say a thing and I wouldn't have.' I've got my chin resting on my chest and telling him 'I'm very sorry'.

'Ah you're only saying that now because you were found out'.

I'm asking him does this mean I'll get fired. He says' I should be for lying, especially swearing on my Grandmothers grave and all belonging to me that are dead in the ground.'

'It's not a nice thing you know to be swearing on the graves of those who are dead whether they belong to you or not.'

He'll walk away and never talk to me again even though I'll say hello or good morning to him, he'll walk by as though I'm not there. I'll feel terrible and wonder what he would do if he found out I was stealing the ten bob every day that I'm getting sick of now. I could go down to Nestor's Sports Shop in O'Connell Street and order a new bike with all the latest gadgets, only Mam would want to know where I got the dosh. I can't even buy some new clothes or shoes for the same reason. The apple tarts at Keane's Bakery don't taste the same anymore and neither do the chips over at the Roma Café. Mam has me into see Dr. Crowe again wanting to know would he weigh me again because she says I must have put on two stone in the last few months. I'll ask Jack if there's anything else I can do between giving the few customers that come for their petrol everyday. He says 'there isn't,' and I don't think I've ever being so browned off in all my life before. But Pop will come to my rescue when he says, I have to give in my notice to Jack and Mr. O'Connell. And the day that I have dreamt about for years has arrived. I am going to be working with my dad.

Jacks say's 'Its an awful pity I am going because they never had anyone stay at the pumps as long as myself'. He wants to know if they gave me a small rise would I stay on, but I have to tell him that I am going to be working with my dad that I've being waiting for years and that I'm bored out of my skull walking around the showroom with my hands in my pocket looking out the window. And if I had to work here another week I would wind up in the mental hospital everyone calls the 'opera house' above in Mulgrave Street.

He said, 'that's an awful pity'. And when the time comes he wishes me the best of luck in my future with a big hand shake and hopes the next young lad will be as honest and diligent as myself what ever that means.

Tony Cronin and myself

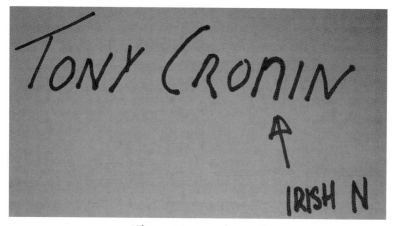

The writing on the wall

There's no sign of Mr. O'Connell coming to say goodbye, he must be still mad at me over Tony Cronin and I can't wait for Monday to come. I have Pop pestered over the whole week-end with questions like, 'Where will we be working?' 'What will we be doing?', and 'What kind of a job is it that they are working on?. How much will I be getting a week?, and a dozen more questions.

CHAPTER 4

Mr. O'Dwyer lives across the road in number 40 and has a beautiful garden with mature hedging all around the front of his house, he's a lovely man whose wife died years ago, and every year when the spring comes he will be out in his garden trimming weeding and keeping everything ship shape. Mam will go over to him every few days looking for a slip of this and a slip of that, that he has in his garden. She'll dig a small hole and put whatever he has given her into the ground and a week later it will hang limp because it has gone dead. Mr. O'Dwyer tells Mam that there are green fingers in every family and that there are more slips for Pop, Jetta, James and myself to put in the ground and wait for a week or two to see who has the green fingers. After the week or two mine will be the only one still in an upright position looking for the sunshine to keep it healthy and growing and now Mam has me sticking all sorts of stuff she got from Mr. O'Dwyer into our front garden and my weekend is gone and when Monday morning comes I'll get the bus into O'Connell St, walk to Whelans Chemist and wait for Pop to arrive on his bike, and when he does he'll take me upstairs to a hairdressing salon for women. It's huge and there are girls my age working here and things are looking good. Pop says himself and Lar have being putting an extension on to the back of the salon over the last two months and now its time to do the decorating work.

A few minutes later Lar comes in, takes me to one side, and says he has two new white overalls for me, and that he will take the price of them out of my wages over the next eight weeks, he explains how important it is to look the part in our work.

'We won't want people to think we are unprofessional in our appearance,' there's a laundry in Sarsfield Street, called the Phoenix and every Monday each of us will call in and give them the overalls we have been working in all week and collect the ones we left them the week before.

He shows me two large cans of brushes that are all shapes and sizes and tells me my first job every Monday morning will be to take out every brush and clean it thoroughly, that I'm to use paraffin oil and I'm to throw the old stuff out. That he wants us to start every week with brushes like they were new. He says my wages will be two pounds per week and that I will have to start just like any other apprentice even though he knows, I am able to do lots of things, that I learnt from Pop. I'm shocked because I thought I'd be able to earn four pound a week at least, because I am able to do so much, I thought I would have made enough money to buy a car in no time at all, but the smell of wood, cement and other building materials is making me forget. I am just happy to be here at long last in this kind of environment.

The man with the dickie bow and black suit who has an English accent and speaks a hundred miles an hour is talking to me and I haven't a bloody clue what he is saying, I'll guess and say 'thank you', because I think I heard the word that sounded like 'welcome'. Pop says he is the owner called Mr. Ferris but that the salon is named Richard Hate Cofferier and he is a very jolly decent person.

Over the next six years Mr. Ferris will help Pop make 36 Claughan Court a palace with left over rolls of wall paper imported from Italy, France and other European countries, paint especially mixed above in Dublin by the manufacturers, and the very latest in taps, mirrors, lighting, water fountains, dried flower arrangements etc,when there going to be trown out, because Richard Hate Cofferier will want the posh ladies that come to him from all the snotty areas of Limerick, to be sitting in his salon surrounded in luxury and feel good about paying the extra few bob for the hairdo that they'll get from the master himself, and when the posh ladies are having their morning coffee across the road in the 'Stella restaurant', Mr. Ferris, who only arrived in Limerick a year ago will be famous in no time at all.

And the women who came to him months ago who could walk in off the street and get their hair done there and then now have to ring or call in to make an appointment a week or two in advance because Mr. Ferris and twenty five of his staff are up to their eyeballs six days a week, and that means more work for Pop, Lar and myself. Over the next twelve months I'll see Pop handle all kinds of construction difficulties, I'll watch his customers and the confidence they'll put in him, the way Lar will get involved and throw in his tuppence worth to be told it won't work, and listen to Pop explain why it won't. I'll realise that Lar is learning too even though is he is twenty five years of age. At the end of the year I'll understand how these two people are a great team and my brain will tell me how little I know and how much I have to learn that the weekend and holiday periods I spent working with Pop over the years only taught me a fraction of what I need to know. But I'll learn fast because I 'm interested. I'll be full of questions. I'll never get side tracked because I'm loving every minute of it. And Mam says she can't understand why I am eating my dinners everyday at 1 o'clock now and looking for more when I come home in the evening since I started working for Pop and she's asking him everyday, 'what the hell kind of work am I doing at all', and makes him promise that he'll not make a slave out of me and how she was sick with worry about me putting on so much weight and can't understand why I'm losing so much now. She'll walk out into the kitchen saying 'Jesus, Mary and Holy St. Joseph when does the worrying ever stop, I thought when he grew up the worrying would be over'.

It's hard to see her upset and worrying about me all the time especially when I could put her out of her misery and tell her the truth about the money I stole that must have been a couple of hundred pound but if I tell her I'll be dead and she'll worry more. She'll want to go down to Mr. O'Connell and tell him what I did and give him the money back out of her house keeping and I couldn't do that to her so what can I do? I'll be laughing every day with Pop and Lar from the things they'll say and do and being late for work any day won't happen because I might miss something. Its my second day at Richard's and two men that weren't here yesterday have arrived with rolls of electric cable, a large tool box and other bits and pieces.

'Good morning, Harry, and how are you this fine, lovely morning,?' 'Asked one, whose voice and accent sounds very grand and posh, I am surprised because I didn't think people who spoke like that worked with their hands.

'Mind your own business', says Pop and everybody bursts into laughter.

'My goodness Harry you never lost it, always a man for a quick funny answer, harr! harr!

The laughing is hardly over when Pops says 'I hope the two of ye aren't going to be knocking fupping holes in all our work because if ye are ye can fupp off out of it,'and Mr. Ferris is out of his office joining in the laughter with all the girls who work in the salon who are sticking their heads into the extension to see what's causing all the laughter. The other fella who hasn't opened his mouth since they walked in the door looks like a half-wit, he has no teeth like Pop and just stands there with drooped shoulders laughing away and shaking his head up and down all the time.

'How are you Barney', says Pop, and Barney answers back 'I'm grand Harry,' and I realise he is not a half-wit he just looks like one. The hours pass and everything is normal, Barney is downstairs under the new timber floor we are all working on. He's made a small 1 inch hole over by the wall and is shouting up to his partner Edmond to catch the cable he is feeding up through the hole, Pop walks over to were the hole is with a big four inch concrete block in his hands and shouts, 'is that you Barney', Barney has his head stuck between the floor joists where the hole is and shouts back up through it, 'Yes Harry, that's right its me'.

Mr. Ferris is back in the extension because he heard Pop shouting, Lar and myself have stopped working because we know Pop is at it again. He has his hands high in the air with the block and shouts 'Are you still there Barney?', 'Yes Harry, I'm still here', and Pops lets the block fall flat on the floor right above Barneys head when the block hits the floor there is such a bang it breaks in two. The women in the salon including the posh ladies that are having their hair done all shout in unison, 'Jesus, Mary and

Holy St. Joseph what was that?' and the place is in an uproar again and there's Barney up from the basement thumping his ears with both hands because he thinks he has gone deaf.

When the laughing stops the farting that started ten minutes after I came to work on Monday, and hasn't stopped since is back again mostly from Pop and Lar. Lar and myself will run out of the room and come back five minutes later when the smell is gone. And when we're back in Lar is at it with farts that have no sound at all. Pop calls them silencers.

Mr. Ferris will get involved too with farts that Pop says aren't farts at all only squirts and there I am in the middle bursting blood vessels trying to fart and can't even spit. I'll ask Mam when I go home for the dinner what can I eat that will make me fart. She'll laugh and say 'beans', so I'm stuffing my face since Mam brought them home for Tuesdays dinner and I haven't been able to drop one silent or otherwise and its making me depressed. Pop says, I should try Brussels sprouts and when I ask him what they are he says, 'small heads of cabbage', and I'm pleading with Mam to get me the sprouts. She'll come home every day and say how she tried half the shops in town and can't get any and that she'll try again tomorrow. Nan says that I should drink a pint of porter as quick as I can because 'your granddad could fart for Ireland, minutes after drinking one of Arthur Guinness brews'. I'll go to the pub on Saturday to buy a pint of porter with my half of the two pounds wages but they won't give it to me because they say I am too young.

When Monday comes there is still no sign of the Brussel sprouts, I'll ask Lar to buy me a pint of Guinness when the pubs open. 'What the hell do you want with a pint of porter?', he asks. And when I tell him I want to fart like him he can't stop laughing and over he goes across the road and brings me back a pint bottle, he wants to see me drink it and so does Pop. When I put it to my mouth and take the first gulp I'm spitting it out straight away shouting 'Oh Janey, that tastes horrible!' Pop and Lar are having a right good laugh at the faces I'm making and Mr. Ferris is in wanting to know what all the laughing is about and what he's missing.

Lar tells him I'm trying to fart like the rest of them and there they are looking at me gulping the awful black stuff that has me wondering why Pop or anyone else could love this stuff and keep drinking it until they could hardly walk. But my determination to join the choir of the farting club is so strong that I am prepared to do anything. The pint is gone, the whole lot and I'm gasping for air and panting like a dog. All I have to do is wait minute I'll be exploding just like Pop or let the odd one off just like Lar. But instead of ripping I'm a bit giddy and my stomach is starting to heave. Lar, Mr. Ferris and Pop are huddled together talking under their breath, and sniggering away like they are waiting for something.

I'm starting to sway a bit as I walk past them. Pop asks, 'Well Pa, any sign of a fart on the way?' I look back to answer and fall over a box on the floor and the girls from the salon are back again to see what has them laughing so much. I can only get back on my knees I can't understand why everything is spinning. Pop and Lar put me into a chair while they are killing themselves laughing. I have my head in my hands and the only wind I can manage to make is coming out my throat. I don't feel well at all and Lar wants to know would I like him to go across the road to the same pub and get another pint which causes more laughing. I swear to God that I will never put another drop of that stuff to my mouth as long as I live. I'll go home that evening on the bus with a terrible headache. I won't eat my supper either I'll go straight to bed and listen to Jetta and James laughing at Pops account of my attempts to enter the farting club.

When Monday morning comes, Mr. Ferris, Pop and Lar are at it again. They want to know when am I going to drop one because if I don't start soon they might give me the sack. Mam has a surprise for me when I go home for my dinner at 1 o'clock, its the Brussels sprouts I have being waiting for but they taste bloody awful, they're like tiny rocks as well but down my throat they'll go, the whole lot, just like the Arthur Guinness. I know I won't be getting dizzy or even sick from this stuff. When 3 o'clock comes out comes the first fart, it's a rocket. Then Lar says 'Jasus, Har was that you?', 'No', I reply with a big smile and my chest out. Before I can say another word there's another building up steam and I know its going to be even better. But a good fart is no use without the body gestures the way Pop does it, like leaning to the left or right while at the same time lifting one of the legs slightly off the ground just before the explosion, the timing must be perfect.

Mr. Richard Ferris in his hairdressing days

Mr. Ferris has arrived just in time to witness the next one. I want it to be a unique one that I haven't seen Pop, Lar or even Mr. Ferris do before, so its up with the right leg nice and high and a fast downward thrust and out it comes with perfect timing along with the words, 'try and better that', I have arrived at long last I'm part of the choir.

Mr. Ferris says 'Jesus, Harry he is better then you' and I am blowing away for the rest of the day I have them all in the shade. I'll be at it when I come home as well. Nan will be asking Mam not to be giving me any more Brussels sprouts because the house will have to be fumigated. Mam will be opening the windows every five minutes giving out about the smell saying ,'Jesus, Mary and Holy St. Joseph why the hell am I giving that fella ammunition every day so he can come home, in the evenings with his father and between the two of them have my house smelling like a septic tank. Other times she'll have a look of pride after hearing a rasp saying 'That's the sign of a healthy stomach'. But I have pestered her into giving me the sprouts everyday so I can keep up the high standard that I've started. She will and I am a happy chappie now the leader of the pack because none of them can fart like me.

Mr. Ferris today

I'll ask Mam does she ever do it. Nan will laugh and say its not polite for ladies to break wind in public but I want to know has she ever left one off when she's on her own, she laughs again and tells me to mind my own business. ' Ah, go on Mam tell us, have you ever dropped one?' 'You shouldn't be asking a woman if she does something like that'. Here's Pop and I'm asking him why and out it comes again the same bloody answer to every question. The answer I have being getting all my childhood and that's 'shut up or that's the why', but I'm older now and I can insist, 'Oh, come on Pop, tell me why I shouldn't ask a lady if she ever farted'. 'Because its none of your business that's why', Did you ever fart Mam?, Mam laughs and says 'a lady wouldn't do things like that', 'ya, I know that, but I mean I never heard you let one off, but what about when you were on your own, have you ever done one then?' We are all having a good laugh because I've just dropped another one after I asked the question. 'Never you mind', she says, 'You do', I shout, 'you do I know you do, are they good ones Mam?'

She won't answer, she just laughs away.

After another two weeks the sprouts I'm getting all the time are starting to taste nice and its no trouble at all to take the fuel into my body that will do its best to keep me floating and sailing every day.

Mam says I've got the best set of teeth in the whole family. She's right. Snow white and not a sign of yellowing even though I'm smoking fifteen a day. They don't know about it yet, not a tooth out of place top or bottom, except one in the back of my top set, the one that started with a tiny hole and worked its way into a volcano after four years because I neglected it. And its now giving me hell, I can't go to work with it, I cant eat or sleep either and Mam is begging me to go to a dentist and have it pulled. I've never been to a dentist before and I don't want to go either. But the five days of hell and no sleep is too much, I'm dosed up to the eyeballs on tablets that won't or don't work anymore. So it's down to a dentist in William Street the one Mam said is very good, Dentist O'Callaghan, when I arrive at the reception area and get that awful smell, I'm so bloody nervous I think the pain has gone to sleep. I'm only waiting ten minutes when I'm told I can go in. I'm terrified. When I see who is going to be taking out my tooth I want my legs to take me out of here as fast as they can. But they won't. Before me is a very small baldy headed man who must be well over his eighties. He has got glasses and his eyes are like billiard balls because the lenses in them are so strong.

He says everything three times, 'Come on, come on, come on, sit, sit, sit', he says pointing to the chair. And I am wondering why he is saying everything three times. 'Open, open, open', his hands are shaking badly. I want to tell him I have changed my mind but he has one of them half way down my throat poking away at all my teeth. I want to tell him I just want the one out now and not all of them. He has got an injection in the other hand that's shaking like an alcoholic who hasn't had a drink in days. His assistant is holding my forehead back against the chair. He sticks the needle in my gum three or four times and the pain that I had for the last five days its going and what a relief. I'm only in the waiting room three minutes when they want me back again I'm trying to tell him I am not ready yet that my gum isn't frozen completely but he just says 'sit down, sit down, sit down'. Now he has a silver pliers in his hand that is wobbling all over the place, he puts it into my mouth and says 'Open, open, open', and shouts 'Wider, wider, wider,' and in he goes. He's rooting away pulling and dragging just like Pop trying to pull a crooked rusty nail from a piece of wood with a crow bar. And every time he pulls, my head is following his hand and I'm panicking. I'm starting to roar like the pigs in O'Mara's before they get their throats cut. 'Sit down, sit down, sit down', he shouts but I won't, he puts his knee on my lap and tells his assistant to hold my head against the headrest. I've got my mouth closed and both my hands on his wrists that's holding the pliers he's still trying to pull the bad tooth. He's shouting at me to take my hands away. The pliers is pinching my bottom lip and I am thinking if there is anyone out in the waiting room listening to all the commotion going on, they are well on their way up William Street by now. And then its out and so am I. He is shouting, 'Wash your mouth, wash your mouth, wash your mouth', but I'm well on my way down the stairs after paying the receptionist with a hole in my gum and a big red lump on my bottom lip that's beating to my heart. It will be a long time before I go to a dentist again but when I do I'll have a whole new attitude. A couple of weeks later, one of my eyes is getting sore and hurts when I blink, and after a few days I cant open it at all. Its like someone has given me a hiding and the training that Lar is giving me is hard to put into practice with only one eye. Two days later I'll wake up with the soreness gone and I can't open my eye because its stuck to the pus that came out it and has the hair on my eye lids welded together and its agony forcing my eye lids apart. Two weeks later there's another one coming on the other eye and Mam has her fifteen year old son down at the City Dispensary telling Dr. Crowe about it. I am asking Mam why she has to come down with me, sure aren't I big enough to go down myself now that I'm working and bringing home a week's wages, she says she wants to be sure that I tell him everything.

Dr. Crowe says I must be 'run down', and gives Mam a prescription for her to stand in the queue behind another twenty mothers who have children balling their eyes out with snotty noses. And Mam is shoving the purple coloured liquid down my throat three times a day for the next seven days, and its no bloody use because after another two weeks the other eye gets a second boil in it and I might as well have only the one eye. Nan is in from Cappamore and says Uncle Peter used to get the same thing when he was my age and that they are called stys and I could be getting them every two weeks, for the next two years just like Peter. Mam tells every woman she meets about the state of my eyes. How every fortnight I look like a fella that had the living daylights beat out of him. She'll come home with a remedy every time that's sure to work. Like I should put a spit on the sore eye every morning after I wake up and Mam is knocking on my bedroom door every morning at eight o'clock standing over me saying she wants to see me rub my eyes with my spit and after two weeks of hawking up a spit every morning, there's another sty on the way, then she'll have me look through a wedding ring that's more than a hundred years old and it's Nan to the rescue with the ring her mother gave her who got it from her mother a thousand years ago. Mam is at my door again every morning making me look through the wedding ring, not with the good eye, it must be the bad one, but I am telling her I can't open the bad one because it's too swollen. 'you must', she says, 'otherwise it won't work', I am getting really cranky because this is stupid. I'm asking her how could looking through a bloody wedding ring that's over a hundred years old cure a boil in my eye. She says 'she doesn't know', that the woman that told her about it said it never fails. And after another seven days of looking through a stupid ring I have to tell Mam she can go back to the woman that told her about the ring, and tell her what to do with it. Now she's praying to a saint I have never heard of before, she says he's not a saint yet but at the rate he's going with miracles and cures it will be only a matter of time before her prayers will be answered. It won't be answered at all unless she puts it in the Limerick Leader and I am asking her 'do I have to say a prayer to the man that has been dead for the last two hundred years to get the boils in my eyes to stop that could last for another two years'?, and if they do I'm goosed because Phonsie, Noelie and myself will be chasing the girls and what chance will I have of getting a girl that I can only look at with one eye and the other closed and looking like a tomato. If I get a chance to have my first kiss, what girl is going to want to be inches away from a yoke like that on my face, so the only chance I'll get to kiss a girl is in between the two week period of one sty coming and the other going and get involved with the three girls that come to Careys Road sussing out the talent and Phonsie, Noelie and myself are the talent.

I've never kissed a girl. I've no idea what it's like but I'm about to find out and it will be an unforgettable experience!

Phonsie and Noelie will want the prettiest but I'll look for the cleanest; the one with the nice perfume, the best dressed. One that looks like she comes from a nice clean home and it's all because of Mam drilling it into me ever since I can remember. It all seems so natural the way it happened. "Will you come up the lane?" we'll ask. "For what?" they'll want to know. "For a walk" we'll answer. They'll answer and say they don't mind and we'll go up in three pairs. I'll shove my one against the stoney wall that separates the railway line from the quarry that's filled with dogs and cats in canvas coal bags and go in for my first kiss. I'll take a deep breath like I'm going underwater and plant my lips on her pink lipstick. And the softness is beautiful. Everything I'm doing is clumsy, awkward and wonderful. My nostrils taking in all the smells that make a female beautiful. I won't move a muscle. I want it to be just like the way they do it in the pictures but I need to take a breath before I pass out. I'll move away. She'll ask do you know such a fella and I haven't a bull's notion of who she's talking about. But I'll pretend to

The lane way at the bottom of the hill were I got my first kiss

think about it because if we're not talking about this fella I don't know what else we're going to say to each other before I move in for the second kiss and take the rest of her pink lipstick away. When another breath is needed, she will be at it again for the rest of the night against the stone wall with do you know this fella, telling me where he lives, where he works, his brothers and sisters, if he has any, mothers, fathers, uncles and aunts. I think she is making the whole lot up just to have something to say between the kisses. And I thought I was a talker. We'll be at it again for another two nights before they get fed up with us and want new mouths to suck. I'll be up in Carey's Road every Saturday night and all day Sunday. I won't bother going to mass because I don't see the point and Mam and Nan are giving out when I tell them, saying "It's a mortal sin, not to go to mass".

Mam will stick her finger in the holy water font, in one of the half dozen that hang in every room of the house and that are topped up every day from the bottle she'll bring to the tank at the side of St. John's Cathedral after every Sunday mass. She'll tell me to put the sign of the cross on my forehead and tell God that I'm sorry, and gives me a spatter of water in the eye that was meant for my head. She'll bless herself three times while putting her eyes heavenward that's followed by the usual comment "Jesus, Mary and Holy Saint Joseph! What's the world coming to at all?" "I'm doing my best. I brought him up as best I could but he is old enough now to make his own decisions". And Nan will say "No. he's not. Jesus, he's only fifteen". I'll put the sign of the cross on my forehead just to keep Mam happy and listen to the two of them going on about the youth of today, how they have too much, not like their day. I'll walk out the hall and close the door behind me and hear them at it because the windows are open. I'll head up to Carey's road in my best rig out: a dark grey suit, white shirt and a tie and black leather shoes. I'm not going anywhere special. It's all I have. I have one of everything. The same as my work clothes. I'll hang around Lynch's shop that's called the Railway Stores in Carey's Road with Phonsie and Noelie, Anthony Hartigan, who I went to school with, Johnny Egan and Pat Stubbens. Noelie will have a ball. We'll play against the long stone wall on the right side of the hill that takes you under the bridge at the bottom of the road for two hours. I'll bring some white paint and a brush and paint the goal on the stone wall that's still there today. We'll play against the wall for hours before we go to the green just beyond the bridge where other lads will join us. We'll finish at six o'clock. Mrs. Meade will tell Phonsie to be sure and bring me in for a cup of tea and a few slices of bread before we head to the pictures at seven o'clock. We'll be sitting in the back stalls of the Grand Central Cinema eating crisps, drinking Fanta orange, sharing a fag

Forty years ago and the painted goals is still clearly visible.

if the funds are low, and be completely unaware of the stench that's wafting its way from the shoes and socks, shirts and vests we've been running around in for the last five hours because they're the only good clothes we have.

*The green were we played football on the summer
evenings and weekends*

When another Monday comes, Pop and Lar will be asking me to go down to Johnny Cannon in McMahon's for things I never heard of before. "Go down and ask him for a long weight"; Johnny will leave me there for two hours. He'll serve every customer that walks in off the street. They'll look at me and tell Johnny that I was there before them and Johnny will say it's ok, he's been looked after. And when the two hours have gone, Johnny will ask me what colour did I want. I'll shake my head and say "Pop never said". I'll go back and ask. Pop what colour he wants.' He says it's alright, he found one in the tool box while I was gone and I'm asking him to tell me what a long weight looks like but he just tells me to go back to work. The next day Lar is sending me back down again for a round square. A couple of days later it's bubbles for levels, then it's glass hammers and other days bags of steam and sky hooks, before it finally hits me that they're making a bloody eejit out of me and stop asking me to go anywhere.

A week later Pop wants me to go down to Johnny again and get a pint of nothing. I'll laugh and tell him to go down and get it himself because I'm not falling for that one. Pop raises his voice and says "I'm not going to ask you a second time". I'll raise my voice and say "Well I'm telling you a second time I'm not going down". "Do you want a thick ear?" he'll ask. "No", I'll answer. "Well go down to Johnny and ask him for a pint of nothing". 'I'll tell him I'm not falling for it'. "Will you go down", he shouts. I'm down at Bedford Row again, telling Jonny my father is trying to make a fool out of me but I'm not falling for it. "What's he looking for now?" he asks. 'A pint of nothing'. 'How did he think I'd fall for that' and Johnny says 'right you are', walks over to a ladder, takes it in his hands, puts it against the shelves that reach at least ten feet up to the ceiling, climbs all the way so he can reach the tins that are on the top shelf, takes a plastic tub out, climbs down the ladder and bangs it on the counter with a smile and says 'One only pint of nothing, Mr. Taylor!' I'm smiling at Johnny asking 'What's that supposed to be?,' 'You did ask me for a pint of nothing, didn't you?,' 'I did', 'Well there it is'. He turns the bottle that has a brown liquid inside it and there on the cover is the word "Knotting".

I'm asking Johnny what's "that" for. He says "for knots". I'm asking him why would you need a liquid for knots? He says because no matter how many times you paint over them, knots will keep soaking the paint but if you paint over it with this stuff, it stops the soakage. I'm walking up to Pop saying "he's caught me again". A couple of days later Pop will park his bike outside Whelan's, lock it, walk up the stairs to the salon and tell us all there's divers with air tanks jumping off Sarsfield bridge into the Shannon river and I'll be the first to ask why and he'll say 'they're looking for fishes farts to make bubbles for levels'.

After we'd finished Mr. Ferris's ladies hair salon, we're up in Mallow Street to a place that Pop calls 'The Church' that doesn't look a church at all from the outside. But inside, it's just like St. John's Cathedral or any other church in Limerick, except there's no holy pictures or statues. Just plain painted walls everywhere with long timber seats just like they have in our own church. Lar and myself will be on ladders working away and Pop will make his way up to the podium where he says the preachers do their talking. He'll say things like 'The Lord be with you!' and Lar and myself will say 'And also with you!' He'll pound his hand on the rostrum and say 'Ye're all sinners and ye'll all be damned and burn in hell forever!' And Lar and myself will shout 'We're sorry Lord, we're sorry! forgive us, forgive us!' we'll be laughing all day, everyday, for the six days we'll be here.

Another day Pop will go back to the podium and say something that doesn't make any sense at all like 'At that time there was no buses and Joseph had to walk to Jerusalem after another five minutes'. He'll go back to the podium and say 'This is the second Sunday after last Monday. Next Tuesday is Ash Wednesday. The gates of the church will be open but the doors will be shut. You can book your seats but you'll have to sit on the floor. There'll be high tea but it'll be on a low table'. And on and on it'll go. And then the two of them will start at me. Lar will pretend he's Mam and Pop will pretend he's a neighbour as they meet on the street. And Lar will say 'Jesus Mrs. Taylor! Is that your son Paddy isn't he after getting very big, God bless him? I hear he is working with your husband Harry. He must be making a fortune. I bet he has to bring all the wages home every week in a wheelbarrow'. And off they'll go doing their level best trying to wind me up but it won't work because I'll be loving every minute of it. I'll be laughing as much as they are and I'll be hoping every day will be longer and when it does end, I can't wait for the next one to be back there in among the laughing the slagging and the joking.

After finishing the church at Mallow Street, we're off up to O'Connell Avenue to a three storey house that Lar says is going to be a new bed and breakfast, and that we'll be only doing the decorating; that the carpentry will be looked after by two other lads because the woman who owns it needs it ready to start making an income. So, it's up to the top floor. The woman who owns the house is a widow and has moved from the north of Ireland to set up home again in Limerick, and is no spring chicken. Everything is wee this and wee that and when eleven o'clock comes the five of us will be down to the table that's well laid out with beautiful cups and saucers, plates of ham, tomatoes, white and brown bread and right in the middle, a plate with five slices of home made cake. I can't wait to get started on the cake but I'll have to leave it and take a slice of bread first. Pop and Lar do the same along with one of the other carpenters. The second one puts his hand out and takes one of the five slices it's obvious that the five slices means there's one for each of us. He has it gone in seconds and the hand is out again for a second slice, the dirty louser. But instead of taking one, he takes two. He butters each and puts them together and takes a big bite out of it. I can't believe there's only two slices left and I'm still trying to finish off the slice of bread that I buttered. I'm nearly choking myself trying to get them down my throat, when your man puts his hand out again and takes the other two, butters them just like the other ones, puts them together and has them gone in seconds. Pop, Lar and myself will spend the rest of the day talking about the louser. We'll ask each other questions like: 'Why would anyone be so selfish to stuff their face and be in such a hurry to make sure nobody else got a slice?' But we have a plan for tomorrow's tea break. And I'll have a part to play in it.

When tomorrow comes, Lar has me working in the hallway downstairs by the kitchen so I can keep an eye on things. Its ten forty five and Mrs. Mills is starting to set the table and by eleven o'clock, she sticks her head out the hall and shouts to the lads upstairs that tea is ready and that's my cue to go in first. And there they are again, the five slices of cake. But they're gone now because I have two on my plate, two on Lar's and one on Pop's. Lar and Pop are down next and each give me a wink of approval. And there's the two boys behind with your man looking at the empty plate and making comments like 'Jesus lads! Ye took all the cake and you never thought of leaving a slice or two for myself.' And it's time for Pop and Lar to go into action. Pop starts first and says 'Jesus, sure you must be sick of cake, you ate so much of it yesterday'. Then Lar adds 'I fupping hate currant cake' as he puts a slice into his mouth, then adds in a whisper 'This fupping thing tastes awful'. There's so much talk about the cake that Mrs. Mills says that that's the last of it and she won't be baking again until next week and your man has an awful face on him and says to me 'Can't you give me one of your slices?', But Lar answers him saying 'Would you ever go and take a fupping jump in the river? You came down here yesterday and gulped the five fupping slices on your own and didn't bother your arse asking any of us if we wanted any. so you can fupp off now and have the rest of the stale fupping bread we had yesterday'. Lar looked around to see if Mrs. Mills was still in the kitchen before he left your man have it and the laughing and the joking that involved the five of us is gone because the other two have got the hump over the cake and when Mills shouts 'Tea up' the next few days the two boys won't be down until we're gone.

Mrs. Mills will call Lar and Pop and tell them she doesn't want any trouble between the workmen over a few silly slices of cake. That she needs the five of us working together in harmony so as the work can be finished as soon as possible. We're on out third week here at Mrs. Mills' and she wants to know if I could make her a small press with two doors under the Belfast sink in the kitchen. I can't believe that someone wants me to make something for them. I'll be able to make extra money after six o'clock for the next two evenings.

'Go handy with me now', she says, 'I'm only a poor widow woman' and I'm telling Pop and Lar I've got a tommer off of Mrs. Mills and Pop says be careful with that one because she's as tight as a duck's arse. I'm asking him has he got any spare hard board; 2x1 wood, that I have to make two small doors. And that I need some 3x2 plain wood for the frame but he hasn't. Now I'm asking him for the loan of a pound so that I can buy some for the next two nights, I'm working in Mrs. Mills' kitchen next to her Waterford cooker that will have the sweat pouring out of me. I'll take my time because it's the first job I've ever been asked to do and if I don't do it right I mightn't get another one, I'm sick and tired of sanding wood and filling walls with polyfilla that has the top of my fingers cut and scrapped because Lar says I have to learn to prepare walls and wood properly before I can put a paint brush into my hand. Mrs. Mills will watch me each night and tell me I'm a great young man for my age, that I'll be a great asset to the girl that gets me and she's sure my home will be a castle.

When the second night arrives I have it finished and I'm dead proud of what I've done. Mrs. Mills is opening and closing each door with comments like 'Good man yourself! That's a great job. How much do I owe you?' She's looking for her purse and my heart is hoppin because I have to tell her how much I'm looking for. I should have told her before I started. But I mightn't have got it then. Sure I've made it up on a piece of paper twenty times. The price for the wood, the hinges and handles plus the amount of time I spent on it at the same rate that Lar pays me per hour. That's fair isn't it? 'Two pound, ten shillings Mrs. Mills please'. Mrs Mills has stopped in her tracks. 'How much did you say?' So I repeat: 'Two pounds ten shillings please Mrs. Mills,' thinking she feels it might be too little. 'Jesus, Mary and Holy St. Joseph! That's very dear. Are you charging me that much for two tiny little doors? Sure if I knew it was going to be that much, I could have got one of the two carpenters upstairs to do it for me'. I'm stuttering all over the place trying to explain how much everything cost. She says 'You'll have to go home and talk to your father. I couldn't afford that much'. And there I am walking home in the dark thinking Pop is going to give me hell because I've upset one of his customers. He'll be giving out that work isn't easy to come by and the last thing he needs is me working for them and upsetting them too. When I arrive home he's watching the news and I have to wait until it's finished and get the head blown off me. It's a long fifteen minutes before I can tell him what happened. He wants to know what I did, how long I was at it, and how much did it cost me for the materials. After I've finished telling him, he's not taking the head off of me. Instead, I get the best bit of advice, the best bit of wisdom that I'll never forget for the rest of my life. 'Go back down' he says 'and tell her that it isn't for doing the job you're charging her but for knowing how to do it'. 'Do you think' he says 'if she could do the job herself she'd have asked you to do it'? I'll never forget that night and those great words of wisdom. I'll use them for the rest of my working life, even when I'm giving estimates. I'll go to work the next day and wait for Mrs. Mills to ask me what my father said when I told him how much I was charging her and when I told her what he said she has no answer, just mumbles away under her breath while taking out the two pound notes and the ten shillings in coins. Pop was telling Lar about it and Lar tells me about the time a woman in Janesboro asked him to call over and look at her gas cooker that wasn't working for two days and that she hadn't been able to cook a dinner since. Lar says he pulled the cooker out from the wall, asked the woman for a sewing needle then a match, did a bit of fiddling, making sure he had his back to her and the husband who couldn't put a nail in the wall and Lar adds 'You don't want people knowing how to fix things. You want them to think you're a fupping genius so you'll make sure they can't see what you're fupping doing'. He says he struck a match, turned on the gas and off it went. 'Oh that's great' says the husband; 'I'll get a dinner now. How much do we owe you?' 'Ten bob' says Lar. 'Jesus Lar, that's very dear. Sure you were only at it a few minutes' And Lar says 'Well, its like this now Mrs, it's five bob for knowing what to use and the other five bob is for knowing what to do with it'.

Mrs. Mills house in O'Connell Avenue

CHAPTER 5

My lovely pearly red accordion that Pop and Mam bought me, and got into hock for, is going because a city slicker like myself doesn't want to be seen dead with one of those country culchie things around his shoulders anymore. So it's off to Peter Dempsey's for a guitar. 'I'll give you this one and an amplifier in a straight swap' says Peter, and I'm gone out the door leaving behind the lovely pearly red accordion that I thought years ago I'd die if I didn't get. It will be back on the window again for another young lad to rest his elbows on the window sill and dream away. I just want to get home and start walloping this thing that has the amplifier. I'm upstairs in my bedroom making an awful racket when Mam comes up the stairs with her hand on her head shouting 'Jesus, Mary and Holy St. Joseph! What's that bloody racket?' Then she wants to know where I got it. I'm telling her I swapped the accordion because I want to learn to play the guitar. She puts her eyes up to heaven, turns and walks away, muttering about the awful days in Upper Carey's road when she had to listen to the racket I was making with the yoke that Pop brought home on his bike from the attic in O'Connell Avenue, and that the same bloody thing is starting all over again, only this time he's got an electric yoke that's four times as loud. I should have given it a bit more thought before I went running up to Peter Dempsey's because this is hard work, much harder than learning the accordion. First, I have to learn how to tune it. That takes me a week at least. Now the tips of my finger on my left hand are killing me from constantly pressing the steel strings. Peter Dempsey told me it'll get easier as the skin will get hard on my finger tops the more I press them. I have a book that he gave me with pictures showing where I should put each finger on the guitar handle. He said if you can play three chords that will do for most songs. But I won't give up. The fingers that I use everyday for the painting are getting harder now and trying to change the finger from one position to another is getting better and after a month of practice every night and Mam closing every door in the house, I can play Elvis Presley's Wooden Heart using my own words, making sure they rhyme with wooden heart because I don't know the words to the song. And I'm wondering why I'm playing Wooden Heart by Elvis when I can't stand the sight of him or his voice, because Jett wanted a dancing partner when she heard him for the first time in Upper Carey's road and had me out in the street, teaching me and herself how to jive with the threat that if I didn't do it, Dinny, Phonsie and Noelie could thump me all they liked and wouldn't come to my rescue. And giving me hell because I'm not doing it right and telling me to stop pussing or else. But then I started to like it, the dancing, not Elvis, because we're getting good at it. Mothers would be out on the road standing longside each other with the arms folded commenting on how good we are. And now she's taking me to the hop for the first time up near the Dublin Road at St. Patrick's scout hall for two bob a head. I'm walking up behind a bunch of her friends because none of the lads in Garryowen want to go to a dance because they say they haven't a clue how to do it. I'm keeping well behind the girls; I won't want to look like a right wally but they'll keep calling me up, and I wish they'd stop doing that because they're drawing attention to me and this is one time I don't want to be noticed. The scout hall is tiny; not a bit like St. Joseph's in Reeves' path. It's just like Jett said; girls on one side and fellas on the other. There's one loud speaker at the corner of the stage that's at one end of the hall. All the girls have cardigans and frocks with white ankle socks. The lads in their one and only suits, sucking a fag and taking a comb out every few minutes, fixing the quiff that's soaked in Brill Cream and the hand that doesn't have the comb is used to pull the quiff out over the forehead. Then it's up with the shoulders; and the heads sunk into their chests while the fag is put in the side of the mouth and sucked in with the jaws as far as they can go.

When the smoke gets exhaled, there's all types of gestures with the mouth and head giving the onlookers, mostly women, a gander at the tough male who's doing all he can, with everything he has, to attract the female species that might think he's a desirable hunk. The music is blaring away for the bones of an hour with The Shadows, The Beatles, The Rolling Stones, Billy Furey, lousy Elvis, The Everly Brothers, The Fortunes, Billy J. Kramer, Manford Man, The Hollys, The Tremeloes, The Searchers and many more. A voice from the loudspeaker will appeal to the young lads saying 'Come on now lads, who's going to break the ice and get the dance started?' The lads are there smoking away, throwing all the shapes and the girls waiting to see what kind of amadán is going to walk the six feet across the floor and ask them to dance. God help them if he's a right gobshite and, if he is, she'll be stuck with him for three dances and will have to talk to him in between the time it takes to change a record. And if he's shy or has a stutter because he's with a girl, it will be bloody unbearable. And if he thinks she likes him, she'll get lost into the toilets for fear he might ask her again and that means she won't be available for the guy she likes that she hopes will walk across the floor and say the magic words 'Will you dance please?' The lads will be there pretending they're not really interested but are all watching each other because they might have come here with a girl they're going out with. But you can't hang around in this hall with your girlfriend; it just isn't done. And God help them if the stampede of male legs starts before they are ready and now their girlfriend is dancing with a gobshite and she's not a bit happy about it and it will be all his fault. Now his head is in a muddle, he'll go over and give your man a box and all hell will break loose. There'll be fellas here like Bashers Kelly, Cyril Tynan, Tom Hickey and others who'll be jumping over bodies throwing punches at people they've never seen before. They won't know why it started or care either. The loudspeaker will be calling for order and the scoutmasters who are there to keep order are gone like they will every Sunday night when the fighting starts and the whole thing will be over in a matter of minutes and it'll be like it never happened at all.

St. Patrick's Scout Hall,
how we all fitted in here, I'll never know

There'll be other lads here who don't have a girl and that's why they're here. They'll have their eye on a girl at the front of the seventy or eighty that's lined up against the wall, four or five deep, and when the music starts for the next three dances they're out of the block. They'll have their hand out to a girl that's only two four feet away and someone else has got there before them. Now, they can't turn and walk away; that would be too humiliating. But all is not lost; there is another three or four behind where his first choice was standing and, if he's good at it, he'll make it look like one of them was his first choice. And there has to be no sign of disappointment on his face. And this poor girl mightn't have had a dance all night and if it wasn't for him she wouldn't have been asked at all. And when the three dances are over she'll be looking over at him smiling away wondering when he's going to come over and ask her for another dance. I'll come here every Sunday night with or without Jett. I'll get the guts to ask a girl to dance because I have the bug and love every minute

106

of it. When ladies choice comes once or twice every Sunday night, I'll be bricking it like all the other lads, hoping that one of the eighty females will ask me to dance. There's only fifty lads here and if any one of us are left here looking at the other guys throwing the legs around with the ladies who thought they were good looking and asked them to dance, we'll want to dig a hole in the ground and jump into it. It was bad enough not being asked but there's another thirty frocks across the other side who didn't think we were worth the trouble of asking.

Monday mornings can be hard to handle, especially if we're working on a Georgian house in O'Connell Avenue. The hand cart made of two large iron wheels, wooden frame and handles, that sits behind the Grand Central Cinema in the open yard waiting for me to load it up, with ladders, dust sheets, the fold-able table for pasting paper plus other tools, and paintbrush-es. Pop will be in McMahon's getting the paint and Lar up in Lower Thomas Street at Geary's wallpaper shop collecting the paper that might've been ordered in 'specially from Dublin or England. By eleven o'clock we're there at the job taking every-thing in and getting ourselves organised. Lar and myself will be on the one plank that's resting between two ladders in a large downstairs room. All the ceilings in O'Connell Ave have cracks everywhere, so it's a case of cleaning it down and covering the ceiling with lining paper. Pop will have two or three lengths of paper pasted and soaking away for ten minutes. I've a twenty one inch piece of roundwood in both hands. Lar and myself will start at one end and Pop will hand me a length that has four folds on it, I'll let it hang over the stick. I'll hold it to the ceil-ing for Lar to take the end and place it up to the ceiling while he's telling me to pull it tight. He'll apply the outstretched piece to the ceiling and brush it out and then we'll move forward to another section while I have my eye as close to the ceiling as I can get it and find what he's left out of his backside two minutes earlier and it's bloody awful. Sure, he's only been telling us, as we walked up O'Connell Street, what he tells us every Monday; how he went out last night in his lovely brown suit with the creases perfectly ironed, not a wrinkle to be seen, a beautiful snow white shirt, spotlessly clean, collar and cuffs, with a tie to match the cufflinks that are made from fourteen carat gold with a tie pin to match that his girlfriend gave him. He'll talk about the pair of pure leather brown shoes that he paid ten pounds for that has the steel studs in the heel that makes the clicking sound when you walk and gets you noticed that have a dazzling shine. 'Hands beautifully clean and scrubbed leaving no sign that I'm a fupping painter. When people look at me they'll think I'm a businessman. I am a businessman, myself and your father are fupping businessmen, aren't we ,for fupps sake? My face will be clean and well shaved with no fupping cuts or gashes. From the steady hand that paints the straight lines every day with the brush that's doing it, and I'm off down the town on my own because Sunday nights are my nights. It's into the Bedford where I'm well known and everyone there will say 'Jaysus Lar, is that you? You're looking like a millionaire.' I'll have my four pints and it's off to the Hong Kong Chinese Restaurant in William Street for a feed of curry and fried rice. Then back down to the Bedford for another four pints of the black stuff and home to the bed for a good night's sleep'.

And I saying to Pop 'Yea, and the whole lot souring away in his stomach, turning into gas, and plenty of it too, that will erupt around eleven or twelve o'clock every Monday morning'. It would be grand if he gave us a warning but that's not Lar's way of farting. He'll just let them crawl out of his backside nice and slow with no warning at all. I'll be begging him to stop because my nose is so close to the ceiling. He'll just laugh away with the plank we're both standing on waving up and down. My hands will be killing me trying to keep the stick with the folded paper that's hung on it as close as I can to the ceiling. I'll be holding my breath keeping my mouth closed. I won't want any of that stuff he's releasing into the air in my mouth. But he'll just keep doing it every five minutes. But I can't keep my mouth closed because I'm laughing so much. When the gas goes and the laughing stops they'll be talking about something else over a cup of tea and biscuits that will come on a tray in the mid afternoon from the young girl who lives in the country, and looks after the house for the swanky woman who'll be out in the town meeting all her rich friends with a dead fox wrapped around her shoulders, whose skeleton and insides are gone and just hangs there with its head and legs resting on her breasts.

And if Pop is in the mood, he'll start telling Lar and myself about his childhood days and the tailoring shop in Bedford Row. How his brother Paddy was a beautiful tailor, a perfectionist. And you daren't walk in on top of Paddy while he was hand stitching a garment. I'm looking at Lar thinking how he's taken after my uncle Paddy because he's the same; he'll have my heart broke every day repeating the same bloody thing, over and over, until I'm doing it automatically. He'll be saying 'Before you start working anywhere, clean the place first. Always work in a clean environment. You don't want to be falling over tins of paint or buckets wondering where the fupp did I leave this or that. You have to be properly organised to do the thing right and when all your preparation is done sweep the floor again. Feel the woodwork that you're sanding with the palm of your hand just to make sure the surface is right. Don't be trusting your eye all the time or guessing. When you're painting the skirting board get your head down on the floor so you can see the bottom.' I'll be saying 'Sure you won't be able to see the bottom when the carpet goes back'. And he'll say he doesn't give a fupp about the carpet. How he wants it done right for the customers when they come in here on Friday evening and inspect the work. 'I don't want them looking at lumps or fupping bubbles of paint anywhere; I want everything painted properly. I don't want the embarrassment of having to make excuses to customers if they point out something that's wrong and say 'Ah sure you won't see that when the carpet goes down or the curtains are on the window or the fupping couch is against the wall or the big fupping Georgian mirror is hanging over the fireplace. Because when the customers come in here on Friday evening, I want them to see a professional job carried out by professional people. I want to hear words like 'Oh my goodness! That is such a beautiful job. I'm delighted. Thank you very much!' I want them to be telling the rich women they hang around with about the guys from Bedford Row and the beautiful professional work they carry out. I want them to be talking about how well we look in our white clean overalls with a clean shirt and tie. I want them to feel like they're employing the best there is. I want them to say to their friends, if they want us to work for them, they'll have to get in the fupping queue and wait .

He'll be saying the same thing again next week; only the speech will last an extra five minutes. I won't know whether to laugh or have the serious look on my face because when Lar uses the F word it's very funny. Pop doesn't do it very often, maybe because I'm around, but when he does it's not as funny as Lar. But Lar will take the lecturing too far. He'll be giving out if I put too much butter on my bread if we're outside the city and the customer gives us our lunch. I love butter but he says I'm putting it on with a fupping trowel. He won't say it in front of Pop because he knows what Pop will do. So I'll get it in the ear if the two of us are working together in a room on our own. If I meet him in the town on a Saturday or Sunday he'll be talking about the job that we're going to in the morning, the first thing we'll do is get the fupping furniture out, then the carpet up. After that the two of us will strip the paper off the walls so when its time to go home the whole fupping place is ready for filling and sanding. I'll think he's finished but he'll want to talk about what we're going to do on Tuesday, Wednesday, Thursday, Friday as well and when we say goodbye, I'll look at my watch and realise half an hour has passed. I'll be only with him six months and hate his guts because he'll tell me the kind of clothes I should be wearing, giving out about the food I'll turn my nose up at when we're in people's houses like: eggs, lettuce, tomatoes, onions, carrots, asparagus and other things I've never seen or heard before. He'll look at Pop and say 'Jaysus Harry, you have that fupping fella spoiled' and off he'll go about how hard things were when his father Lar died and left his poor mother with five children to rear. 'And you can be fupping sure we ate every fupping thing that was put in front of us and we didn't give an fupp if it was cooked or not' and it's like being at home listening to Nan, Mam and Pop. I'm wondering why do grown ups always have a story to tell about how hard things were in their days. Years later I realise how blessed I was to have this man train and give me habits I still have today. I'll become very fond of him and laugh at the things that he said and did and see this man's insistence on giving me the best training I could ever get.

When Pop starts with the stories that are always worth waiting for I'll try to get him to tell us something about his past every day but he has to be in the mood and today he is in a good one. He doesn't need much encouragement and off he goes about his Dad's tailoring shop in Bedford Row. The shop that so many of his customers are familiar with. Taylor by name, tailor by trade and used to live in Taylor Street. He tells us about the time he wanted to impress the girls in the gang of twenty he used to hang around with. 'My brother Paddy, the perfectionist, had been working for days on a Cavalry Twill trousers.' And I'm asking 'What's a Cavalry Twill trousers?' and Pop says 'Cavalry Twill was the most expensive material a tailor could work with in those days and, also, the most difficult. And when Paddy was working with that material you wouldn't want to be around him when he was on the table with his legs crossed, hand stitching a garment'. 'Anyway', 'I went into the shop on Sunday morning during the summer as the gang were heading out to Corbally for a swim,' everyone in the house were over in the Franciscan church for mass so I had the shop to myself and there on the counter ready for collection on Monday morning was a brown paper parcel with a string wrapped around it and when I opened it up there it was, the beautiful cream coloured Cavalry Twill trousers. I tried it on and it was a perfect fit and I thought boys, but the girls in the gang would be fair impressed with me when they clap eyes on Harry Taylor in a Cavalry Twill trousers'. And I'm thinking 'Janey Pop, you'd want more than a cavalry twill trousers to impress the girls. Maybe you should have looked for a face covering garment as well'. Pop says he put another pair of pants into the brown paper and left the parcel to look like it hadn't been touched, just in case Paddy came into the shop when he came back from mass. 'So there I'm, 'prouncing around the place all the way out to Corbally and the girls saying 'Oh Har, your pants is gorgeous!'. Pop says when they arrived at Corbally he was halfway through a fag, the only one he had. So before he togged off for the swim he flicked the top of the fag and put the rest of it into the pocket of the Cavalry Twill trousers, folded it up carefully, laid it on the ground and jumped into the River Shannon out in Corbally with the rest of the gang. An hour later, dried himself off, unfolded the pants while talking to his friends, put his foot into the right leg of the pants and there around the arse area of the pocket was a great big burnt hole from the fag end that wasn't quenched at all, and had to listen to remarks from all the gang on his way back home about what his brother Paddy was going to do to him when he found out. And how he had to figure out a way of getting the pants back into the shop without being seen and then into the brown paper parcel as well. He said he had to wait until everyone was in bed late that night before he could creep down the stairs at twelve o'clock to put it back. When Paddy's customer arrived the next morning to collect the trousers, Paddy wants the customer to try it on. The customer says its ok, 'sure haven't you been making clothes for me for years and don't they always fit perfectly?' But Paddy insists. The customer reluctantly agrees and when the parcel's opened and the lovely cavalry twill trousers is shown to the customer, Paddy lets a roar out of him shouting 'Harry!' And Pop says he had to stay at a friend's house for a week before he could go back home.

Lar and myself want to know has he any more stories, and Pop tells us of his other brother who was also Lar's father. How the three of them used to sleep in the same room every night. Pop says his brother was so mean he used to wake up every night to see if he lost any sleep. He said 'The three of us all smoked, but the second eldest brother Lar was the only one who could afford to have extra fags and would never take one out in company in case he had to offer some. Every night before he closed his eyes, he'd open his packet of fags, count the number inside and write that number on the back of the inside and when he'd open his eyes the following morning count them again and, if there was any missing, he'd kick the shit out of Paddy and himself . And Lar isn't a bit happy, 'Sure, you're the fupping same' says Pop and Lar wants to know how he's the same. 'Sure you're worse than your father'. Now they're shouting at one another. I can't believe it; a minute ago we were all laughing. Now they're not talking and there's a terrible atmosphere in the room. No conversation of any kind, Lar will turn to me and say 'Ask your father where did he leave the seven inch brush'. I'll turn to Pop and say 'Lar wants to' and, before I can finish, Pop will say 'Tell him it's outside in the hall in the blue bucket'. I'll turn to Lar and start to say', 'it's outside.' and Lar is gone out to the hall and I'm thinking: this is bloody ridiculous. Sure they're only a couple of feet away from one another and it will go on for the rest of the week when the same bloody sentence will be said three times, every time, and, now, I don't like coming to work anymore because there's no laughing or farting either. But when next week comes it's all forgotten it's like it never happened.

We have a selection of buckets of all shapes and sizes. Lar says they're buckets that customers give them and they don't get them back so, 'if a customer ever complains about not getting their bucket back, you'll get the blame. We'll tell them it's all your fault. That you are only with us a couple of days and that you don't know what belongs to whom.'

Mr. & Mrs. Lynch are good customers of Lars.' They have a fish shop in Thomas Street and a hairdressing salon overhead on the first floor and another one in the basement. They have buckets of money and we'll spend a good three months here every year. Mr. Lynch has elderly parents living over on the North Circular Road and Lar says we'll be there for the bones of a month, redecorating the whole house. They're lovely elderly people and great to work for. Pop says Mr. Lynch in Thomas Street is paying for everything and wants a good job done. I'm six months working for Pop and Lar now, and a month ago Lar let me use a paintbrush when he put it into my hand for the first time. It's great because I've started to get a few small painting jobs on the weekends and evenings. I'll be in and out of the back kitchen door of Mr. and Mrs. Lynch's house, the door that has a latch on it, and every ten minutes I'll go to the old galvanised shed at the back looking for things that Pop or Lar will want, because I'm the gopher around here. Sure, didn't I bring all the stuff out here in the handcart when we arrived on Monday morning? Mrs. Lynch will be giving out to me because I'll knock on the door every time I want to come back into the house from being outside in the shed. 'For goodness sake, Pat!' she'll say. 'You don't have to knock every time you want to come back into the house. Just lift the latch and walk through'. I'll apologise and say I can't help it, that it's a habit I just can't get out of. She'll say how well reared I am and that I'm a credit to my parents. But I'll keep doing it every day, twenty times or more and keep telling her I'm sorry once I'm inside in the kitchen. She'll laugh and say it's ok. But my brain and it's lack of taking in what's going on around me is going to walk me into trouble again very soon and I won't want to come back to this house to these lovely people again because of what I'm going to walk into later on this evening.

Lar and myself are working away upstairs on the three bedrooms while Pop is putting a toilet and washbasin under the stairs that used to be a storage area. There's a lot of talk about Mrs. Lynch getting too old to climb the stairs, even to go to bed and use the toilet and how one of the downstairs rooms will be used for a bedroom once we're gone. And if poor Mrs. Lynch, who's small and massive in size, wants to relieve herself and can't go upstairs, then she has to do it someplace else. But not while there's three men working in the house from nine thirty to six every day. I have a job to finish that evening; a small tommer I'm working on, I have no money to buy some bits so I'll have to knock off a few items belonging to Pop and Lar that will be outside in the small hut where all our gear and materials are. Items like polyfiller and sand paper, some white spirit and a small bit of white gloss paint. Pop won't mind if I take some but Lar will crib and moan. I'll pretend I forgot something as the three of us cycle home on our bikes that evening around ten past six. It works perfectly, I'm on my way back, leaving my bike against the wall of Mrs. Lynch's house and make my way to the hut. But

I can't find what I want. Then, I realise, they're upstairs in one of the bedrooms. So I make my way to the kitchen door and, instead of bloody well knocking like I've been doing for the last few days, I lift the latch, and put my two feet into the kitchen floor and there, right in front of my sixteen year old eyes, is a female's arse, the size of which I have never seen before. It's poor Mrs. Lynch holding a white enamel potty between her knees, firing away into it with a force that sounds like she's getting a great relief like she's been holding if for hours. I can see her upside down head looking at me through her thighs. 'Oh Jesus, Mrs. Lynch. I'm very sorry'. And as calm as you like Mrs. Lynch says, while looking at me through her legs with the flow as strong as ever 'That's ok Pat love. Don't be one bit sorry. Sure it could happen to anyone'. And I'm thinking 'Jesus, no it couldn't. It could only bloody happen to me'. I'm trying to take one of my legs off the floor to get me out of here as fast as I can but it's like it's stuck to the ground. I can't take my eyes away from the bare arse either. An arse that I have never seen anything like before and don't ever want to see anything like it again. After I managed to get my legs to take me upstairs for things I can't remember, to have the stuff I need that should have been out in the bloody shed and if it was I wouldn't be the mess I'm in now. Mr. Lynch is there and knows I have walked in to his wife's bit of privacy. We're in the room talking away and I haven't a bloody clue what he is saying because I am trying to think how am I going to get out of here without running into Mrs. Lynch's arse again. I'll have to go back downstairs and try to sneak out the front door without being seen, I'm there in the room talking to Mr. Lynch jabbering away about nothing, looking at my watch waiting for a good 30 minutes to pass before I jump down the stairs three or four steps at a time get on my bike and tear down the North Circular Road forgetting all about the few bits of things I need for work that night and forgetting about work too.

Before I know it, I'm home, panting and gasping for air. Pop says he thought I was going to finish a job tonight. I'm telling I'm not going back to work tomorrow, that I'll go looking for another job instead. Nan is there sitting in the chair by the fire that has the extra cushions with the face she'll always have. The curious one that is going to stick its nose into other people's business any minute now. Pop is giving me a look with one eye closed and an expression of what the hell are you talking about?

'I am not going back to that house over on the North Circular Road any more and I don't care what you say to talk me out of it,' 'why not' he asks and out it comes, that same stupid answer he and Mam had been giving me for years: 'That's the why'. 'What do you mean that's the why', asks Mam. I don't want to talk about what happened because they will fall around the place laughing when they hear the reason, so I am telling Pop again that I am going to look for a job tomorrow. Pop asks me a second time what happened but I am not answering and off goes Nan with the 'Why don't you answer your father when he's talking to you? Have you no respect telling him you're giving up a grand trade that many a young lad would be bite your hand off for'. And on and on she'll go until Mam puts her hand on my shoulder and asks me kindly 'Pa, will you tell us what's wrong?' When Mam talks to me like that, showing me kindness and consideration putting her hand on my shoulders, I can't resist it and out it comes, the whole lot. And there's Pop's shoulders slowly starting to go, up and down, before they're going out of control. When Nan sees Pop starting to cough, off she goes repeating what I said with the usual 'Jesus, Mary and Holy St. Joseph. He walked in on top of the poor woman with a potty between her legs.' I know Mam is trying not to laugh but it's only a matter of time before she is at it as well. She'll say 'Ah, don't be laughing at him' in between a few giggles. I can see the funny side of it now and join in the uncontrollable laughter that can be heard out on the road that has Jetta and James in wanting to find out what's so funny. But no one can tell them because we are all bending over holding our stomachs and when we can't laugh no more there's more questions like 'Why didn't you knock before you went in? Why was the woman using a potty? Is there no toilet in the house?' and, 'Are you going back to work tomorrow?' I am telling them that I haven't a bloody notion of going anywhere near that house, not for the rest of my life. And off the laughing goes again before they will all give me reasons why I should go back. Nan is at it again with the 'I should be so lucky to have a job'. Pop will be making funny comments like 'Did you get to see if she wiped her backside before you went upstairs?' And off we'll go again with the laughing. But it will be Mam's words that would give me the courage to think about going back tomorrow when she says 'I can promise you Pa that that will be the last thing on that woman's mind tomorrow when you walk in the door. Just pretend it's another day'.

I'll go to bed that night with the image of that woman's arse and the size of it in my head that won't go away and her thighs like porter barrels and flesh hanging all over the place that has lumps and hollows as well as veins of all colours and sizes. I have never seen a naked woman before and, if they are all like that, I never want to see one again. I can't sleep trying to get that awful image out of my head and I am trying to figure out will I or won't I go to work tomorrow and before I know it, the morning sun is coming in through the bedroom window.

It is time to get up. I can feel that lump in my gut. The lump that has me feeling light in the head. I can't eat my breakfast and Pop is across the table with the shoulders up and down again every few minutes and Mam giving him a thump, telling him to shut up and leave me alone, saying, 'Can't you see the state he's in, having to go over and face that woman'. But it only makes him worse and now he has me at it with a laugh that is only half hearted because one minute I am saying I can't face that woman and the next minute I am wondering will I get another job and before I know it, I am heading across Sarsfields bridge and the closer my bike takes me to Mrs. Lynch's house, the louder my heart is beating. I'm asking Pop will he walk into the house in front of me to give me a chance to get up the stairs as fast as I can. Pop is knocking at the kitchen door that we are standing outside waiting to hear the voice that will tell us to come in and wish us a good morning. It's Mrs. Lynch. She's there at the sink talking to Pop about the weather, like nothing happened and looks at me and says 'Good Morning Pat. How are you this lovely morning?' I am looking at the floor while answering her with the words 'I am fine thank you, Mrs. Lynch' and I'm gone upstairs while herself and Pop talk away. I am trying to figure out how a person can act so normally to me when I was only looking up her bare arse last night and how did Mam know she would be the way she is this morning? Lar is on his way up stairs and tells me what to do. I'm on my knees painting the skirting board and I can hear Pop whispering to Lar and it is only seconds before the two of them are on their knees, snorting and hissing, with hands over their mouths, trying not to laugh out loud and I'll be listening to smart remarks for the rest of the day.

Lar comes into the room I'm working in and asks in a whisper if I'd go down to Mrs. Lynch and ask her will she have a loan of a pot to mix some paint in. A few minutes later he'll ask me was her knickers clean and then Pop starts with: 'Does Mr. Lynch know you were looking up his wife's arse last night?' and on and on it'll go, all next week as well. When the call for tea break comes from downstairs I have to face Mrs. Lynch again. She's telling me to sit down at a certain chair at the table, would I like this or that and to be sure to take what I want. And there we are the five of us sitting around the table talking about everything and nothing while we all have it in out minds that I was looking up at Mrs. Lynch's bottom last night. And Lar opens his mouth, with a smirk on his face, and says 'I hear you were doing a tommer last night Paddy. I know I have gone red in the face. Before I can answer, he asks: 'Did you go straight from here to your job or did you go home first?' He's a dirty rotten louser. I know he is doing it on purpose. I'll ignore him but he'll keep at it with more comments one after another.

In another few days I've forgotten all about it and, before we leave a few weeks later, Mrs. Lynch is telling the three of us that having a toilet downstairs is going to change her life. Lar and Pop are looking at me while she's saying it and I have to get out of the room before I burst a blood vessel trying to keep in the laugh.

The following Monday, the hand cart is loaded again for an-other job on the Ennis Road. To people Pop says are very posh. Mr. and Mrs. Stokes of Stokes & McKiernan, who have a big motor store in Bedford Row next to James McMahon, Pop and Lar call him 'WW', short for William Walter, and it's the same old story again with the two ladders against each wall, a long plank in the middle with Lar and myself on top of it and Lar dropping silent ones every five minutes and, as usual, my pleas are ignored. Pop says 'The curry Lar got at the Chinese must have gone off before he ate it because the smell is unbearable'. He's telling Lar he is a walking shithouse and he'd better go out-side the door and pull the chain on himself. There's a knock on the door of the room we're working in. It's Mrs. Stokes with a tray of sandwiches, biscuits and tea. She's asking what the awful smell in the room is. Pop's telling her 'It's fungus, Mrs. Stokes'. Mrs. Stokes is horrified that there could be fungus in her house and why she never smelt it before. Lar say's it's because we're taking the old wallpaper off the walls, and the fungus that was trapped for years behind it is now free to waft all over the place. Mrs. Stokes says she thought fungus always came through the paper but Pop says because the old paper was vinyl it can't come through it and Mrs. Stokes says she hopes it has plenty of time to get itself out of her walls, before the new paper goes up and it is just as well she's gone now because the two of them were making it up and couldn't think of another thing to say, and we're all killing ourselves laughing. Lar has to stop dropping any more because, if Lar keeps at it, Mrs. Stokes might want to get the fumigators in before we can finish the job and that means no work this week and no wages either.

Mrs. Stokes wants Pop to fit a mirror on a wall in her hall. It has a hole in each corner to take a screw and Pop says that the wall she wants it on isn't very even which will make the job of hanging it more difficult. But she says she knows she can leave it in his good hands. Pop says he will do it around five thirty, just before he goes home this evening and, when the time comes, Pop is drilling out the holes with an electric drill; the one they bought only a couple of weeks ago. And it is the only piece of electrical equipment they have and it's their pride and joy. Pop is drilling away and, when he is ready to hang the mirror, asks Lar to hold it while he puts a rawlplug in each hole to take a screw. After he inserts each one and gives them a few turns, he stands back with Lar and the two of them are asking each other if it's level. One of them is adjusting it this way, then the other way, before they decide it is hanging level. Pop gives each screw, a few turns, when he gets to the last one, gives it a final turn, the hall door opens and a posh voice says 'Evening all!' and Pop says 'Fupp it!' because he's just cracked the mirror as Mr. Stokes walked in the door. And Pop whispers to Lar 'Of all the fupping times for the boss to walk in the door when you've made a haimes of what you are doing!' After ten minutes, Mr. Stokes is upstairs with Mrs. Stokes and talking about the awful smell. They're sniffing away. Mr. Stokes has a big fancy moustache that curls at both ends, he says to his wife 'Are you sure, my dear?' 'That there was a bad odour in here this morning'.

'I must say I don't get the slightest hint of any kind of a smell whatsoever.'

Mrs. Stokes says she can't get it either but swears it was quite horrible; unbearable in fact. Mr. Stokes wants to know where the fungus is to be found and Pop lets Lar do all the talking because he was the one who was dropping the quiet ones all over the place this morning and is making all kinds of ridiculous reasons why the said fungus was the cause of the horrible smell even though there isn't a damp patch to be seen anywhere on the walls. Mr. Stokes says it must have been something else that caused the smell. That he'll check it again in the morning before he goes to work.

When the next day arrives there's no more talk about the awful smell. Pop is working on a small step ladder all day, up and down, moving the ladder and the bucket around the floor. When five thirty comes, and Pop has just finished the final coat on the ceiling, he's just about to put the paint away when I point to a patch he's missed. He puts the bucket of paint down near the bottom of the step ladder, dips the seven inch destemper brush into it, climbs the ladder four steps, gives the patch a wallop of the brush, starts to descend the ladder, and as he puts his right foot to the ground the front door opens. It's Mr. Stokes again. 'Evening all' and Pop sticks his foot into the bucket of white emulsion, stumbles, and falls to the ground, causing the emulsion to spill all over the dust sheet. There's a mad scatter of three bodies in white overalls trying their best, while laughing their heads off, to get the floor clean and Pop's shoe as well, before Mr. Stokes arrives upstairs to see how the work is progressing. And Pop is asking the two of us, is it his imagination or a coincidence that, when Mr. Stokes puts his foot inside the hall door disaster strikes? But, we will know tomorrow when five thirty comes when Pop is sitting on a plank doing nothing, just waiting for the door to open, at five thirty that evening. There is no sign of Mr. Stokes. It's six o'clock and as we are cycling home, Pop says it must be a bloody coincidence. We've forgotten all about it the next evening around five o'clock. Pop is in the attic putting a new ballcock in the tank. When five thirty comes, he's finished and starts to make his way across the roof joist taking his time because it's dark up there. He has only a small torch and the batteries are nearly dead so he's not getting much light from them. Add to that the problem of his bad eyesight and it's an accident waiting to happen. And happen it does. Just when Mr. Stokes turns the key of the front door and shouts 'Evening all!', Pop's leg comes through the ceiling of the main bedroom and he's roaring for assistance. Lar has gone up to him and shouts down to me to get the stepladder and use my shoulder to push his foot back through the ceiling. Mr. and Mrs. Stokes are there asking is he alright and telling Lar and myself to be careful and to be not one bit bothered about the ceiling; that a person's health and well being are more important. Now Pop is convinced, more than ever, that the minute Mr. Stokes walks in the door he should be on his way home, he'll be gone five minutes every day before he comes. He says he's afraid of what else will happen if he stays in the house after five fifteen for the rest of the week we're working here.

CHAPTER 6

Paddy McCarthy lives out in Clarina at the cross roads on the main road. He is a skin and hide merchant and anyone who works in his yard near the cathedral will go home stinking like a dog's stomach. And I'm about to find out how stingy and tight Lar is. It'll be the first of many experiences that I'll never forget.

Mr. McCarthy will bring us out in his car in the mornings because Pop says half the day would be gone if we were to cycle the five miles to the house every day and that we'd be too knackered to do any work by the time we got there. We'll have to make our own way home in the evenings and that's where the frustration and fun starts. Frustration for me and fun for the other two. Our first evening after work outside in Mr. & Mrs. McCarthy's house, I'm on my own with my thumb stuck out the end of my arm smiling away every ten minutes at the car I'll want a lift home in. They have me on my own because they say it would be much easier for one guy on this own or even two together to hitch a lift rather than the three of us. But I don't mind because they've let me have first choice of every car that passes Mr. McCarthy's house. They'll be a good hundred yards further down the road and, because I'm on my own, I'll surely get a lift in no time at all. Well, that's what I thought. I'm there doing all the things they told me to do like, don't have your white overalls on otherwise people will think you are full of paint and won't want you in their cars. Be sure and have a respectable smile on you face and I'm asking them: what the hell is a respectable smile? They say it's a smile that'll make people sorry for you, and stop their cars to give you a lift. I'm there with the hand out, trying my damndest to have a respectable smile and haven't got a clue what I look like. But it's not working at all and when a car passes me by, there's Pop and Lar getting into it, laughing their heads off getting into a car that should have stopped for me.

When Tuesday evening comes, it happens again, Wednesday as well and I'm getting sick and tired of it. When Thursday comes, I'm asking them to go up another two hundred yards down the road, which they do, and it doesn't work at all. But I have a great idea. I'll ask Lar on Friday morning what work I have to do today before I go home that evening and, when he tells me, I'll ask if I can go home when all that work he says I have to do is done. He says no problem at all. I'll be tearing into everything at incredible speed. I won't even stop for the break in the morning when Mrs. McCarthy calls us in at eleven o'clock and when one o'clock comes, I'm out on the road with the hand out and the respectable smile I've been practising all of Thursday night in front of the mirror at home. Asking Mam if I've got a respectable smile on my face. And she wants to know what a respectable smile is. She laughs when I tell her and says Pop and Lar are trying to make an eejit out of me again. And here I am for the whole of Friday afternoon with a pain in my hand and face, when six o'clock comes Lar and Pop walk out of the gate of Mr. McCarthy's house, look down at the corner with their hands in their pockets and can't believe I'm still here. And of course they're laughing their heads off. There's an old Morris Minor on its way down the road and when it gets near I can see a big fat one at the wheel with a sour face on her. I'm there with the hand out, smiling away, praying she'll pull in and take me away from the constant comments from the two of them like 'The road must be quiet today Paddy seeing you're still here' and 'Is there a particular car you are waiting for?'. But it is no good. She's not pulling in to give me a lift. They're still at the laughing with their hands in their pockets. And what does the fat one in the car do, only pull in longside them and offer them a lift. Pop gets in first and gives me the two fingers as he closes the door. I'm gutted with the injustice of it all and wind up having to walk the five miles home only to find more bad news. Lar has docked me a half days wages even though I finished the work that I would've done in the full day.

But there is more meanness to come from Lar, a month later Mr. McCarthy sends word to the Bedford bar that he needs his new front door painted. The door that he thought would be there when we were doing the house a month ago but wasn't ready to be fitted and that it'd be an ideal job for me. Pop says he will collect me every evening at six fifteen outside the Bedford and will give me my supper and take me home again that evening. My first night going out in his car Mr. McCarthy says when I see the new door he got fitted that it's just as well because it had benefited me in a big way. He says I can give him a price first, and work it out on the basis of pay I get off from Lar. When I tell him it will take me five nights at a pound a night plus a pound for paint, he said that's grand and after he showed me the new door and frame, I'll give it it's the first coat of primer and he takes me home and everything is great because, at the end of this week, I'll have a whole seven pounds. And when I've given Mam half of it, I'll have three pounds ten shillings myself and a great weekend to look forward to, or so I thought. But that was until Lar got wind of it.

We're over in Clancy Strand, painting the outside of an old house for four women Pop called spinsters. He says he doesn't think any of them ever went out with a man in their life because he thinks they were reared in a convent. Lar takes me to one side and says 'I hear you are doing a job in the evenings for Paddy McCarthy in Clarina'. I said 'That's right Lar. I'm painting a new front door for him that he had fitted only last week.' Lar said Paddy McCarthy is one of their best customers, that there must have been a mistake because Paddy McCarthy always leaves a message for himself or Pop when he needs work done at his house. 'You're to tell him tonight when he collects you from the Bedford Bar not to bother paying you when you've finished on Friday night, that we'll pay you instead and you can take whatever paint you need from here as you need it'. When Paddy McCarthy calls and takes me out the Dock Road that evening to his house, I'm telling him what Lar told me. Mr. McCarthy puts his foot on the brake so fast it nearly puts me out the front window. He lets a roar out at the same time, saying 'Jesus, Mary and Holy Saint Joseph! He said what?' Between nearly going through the windscreen of his car, the shout and the look on his face, I'm in total shock. I can't say a word. Mr. McCarthy says 'Are you telling me that big long lanky fupper has told you to tell me that I shouldn't have asked you to paint my front door? That I have should have asked him instead?' I just about managed to spurt out the words 'Yes, Sir! Mr. McCarthy Sir!' He's still shouting 'I don't fupping believe it! That miserable fupper. I've a good mind to turn the car around and go back to his house,' my heart is doing ninety an hour. He's fupping and blinding all the way out to Clarina while his face is getting redder. I hope he doesn't get a heart attack and die on me. We could be killed on the road or, worse still, I'll have no door to finish at all and all I'll have this week is the lousy two pound wages. He wants to know if my father is involved in this. 'No, Sir'. 'Why not?' he asks. 'Because Lar and my father made an agreement before I started work that Lar would have complete control over my training so he doesn't get involved'. Mr. McCarthy says he's pleased to hear it, otherwise, he'd be giving Pop a piece of his mind as well. Mr. McCarthy is shouting in the kitchen of his house and I can hear his wife telling him to calm down before he gets a stroke. He's answering her back saying 'I bloody well won't calm down. The cheek of that lanky yolk depriving a young lad of making an extra few bob in his own time and giving him a message, telling me what to do'. Now Mrs. McCarthy is shouting at Mr. McCarthy to know will he, for God's sake, calm down and eat his dinner. And I'm out in the hall trying to paint around the part of the door that has the glass on it, trying to stay away from the glass with a steady hand that I always have along with the good training I got from Lar. But my hand is shaking all over the place and my empty stomach is scratching my back looking for something to eat and will take anything that's thrown into it. And I think Mrs. McCarthy has forgotten all about me.

I'm thinking 'Is this all my fault?' Sure for God's sake, all I did was to give Mr. McCarthy a message. He's still at it inside, ranting away. Now he's out next to me in the hall with a paper and a pen, saying, 'Now Pat, I hope you don't mind me asking you a question. You can tell me to mind my own business and I won't be offended; but would you mind telling me how much you get paid a week? And the reason I'm asking you is I want to figure out something'. Sure I would never tell anyone to mind their own business, especially a man that's paying me money. So I answer and say, 'Two pounds a week Mr. McCarthy'. He says, 'Thank you for telling me, Pat' and he's gone back into the kitchen.

The shouting has stopped, there's nothing only the sound of a chair being dragged out from under a table. Ten minutes passes, the shaking in my hand has stopped and my stomach is leaving my back alone because I'm too interested in what's going to happen next. Then I can hear it again, the sound of the chair being dragged from under a table accompanied by some footsteps. The door opens and out comes Mr. McCarthy, 'Oh God, he's much worse than he was before'. He's holding the same piece of paper in the air and shouting, 'Would you like to know how much money your boss Lar is going to make out of you because he wants to have this job in the company,?' I answer curiously and say, 'Yes, Mr. McCarthy 'Your boss is going to make a lousy fupping 4 shillings and six pence. He's going to be 4 shillings and six pence richer when you've finished this job on Friday night! Can you believe that? A lousy fupping 4 shillings and six pence.' That's what all this is about. Now Mr. McCarthy wants to know where I'm working tomorrow, because he says he's coming in, in the morning to give Lar a piece of his mind. And I think Mrs. McCarthy has forgotten all about my empty stomach and the noise its making. I think I'm going to fall down any minute with the hunger. When ten o'clock comes, Mr. McCarthy is still going on about the four shillings and six pence and the cheek of Lar to interfere in his business, and he wants to know if Pop will be at home when he drops me off in Garryowen. I have to tell him that he'll be at bingo. So he says he'll wait until tomorrow to see him. After giving my stomach the energy it's entitled to, Pop is back home. I'm telling him everything that happened and Pop says he can't interfere over the promise he made to Lar but that tomorrow should be very interesting.

When 9 o'clock arrives Lar is up on the wooden extension ladder that has three sections and needs two people to get it against the wall. I won't want to go anywhere near it, because I'm terrified of heights. Lar is cleaning the chutes and wearing an old brown coat because he doesn't want to get his overalls dirty. The sun is shining. Pop and myself are looking up towards Sarsfield Bridge every few minutes to see if Mr. McCarthy is on his way over the bridge. It's 9:30 and there he is coming down the road in his black station wagon. Lar is whistling away and up the concrete steps comes Mr. McCarthy with the same head he had on him of last night. When Lar hears the iron gate closing with a bang because Mr. McCarthy stormed through it and never closed it gently behind him, Lar looks down and shouts, 'Hello Paddy, how are you?' Mr. McCarthy shouts back, 'I'll give you 'hello Paddy'. Come down here you big lanky fupper. I want to talk to you'. 'What seems to be the problem Paddy?' asks Lar as he makes his way down the ladder. 'Did I ask you to paint my front door?', 'No you didn't', says Lar. 'Well then would you mind telling me what business is it of yours when I asked this young man to do it, Lar is as white as a sheet and says he didn't think there'd be any problem, that he just wanted everything to be above board and business like. Mr. McCarthy says, your to stay out of my business in future unless your asked. And turns to Pop and says, 'I'm surprised at you Harry, letting him stick his nose into my business'.

He's gone now and Lar is back on the ladder working away and not a word out of him. When Friday night comes Mr. McCarthy says that I made a beautiful job of the front door. He puts his hand in his pocket and takes out a bundle of pound notes, counts out five and then says, 'I want to give you another one, but first I want you to promise me that when Monday morning comes that you'll tell that big lanky fupper that I gave you an extra pound. Will you promise me that?', 'Of course Mr. McCarthy, yes Sir, you bet Sir'.

I'm telling Lar first thing Monday morning about the extra pound I got from Mr. McCarthy. He won't answer and I know why. It will happen again and again and I'll understand what Pop was talking about.

Mr. McCarthys House at Clarina Cross

Mrs. McCarthy and myself outside the front door that I painted
almost fifty years ago

Cormack McCarthy and myself and the old door before it was replaced

Mr. Lyndon, the man that has two walking sticks and a driver to take him around in a car because he can't walk, or sit behind the steering wheel because he's so fat and heavy, is opening a clothes shop overhead Jacky Glenn's Music store in William Street, next to Todd's and right across the road from Boyd's hardware store. He wants the place open by the end of the week. That means carpenters, electricians, carpet layers, and ourselves working on top of each other for the next six days. By the fourth day, there will be bloody mayhem. Pop says that he never asked anyone for a price; that he just said, 'Do this and that, and send me the bill'. Pop and Lar don't know it yet; neither do the other lads working here, that this is a bad sign. But they'll know soon enough. Pop and Lar are painting anything that doesn't move white, and it's killing Lar to have to work in this environment, shouting every minute, 'Mind the fupping wet paint'. But it's no use.

Lar has me painting the inside of four, large wooden windows facing out onto William Street, and right across the road, from the flats that's overhead Boyd's shop. I'm painting away, minding my own business, when I happen to notice a woman inside one of the windows. I think I'm seeing things. She's taking off her bra. Now she's holding her breasts with both hands. I think she's admiring herself in the mirror. She's turning from one side to the other, her head facing the mirror all the time just looking at herself. I'm trying to shout to all the lads, they won't want to miss this, but I'm gobsmacked and can't take my bulging eyes off her. Then all of a sudden out comes 'Jesus, lads, will you look at the one across the road and no bra on her?' Some are over in seconds. Others jumping off ladders there's things falling all over the place with legs tripping and catching on items on the floor, while they're shouting, 'Where?' I'm pointing up to the third floor, now there's silence. As we're all having a good gawk I get a puck in the ear, with the words, 'Get away from that window, its Pop'. I'm really embarrassed in front of all the other lads. But he's gawking away with the rest of them, so I go over to him and say, 'I'm telling Mam'. 'OK' he says, 'but you're not to say a word'. They're all shouting over at your one, things like 'Are you going to take the rest off love?' I'm there in a world of my own, looking at the breasts I thought would be, just like they are when I go to the pictures. The way the women would dress in the Wild West, with their breasts stuck together up high and all lumpy, ready for a pair of good-sized hands. But I'm looking at your one above and hers hanging all over the place. I'm really disappointed. Between Mrs. Lynch's massive arse, with the lumpy, thighs and your one with the hanging breasts, I'm gone completely off the female form; I used to think it, was beautiful under all those clothes. Then the poor girl happened to look out the window and sees below, in the building that has been idle for months, a gang of fellows making all kinds of gestures at her. She freezes for a few seconds; then drops to the floor, and all the lads go, 'Ah shit! The show is over!'

By the time Friday evening comes, we're all finished. The shop will open the following day. Lar and all the other lads will never see a penny. They'll go to a Solicitor. He tells them to 'never trust a man or woman who doesn't ask for an estimate

Flats over Boyd's on William Street, were I got my first pornograpic instalment

before they start'. Pop and Lar say it could have been worse like, 'We could have been taken for the whole job if there was time to do it', and they'd have been in a right fix! Lar says that I'll be working with a German for a month that needs a young fellow of my age. He says he's opening a garage in Henry Street called Precision Motors and I'm off again asking Lar 'What does 'precision' mean?' He doesn't know either, but says he'll look at it up tonight in the dictionary when he goes home. The next morning he says, 'It means exact or accurate' and I'm saying, 'Well why doesn't he call it that? Sure half the people of Limerick won't know what that means'. Lar says, 'You can't call a garage Accurate Motors'. I ask him, 'Why not?' He says, 'because you can't, that's why. Precision sounds much better.'

Pop says that we'll have to put in a lift that will take cars at least seven feet off the ground and we have to put it in a hole in the floor. Mr. Mehil, wants the best of everything in his garage to give his new customers confidence in the place; especially when they see the very latest equipment in his garage. It would be no good having a name like 'Precision Motors' over the door and not a decent bit of machinery inside to compliment the name.

We're digging for days. Pop is worried we might find the tide after four or five feet in the ground. And I'm asking, 'How the hell can you find the tide on dry land?' He says that every spring when the tide comes in down at the Quays, if the water is brown, every basement in Henry Street and Bedford Row can have up to two feet of water. I'm telling him I'm not falling for that load of old rubbish. 'You'll see', he says. After the second day of taking all kinds of earth and stones out of the hole we're making in the ground that's now six feet wide and almost five feet deep, we have to get the wellies on because there's brown water everywhere. And everything has to be done under that water because Pop says the lift has to be in the ground the same depth as it is out of it and that's seven feet. It's a new type, a twelve inch steel pipe sunk into the ground and packed all around with concrete. Then when it's finished, it's only a matter of pressing a button when another shiny steel pipe will come out of it and keep a car in the air while work can be done underneath. 'What about the concrete, I'm asking Pop. He says that it will go off under the water, that it doesn't need air to go hard. He says that cement will get hard under most conditions except frost.

Mrs. Faye has a basement that Lar and Pop use for storage. It's damp, cold and scary. I often wonder why she didn't put a paint brush to it or even scrub out the floor. But I'm about to find out, because I went around the corner with the key to her house to get another shovel. I'll walk down the steps in the darkness before I find the light switch that will help me to see my feet. I'm up to my knees in water. There are all kinds of things floating around down here. Tomorrow, Pop will take me down to the basement of the Bedford Bar next door to Mrs. Denehey, where the table that's ten foot long that Mam and Aunt Nora worked on to feed the many guests that stayed before she got married is now floating around like a large boat. It all explains why the floor is made of large square slabs of stone and never covered. The next day we have the large steel tube sunk into the ground, levelled and ready to fill in. Pop said that the hand-mixed concrete will go off no time at all even though it's underwater.

Now I have to work with Mr. Mehill every day for the next month. He hardly ever talks at all, only tells me what he wants me to do in an English language I've never heard before, like 'I vant you to svveep the floor', 'I vant you to do this or that'. I'm bursting to ask him did he fight in the war and if he did, did he shoot anyone, and where did he shoot them? Did he see them die and if he did, what did it feel like to kill someone? I'm asking Pop and Mam when I go home everyday should I ask him. They say, 'If he did kill anyone, he might not want to talk about it'. But all I have to do is ask and 'if he doesn't want to talk about it he'll let you know'. So I get up the courage and ask him and he asks, 'Fy do you vant to know?' I'm telling him that I never met a German before in my life.

Mr. Mehill is dark skinned, has no hair at all and is very like Yul Brynner the actor. His smile gets bigger and says, 'And now that you have met a German vaat do you think?' I'm telling him that it's a bit scary. 'How do you mean scary?', 'Well Sir, if you killed somebody or blew them up with a grenade, and there's bits of them lying all over the place, I've never met anyone who killed someone before, or worked with one on my own in a big lonely old place like this Sir'. I'm acting the fool and I think he knows it, because he's having a right good laugh. 'You know', he says 'I should be telling you that I've killed lots of people in the var; thirty or forty, or more, and then you'd really be scared vouldn't you?' 'Yes Sir, I would Sir'. 'Well I'm sorry to disappoint you. I missed the var by four years because I vas too young.'

It was the best thing that ever happened asking him about the war, because now he's talking all the time, telling me other stories that's making me laugh; because I'm missing the laughter I've got so used to with Pop and Lar. I'll miss him after the four weeks, when I'm back working with Pop and Lar again.

133

Site of Precision Motors on Henery Street Limerick

I'm twelve months working with Pop and Lar now, and I'm asking for a rise because I can paint as good as Lar, but not as fast. Pop is half blind, he'll stick his brush in the paint and expect the one dip to paint most of the wall. He'll stretch it all over the wall or ceiling of whatever he's painting. It will be full of streaks and will look like it wasn't painted at all. Lar can't say a word because Pop will take offence or give him a dig. Then one of them will be asking me to ask the other for something and on it will go for another week or two.

So Lar will ask me to keep an eye on Pop and go over his painting, which I'm doing. I'm doing the work of two everyday and only getting a lousy 2 pounds a week. But Lar doesn't want to give me the rise because he says that they can't afford it. I'm telling him 'I'm doing the work of two men' and he's telling me, that's why he can't afford it. If Pop would only wear his glasses while painting, there would be no need for me to go over his work, and that would result in more work being done at the end of the week. I'm totally confused, because my father is holding me back from earning more. I can't tell Lar that I'm not going back over his work. I can't talk to my father about it either, because I'll hurt his feelings. I won't be able to tell Mam about it because she'll worry too much. So I'm telling Lar that I'm doing more work than he is. He says that I'm not. We argue about it for the bones of an hour. I'm saying that it's not fair that I should have to go over anybody's work and try to do my own at the same time and that I'm not going to do it anymore. I didn't mean to say it like that, but it came out of my mouth in temper. But it has the desired effect; and Lar the miserable old fupper says, 'He'll talk to Pop about it'.

I know I'll have to keep reminding him for the next week until I get it. When I do, it's great because Mam will have more money to buy herself something. She hasn't bought herself a single thing since I started working and sometimes I'll get cross with her, because every time I ask her why, she says that she wants to put it on the table. She'll say we should eat better, because it was long enough she had to be buying food that had very little nourishment because the work wasn't there. But it's no good, no matter what I say, she won't buy herself the nice coat that won't be a size too big or small when it came from America or England. She's too good to me and the rest of us as well. We're good at accepting it too, all of us. Sure we've been doing it all our lives; we're hardly going to stop now.

My courting days are getting better now, because the Taylor personality is starting to break through and that's the big mouth and the hard neck with the confidence to take on anything to go with it, but without the brains. Girls will look at me and think, 'Janey your man has been around'. They'll think I'm a man of the world with lots of experience. I'm with the lads in Garryowen most of the time now and hardly go to Carey's Road anymore. I don't know how it happened, but we're together a lot and talk about girls. The talk isn't very pleasant. If one of us is out with a girl, the rest of us will want to know did we drop the hand on her breasts or under her skirt. Every one of us will say we did. I'm wondering are they lying like me because I never have the courage to do that to a girl, I'll just want to have a good shift. But I won't want to look like a gobshite when their talking about it, they could be telling the truth.

But I'm about to become a real man of the world any day now and I won't be able to tell a sinner about it because I'll be so ashamed. We're going to 'The Augaa' now instead of The Hop, its right next door to the back of the Augustinian Church. We're going up-market. This is a bigger and better place, and hardly any fights. It's my third Saturday night coming here and I've danced with a good few females that I've got to know since I came here. Mostly with May, she's been giving me 'Ladies Choice' each Saturday night for the last two weeks. I'll be dancing with her the whole night tonight, even though she has the most awkward way of dancing the slow waltz. She has beautiful eyes, gorgeous hair and a great figure. She smells nice too and tonight I'm going to ask to walk her home. I'm sixteen now and trying to act twenty. And thinking I'm making a great job of it. She's a great conversationalist too. I'm trying to figure out why she's always looking down at the ground, after we dance a slow waltz, when she has the awkward way of dancing.

The walk that takes us from the lane off Thomas Street from one end of Catherine Street to the pub in Lower Carey's Road where her house is, is only twenty minutes away. I'm wondering where I can park her to get a good shift from the lovely pink lips I've been looking at all night. There's a dark spot where we can have a bit of privacy and not having anyone gawking at us while we're at it. I've gone past the stage of my first kiss when I took a deep breath before I went in and had to come away for a good inhale of air in case I collapsed are gone. I'm moving my head and mouth all over the place just like they do in the back seat of the Carlton Lyric and Grand Central Cinemas. All I want and expect is to be stuck to her gorgeous mouth for the next thirty minutes. But I'm going to be offered a whole lot more! And the man of the world that this girl has been chasing for the last three weeks is in for a big disappointment and so am I. I'll be on my knees when I go home asking God to forgive me for the terrible sin I've committed or tried to commit, because I was offered something on a plate and couldn't find the strength to say no.

We're up against the wall of Foster's Pub and in I'll go for my first kiss. Before I get a chance to enjoy her lips she has her knee in my groin that takes this young innocent fellow totally off Guard. I mean surely to God it can't be, but it is. And the heart that had so much practice at beating itself to death down through the years is now beating a different tune altogether, a beat of excitement. My brain is telling me I'm going to experience something I used to dream about and wondered what it would be like and I don't know what to do next. But raw nature is going to do everything for me and it's just as well because I'm in total shock. I can hear my voice asking her does she want it. There's another voice in my head asking 'Why the hell do you think she has her knee up your groin you eejit?' And very calmly she says, 'I don't mind'. I'm beginning to realise she's the one with all the experience. We'll go across the road to the lane by the rugby grounds that the Crescent College uses for practice for their college games. She says she doesn't mind going over there and as we walk the short distance my legs are weak with the thoughts of what's coming my way any minute.

There we are, down in the corner in the darkest part of the lane right next to the gate of the Rugby Ground where you couldn't see your hand if it was in front of your face. I'm rummaging through all the bloody clothes she's wearing on the top part of her frame, because it's the middle of winter, and it's very hard to find anything, but then I eventually find her right breast it's beautiful. I'm caressing it for ages, I'm in another world and on my way to heaven I've never had my hand on anything so soft in all my life before. Then her voice says sarcastically from the dark, 'What about the other one?' I better do what I'm told, even though I can't see how holding the other one would make any difference. I'm breathless with excitement, nearly exhausted. She's just standing there calm as you like. Now there's a part of me that's bursting to go to a place it never went before. The place the lads and I used to talk about all the time. The place we called paradise and wondered what it would be like when we got there. Well I'm about to find out. Well that's what I thought! Because I'm huffing and puffin', pushing and shoving and I can't find paradise no matter how hard I try. I thought this was going to be easy! I'm knackered! And she's loosing interest very fast and so am I. She says that she wants to go home.

I'll walk her up to Prospect and feel like a right clown. The mouth that could speak for Ireland has gone mute. It's no good pretending anymore. I've been found out. I'm a bloody failure again I'm a bloody failure at everything. We say goodnight. There's no mention of meeting again. Sure why would she want to see me again?.

I'll walk home through Upper Carey's Road and down the Jail Boreen with a terrible weight on my shoulders. I don't know whether its guilt or sin, but then realise they're both the same. It dawns on me why she had the awful way of dancing, with the lower part of her body pushing against mine all the time, during the slow dances and then looking down at the ground by the way to see if there might be any evidence of excitement on my part. After I turn the key of our hall door, I fall on my knees and tell God how sorry I am for what I've done. I'll tell Him that I never intended that to happen that, it wasn't my fault at all sure I didn't start it, how all I wanted was to go home after a good shift and be happy with that. I'll tell Him that I'll never do it again until I'm married and then I can do it as often as I like and never have to say I'm sorry.

Days later, I'll realise that if I had been successful that night she might be 'in trouble' and if she was would I be the father? Because that was a girl with experience. I don't think I was the first, and I don't think I'll be the last either. I'll realise too that I could have been a father at sixteen and a half, and how would Mam cope with the shame of that. I'll get over it, it will never happen again because the other girls I'll go out with won't have their knee in my groin. I'll bring them home to meet Mam if I like them. She'll make the usual fuss with the spotted dick. But if I don't like them, I'll make sure that Pop is at home. They'll take one look at him and say that they have to go home because they'll have to be up early in the morning for work. I'll never see them again and that's the way I want it. Because if they hang around with me and get married our kids could turn out with looks like Pop and that's why I brought them home to meet him in the first place.

The entrance of the old Crescent College Rugby ground, now Jackman Park were I thought I lost my innocence, but still hadn't a bloody clue about life and its other complications

CHAPTER 7

Hector Newenham is a brother-in-law to Mr. Ferris and owns
the Lakeside Hotel in Killaloe. Pop says that we're going to be
working down there for the next four weeks. We'll be sleeping there as well and can come home for the weekends. Mr.
Newenham will bring us down in his Mercedes Benz station
wagon on the first Monday. The journey of twelve miles will
only take us twenty-five minutes. I've never been in Killaloe before. It's a small town. But the view from the hotel is breathtak-
ing even in winter. We have twenty rooms to decorate and Lar
says that it's the best time to close down a hotel when there's no
tourists around. We'll come here for the next three or four years
around the winter time and every time we come here, it will be
a time to remember for lots of reasons. One of those reasons is
Pop's seven year drought of leaving Arthur Guinness in his bottle that will end down there and will continue every night for
the duration of our time here. He'll leave it alone at the weekends when we're at home and Mam won't be any the wiser.

When six o'clock comes on our first day, we're shown our
sleeping quarters; one room with three beds and a sink between
the first two. The room has a spare-room sense about it and a
musty smell too. It won't stay that way much longer when Lar
and Pop come back from the bar at all hours tonight and sour
the atmosphere with their backsides. The middle bed has five
spare mattress on top of it and Pop shouts, 'I'm claiming that'.
He throws his bag of bits and pieces on top of it. Lar wants
the other one, next to the door and right beside the sink. That
leaves me with the last one in by the window, that cannot be
opened, which I'll find out later tonight, when I'll try to get the
air that's stale and hard to breathe out of the place.

I brought some clean clothes down here with me, to walk
around Killaloe and see what life is like here. I'm back in thirty
minutes and wondering if there is anyone living down here at
all because I didn't meet or see a sinner. I don't know what to

do with myself, only sit in the bar and slowly watch Lar and Pop talk to the few people who are there, and see the alcohol take its effect on the two of them. It's strange, because Pop isn't drinking good old 'Arthur' at all. He's on the new stuff called 'celebration beer'. It will be taken off the market two years later because it was so potent and I'm going to see evidence of this later on tonight. Tomorrow I'll ask for work in the evenings so I won't go off my rocker looking at the two of them every night drinking themselves stupid, otherwise I'll be bored out of my skull.

I'm in bed now in the room with the musty smell. It's 8.30 pm. I'm rattling in the bed with the cold, and can't go to sleep or so I thought. Some time in the late hours I'm wide awake listening to someone fupping and blinding. I'm rubbing my eyes trying to make out whose doing the fupping in the dark. When my eyes finally get adjusted, there up on the five mattresses is Pop. He's on his knees with one hand on the ceiling trying to keep his balance on top of the five mattresses that are swaying all over the place. How the hell did he get up there in the state he's in? He's in his long johns and fiddling around with the fork trying to find his penis. Lar is on his back next to the sink with a massive snore and the mouth wide open. When Pop finally succeeds in finding his instrument he's pointing it in the direction of the sink that's four foot below him. With his left hand still on the ceiling, the flow starts and there's fair pressure behind it. I can hear it spattering inside the white sink that we'll be washing our hands and face in, in the morning. I won't be doing it now because of the celebration beer that has gone through Pop's insides and is on its way into the sink and not going down the waste because its coming back in a spray and finding its way all over Lar's face and into his mouth. On it goes. I don't think the flow is going to stop at all.

When Lar's face is soaking wet he wakes up, sees Pop's flow on its way into the sink, and back out again. He shouts, 'Jesus, Harry what are you doing?' The shock and the sudden movement of Lar moving up and out of the pillow gives Pop such a fright that he changes his position which causes the flow to change direction and straight into Lar's face. I've got a pain in my stomach from laughing so much. Lar is up at the sink washing his face, over and over. He's washing his mouth as well and fuppin Pop. Pop is telling him to 'Fupp off' that it's his own fault for taking the living senses out of him. And Lar wants to change places with me and I'm telling him what to do with himself.

When the morning comes Lar is exhausted with a hangover. On top of this he says that he never got a wink of sleep, worrying that Pop might fire down on top of him again. We're sitting at the staff table in the hotel restaurant where Mrs. O'Reilly will come in every day just to give us our breakfast, later on dinner, and then supper in the late afternoon. Pop says that he has a terrible headache and can't understand what was in the stuff he drank last night, and that he can't remember a bloody thing.

'Do you remember pissing on top of me last night Har?' asks Lar.

Pop tells him to 'Fupp off' that he's not falling for that.

I'm saying, 'You did Pop, you did. Sure you woke me out of my sleep with the racket you were making'.

Pop looks at me really cross and asks, 'Are you looking for a thick fuppin ear?'

'No Pop'.

'Well shut up and mind your own business.'

There's silence for a few minutes. Then he says that he wishes he'd never touched the stuff at all and starts talking about the first drink that he ever put to his mouth around the time of the Second World War, when he was only seventeen. How one of his friends, who was a couple of years older than the rest of the gang, came back from the States talking about how great things were over there, with lots of work because of the War. And spoke about the kind of food you can buy for next to nothing. And showed them all the dollars that he had in his pocket to prove it. They wanted to celebrate the home-coming with the Yank ready to splash out and pay for all the drink. It was the time of the Emergency when drink was hard to come by; but not for this gang because two of them, Tadhg and Denis Dennehy, were the sons of the owner Mrs.Dennehy, of The Bedford Bar and kept asking her for the drink, it was only a matter of time before she'd give way and consent to all the begging from her two sons. 'I'll give you three trays with three pints for each of the five of ye', she says. 'Ye're to take them upstairs when I give you the signal, because if you're seen down here in the bar with that much drink I'll loose all my customers'.

'We're upstairs' says Pop 'listening to the man who left Limerick three years ago and now has the American accent. We're listening to his stories for hours, and everyone nursing their pints, trying to make them last the evening. But because the stuff tastes bloody awful, I'll gulp mine down, all three pints no time at all. It makes me look like the hard man because all the lads are saying, 'Jaysus, lads will you look at Harry the way he's throwing down the porter! Never knew you could drink like that Har! Good man yourself and we're not even half way through our first pint'. And on will go the stories about America, along with the invitations for all the gang to come and visit whenever they want. Work and accommodation would be no problem at all, and if they need a few dollars for the fare, he'll give it to them. Pop says that he started to get awful sleepy, and after another thirty minutes was stoned out of his skull and sprawled across the timber bench that's right in front of the table that had the other two trays with three pints in each one.

'When another fifteen minutes passes by I'm on my dodgy legs opening my fly, looking everywhere for my yoke; the boys are all still huddled together listening to the stories about America. I must have disturbed the lads, because as I'm about to fire into the two trays of Guinness when one of them shouts, 'Jesus Harry no! Not into the fupping pints'. I'm looking at them out through my unfocussed eyes and shout, 'what fupping pints?' But it's too late, one of them has his hands out in front of the flow, but it's no good. Another is pulling me away. I'm spraying everything I can't stop.' Lar is asking Pop what happened next. 'I don't know', he says. 'I just remember waking up at the steps of the Franciscan Church with a black eye, two missing teeth and a swollen testicle'.

After a good laugh Lar says that he remembers one of his pals who worked out in the Shannon Industrial Estate, how he came home to his one-room flat in Patrick Street on a Sunday night, scuttered drunk, and was too lazy to go to the toilet on his way up the stairs that was shared by everyone in the building. How the ESB cut the power off the Friday before. So he kept feeling around for the cold Belfast sink because he couldn't see a bloody thing in the dark. When he found it he fired away. The next day he opened his lunch and found his sandwiches sopping wet. What he found the night before wasn't the Belfast sink but the cold Formica top on the table where his wife had prepared and left his lunch.

Then the two of them will talk about the guy who, every time he got drunk and went to bed, would get out of it late in the night, walk around the bed to where his wife was sleeping and start firing in on top of her. How she'd scream the house down saying, 'No, no, no', and he'd say 'FUPP you!' open the door of the wardrobe and fire into it.

The next day won't be a good one, not with the mood they're in they're sick as dogs because of the drink. And it's a long day too. There's no laughing at all which makes the day a whole lot longer. But back they'll go to the hotel bar and do the same thing all over again tonight. I have plenty of work to do, because Pop and Lar are too sick to get the amount of work they're supposed to do during the day, and I'm going to be richer come the end of the week. The five extra mattresses are gone into another part of the hotel because Lar says he's not putting down another night of being drowned in Pop's pee again. But they'll be up every hour to pee in the sink and empty their bladders. I don't know where I can wash my face and hands in the morning, because I know that I won't be washing them in that.

The head chef that started his new job at the hotel the same day that we arrived, and needs to be there before the hotel opens in six weeks, says that the place is walking with 'Queers'. He's telling me, who still doesn't know what a 'Queer' is and won't ask either because I'll look like a right idiot. He says they're knocking on his bedroom door every night wanting to come in but he's telling them to 'Fupp off' and leave him alone. I'm bursting to ask him what are queers but instead I'll ask, 'Who are they?' He says, 'The fupping waiters that started here yesterday, the same as myself. They're like fupping vampires. If they keep it up, I'm out of this fupping place by the end of the week'.

Pop and Lar are laughing at him. The following day the 'waiters' are asking me to come and paint their rooms in the evenings after work that they'll give me lots of drink and cigarettes. I know they're up to no good, even though I haven't a bloody clue why they would want me in their room painting it and giving me alcohol and cigarettes that's stolen from the hotel. I'm staying well away from them. Pop and Lar will come to the breakfast table every morning, as sick as dogs. I don't know why they're here because they're not eating a thing, and not one bit prepared for what's coming a few hours later.

We're upstairs painting away and not a word out of any of us when there's an almighty explosion that takes the living senses out of us. We're in total shock. We're looking at one another wondering was it a gas explosion? Our eyes are wandering everywhere in the room for some kind of evidence and can't understand what caused it. I notice and bring it to the lads' attention that a paint tin is jammed between the door and frame of the bedroom, we're working in. We can hear laughing out in the corridor and wonder why anyone would be laughing after a terrible explosion. It doesn't make sense. When we make our way out to the corridor to investigate, with faces of complete and utter confusion, we are greeted by five other construction workers. One of them asks, 'Well lads did ye enjoy that?' Now we're more confused. One of them picks up an empty paint tin, spits in it, walks into the bedroom, picks up the lid off the floor, puts it back on the tin and puts it between the door and frame, waits a minute or two, then puts a match to a tiny hole at the bottom end of the tin and then there's a thunderous explosion just like the last one. We can hear the lid that was on the tin hopping off one of the walls. Now we're full of questions, like 'How the hell did you do that? Is it dangerous? Show us again!' One of the lads shows us the tin that has a small piece of charcoal type stone in it. He says that he found ten tins in the attic of the hotel. He says the tin is very old and explained that is how they lit up the coach lights back in the 1800s, once the charcoal stones were wet, they released a gas which, when lit with a match, would cause the lamps to shine. They then gave us a few stones and before the day was out everybody had some. You daren't be in a room on your own because someone was gently opening its door and putting a tin between it and the frame. It's a good thing Mr. Newenham the owner was not around because if he was, he might think that his hotel was going up in smoke, with all the explosions that were going off every five minutes. All this talk about drunks and where they pee and explosions is making me nervous about tonight and the rest of the time we'll spend down here in Killaloe.

The Grand National is coming up next Saturday and we'll be here because half the hotel is opening soon. We have to work the weekend, and Pop says that there's just enough workers on site to have a sweep. I'm off with the questions, asking him what a sweep is. He says that if everyone here puts a half crown into a hat, there will be forty horses running and there are just enough workers to pick a horse out of the hat. There will be five pounds in prizes, three for the winner, one for the runner up and a pound for the third horse. I'm saying that I'll have some of that. I'm all excited waiting my turn in a queue to give my two and six and put my hand into the hat and take out one of the pieces of paper that will have the name of my horse on it. I don't know why I'm excited; sure I never won anything in my life, not like Pop who can win anything with his eyes closed. If there was a draw for something else and I was the only person in it, I still wouldn't win! Pop, when he wins, doesn't even have to try. He is sure to get a good horse. He does, the one he picked is second favourite. How the hell does he do it? It looks like luck sticks to him and won't let go. Why can't I just once be lucky and win something? My horse is called 'Mr. Dependable'. He's 100/1 a complete and total outsider. Every worker is in the lounge sitting in front of the only black and white TV, waiting for the race to start. I'm keeping an eye out for my fellow. I don't see any sign of him at all. I can hear an announcement from the telly. It says 'Mr. Dependable has been withdrawn; I repeat Mr. Dependable has been withdrawn'. Everybody around the room is asking 'Who has Mr. Dependable?' And Pop and Lar are down on their knees laughing, pointing at me. Everybody can see who has Mr. Dependable now. To make matters worse, I won't even get my two and six back.

When the race starts, I have no interest in it at all until Pop's horse is out in front. Lar's horse has fallen at the sixth fence. Pop is on his feet roaring at the telly, but there's another horse catching up fast. When it's all over Pop's horse is third. 'The Horse With No Name' comes in first and the two of them will spend the rest of the day laughing and saying what kind of luck would you call it when a fellow backs a horse and the fupping horse doesn't even bother his arse to turn up? They're right, and they won't leave me alone for the rest of the day.

After spending the one day at home, Sunday, it's back to Killaloe again on the Monday morning. The boss, Mr. Newenham is away on business. That means we have to split up and thumb our way to Killaloe with a gallon of paint in each hand, stopping every few minutes to thumb a lift and get a bit of relief. I'm keeping well away from the other two, because I don't want them laughing at me when they get a lift first.

The job we have to do down at the hotel this week is the ballroom. There's carpenters, plumbers, tilers, electricians, plasterers and every other kind of tradesman all working on top of one another. I'm in the ladies toilet working away when Pop comes in looking for something I might have. 'I'm asking' 'What's in that thing on the wall Pop?'. 'What thing?' he asks. 'That thing that says sanitary towels.' 'Shut up', he answers. 'But sure all I said Pop was what?' 'Didn't I tell you to shut up?' 'You did, but I just,' he's gone. What the hell is wrong with him? Later Lar comes in to see how I'm getting on. So I am asking ask him the same question, Lar says ask your father. 'I did', 'And what did he say?' 'He told me to shut up'. 'Well you better do what you're told then'. Now he's gone too. I can't understand why people can't answer a simple question. I'm looking through glass part of the machine, at these white cotton things and I'm trying to figure out what would women want with these things. Maybe it's for their make up.

At 6 o'clock everybody is having a break because we'll be here til 10.00 tonight, we're sitting down in what was once the cloakroom. There's a plasterer working on the wall. He says that he can't have his break until he puts a coat of mortar on it first. He's throwing it up and making it look so simple. After a few hand movements, he's gone. I'm saying to Pop, 'Janey that looks real easy'. 'Do you think so? 'Yeah, I think I could do that no problem at all'. 'Well then, why don't you have a go?' So I stand up and take one of the trowels that's on the ground and apply to the wall and it sticks to it. I can't move it around like the plasterer was doing. And Pop and Lar are starting to laugh. So I'll try to take the plastering trowel away from the plaster. I've got my two hands on it, pulling it and then manage to pull all the plaster off with it. The whole lot just flops on to the ground. I'm gone out the door before your man comes back and will want to know what happened to his wall. Pop is back on the wagon again now that we're finished in Killaloe. He'll be back at it again next year around the same time when we're back here again, during the off-season. I'm at home asking Mam and Nan about the white cotton things called sanitary towels on the wall of the ladies toilet in Killaloe and asking them what there for, the two of them are calling down the Holy family again and putting the sign of the cross on their foreheads. And then telling me to shut up and wash out my mouth and I can't understand what I've said, I'll walk away scratching my head, and be more curious about what or where women would do with those things and there's no Jetta to answer my question.

My guitar playing has gone a bit stale and I've become friends with another few lads in Garryowen named Gerry Costello, Buddy Liddy, Steve Sheehan and Seán Carmody. We'll be in each other's houses every night of the week, driving our parents around the bend with our attempts to play the latest songs and some old ones too. We think we're great even though no one is telling us that we are. Only one can tune a guitar, but we'll keep going and learn from each other. Seán Carmody's brother, Tom, is older than the rest of us. He's good on the guitar too and gives us lots of tips. After a few months, the cheap guitars and the battered drum kit that Buddy has are producing a better sound than ever.

The Roma Café has a side entrance at the top of William's Street where you can buy your bag of chips. It has the sound of guitars, drums and voices coming from the basement for the last month that will draw me and others in for the bag of chips, even though we won't want them. Because we'll want to be close to the music. It's gone now, and so are half their customers because Mr. Nadoni's son, Elvio, is no longer part of the band that used to play there. I'm telling the lads that if we could get him to join our group we'd have a place to practice every night and not have our parents throwing us out because they can't hear the T.V, and because it was my suggestion, I have to go and do the talking and put the plan into action. And Elvio is now part of the band. But he can't play anything. That is until Seán's brother, Tom, gets a hold of him for two or three weeks of nights and shows him how to play the bass guitar. Mike Hogan has a music shop in the basement of Sarsfield Street. He'll let us have two guitars and two amplifiers on the weekly, and the sound from the basement of the Roma Café is back again. And so are the customers with business on the increase.

The girls who used to call to the café for their glass of Fanta orange or plate of chips, are back again. They'll drink their orange in sips or share a plate of chips over two hours when they'll go stone cold, because they might have bummed the price off their parents and if they don't make the chips and orange last, they might be asked to leave if there's nothing in front of them on the table. We'll talk to them every time we come up the trap door for a smoke or a drink. We'll stay with them for a good ten minutes. They won't want to talk to us too long because the sound of music will be gone and they'll want us back down there with requests for more. The girl I'm going to marry is here stuck in by the wall and hardly ever opens her mouth; She'll listen and watch everything that's going on around her, making no contribution whatsoever. She is tailor-made for me. She'll be a female partner who will let me talk forever, and like my mother will be spotlessly clean, and best of all, she only lives around the corner. But I am not aware of her, I'm too interested in the other women, the ones doing all the talking and making me the centre of attention and me loving every minute of it. We're there every night, weekends as well and so will they. We'll talk about how the big names in the world became famous; how little they had before that, and talk about where they are now, the money they have, fame and power. God love us, we think it will only be a matter of time before we'll be like them.

Peter Jackson is an artist and lives in Carey's Road. He has a great big curly head of hair with a black beard to match. He's a bit of an eccentric and isn't taken seriously, well not by us not until he says that he's going to have a rock concert at the City Theatre and wants us,to perform there with other acts. Now we're taking him very seriously. It's our first public event and we're all convinced that we'll be millionaires in no time at all. We have to give ourselves a name. After all we can't go on stage without giving ourselves a name. After a lot of suggestions and arguing, it's suggested, The "Koney Kats" after an African tribe. I don't give a monkey's what we're called. I just want to be on the stage and be noticed. We're telling everybody,old and young, that we will be starring in the City Theatre come the weekend and if there not there they'll miss something great. There's endless hours of practicing, worrying about the words, will we forget them, will one of us bottle it and let the rest of the group down. Sure we didn't have to worry at all because when the day arrived there was only fifty in the audience and they were all family members. And our road to fame and fortune has to wait another while.

The beautiful girl that works behind the counter at Power's Small Profit Stores beside the Roma Café won't go out with me. I'll pester her everyday for two weeks because I can't get her out of my mind. I'll stare at her black wavy hair, her beautiful red lipstick, her smile and the pleasant manner she has for every customer. I'll tell her when she's free all the reasons why she should go out with me, until she sighs and agrees and says, 'just for the one night only'. I want to know 'what night?' She says 'Sunday'. 'Where would you like to go?' 'The Savoy,' she answers. 'There's a good film, I'd like to see'. I'm thinking that you won't see much of the film when I get my hands around you.

So when Sunday night comes, I'm there outside the cinema looking my best and wearing the Old Spice aftershave, even though I've nothing to shave except the odd few strings of hair. I'm fixing the knot in my tie every few seconds looking at my watch as well. I gave my teeth a good scrubbing before I came out and bought a packet of hot sweets to ensure my breath was in good shape for the shifting when it starts. There's no sign of her at all and I'm thinking she'd better hurry up or we won't get in at all with the queue that's outside. I want to take her to the balcony. I don't want her thinking that I'm a skin flint. I'm on my third fag and there's still no sign of her. My neck is stretching my head out from my shoulders as far as I can get it. I'm on my toes to look over the heads of people coming down here and there's still no sign of her at all. Hang on, there's her friend who works with her in the shop. She's making her way over to me and tells me that Fionnuala can't make it because she's in hospital having her appendix out. Of course I'm all questions like, 'When did this happen?' There's silence. This is followed by a couple of ams, then a couple of ahs, 'this morning, very early this morning'. 'That's terrible,'. 'Did she have them out yet?' There's another couple of ahs, and more ams, 'I think so, I'm not sure'. 'What hospital is she in?' And off she goes again with the ams and the ahs. 'The ah, the Regional', and says she has to go. I'm thinking isn't she very nice to go to all that trouble of sending her friend down to the Savoy so that I won't be standing outside on my own. She must really fancy me. What a gobshite. The woman is lying out through her teeth, but I won't find out until tomorrow at 11.00 o'clock, when I walk past the entrance of Power's Small Profit Stores, look in and see her working away as healthy as she was last Friday when we made the date and realise I'd have made a right eejit of myself. At 10.00 o'clock I got time off work, and went into Mrs. O'Connor for the bunch of flowers, and walked out over Sarsfield Bridge to the new Regional Hospital that's only been opened a year and every person in Limerick knows that it's a maternity hospital, well everyone except me, and when I got to the reception area thinking how surprised she'll be to see me, with the big bunch of flowers she'll surely want to go out with me when she's better. There I am standing by the reception desk. I have another four months to go before I reach my seventeenth year. I'm waiting for the woman at the reception desk to get off the phone and tell me what ward she's in. 'What's the name please?' she asks. 'Fionnuala', 'No the surname, what's your mother's surname?' Why the hell is she asking me about my mother? 'The name is Higgins, Fionnuala Higgins and she's not my mother'. 'Oh I'm sorry love, it's your sister'. 'No, it's my girlfriend'. I don't know what I've said. I mean its 1965 and you don't walk into a maternity hospital looking like you're just out of short pants and tell these people that your girlfriend is inside expecting a baby. And if she was, you wouldn't go in there broadcasting it to the woman behind the desk. She's taken great offence to my presence. She hasn't said anything yet but with the face she's on her, she's going to let me know any minute. 'Well aren't you the right pup now doing that to a young girl? Does your mother and father know about this?' What the hell is she talking about? 'Do they know about what?' I ask. 'Do they know about this Fionnuala Higgins down here in a ward having your baby?' There's other people waiting to be attended to. They're looking at me like your one. It's beginning to sink in now. How the hell is this happening to me? 'There's no Fionnuala Higgins here,' she shouts. 'Is it possible you got a young girl into trouble and you don't even know her name?' I'm on my way out the door without the flowers, they're on the counter; somebody else can have them. And Fionnuala up at Powers Small Profit Stores, won't be asked out anymore. I've got the message loud and clear.

The owners of The Grand Central Cinema want to refurbish all the seats and drop the timber floor that falls all the way down and then up to the front stalls and gives those who are late a right pain in the neck after sitting there for two hours looking at the screen which is only ten feet away. The owners of the Grand Central won't want to close down because there's a good film on, and many will want to see it. That means we'll have to start every day at seven in the morning and finish at three in the afternoon. There will be a selection of music played for fifteen minutes before a showing every day. Manfred Mann have a new hit out called '*Do wah diddy diddy*' and on our first day here, I've gone to the room that has the large two movie projectors as well as the sound system and I've knocked off the record. I'll play it at home all evening on the record player that Jetta and I bought in Willie Brosnan's at the Top of William Street. When Pop comes home he's sitting down, telling me real nice, that a record was taken from the room upstairs of Grand Central Cinema, and that if I took it, would I please put it back tomorrow? He said I don't have to answer him, just put it back; because if I did take it and got found out, they would lose a valuable customer. I'm not going to fall into the same trap that I did when I worked for Mr. O'Connell at the Standard Garage, so I put it back the next morning when there was no one there at seven fifteen and no more was said about it.

I've got another distraction on my mind today. We're going to be ripping up the floorboards and there's bound to be money down there in the damp earth below the timber floor joists. I want to be the first to get it. Pop and Lar will have a bloody eejit made out of me over the next three or four days, letting me dig a three foot hole in the ground, that takes the bones of two hours looking for money that might have fallen out of the pockets or purses of couples who sit here and suck the mouths off each other through the entire film, because it's the darkest corner of the cinema. It will never dawn on me as to why they're not giving out to me about the time I'm wasting. Every hour one of them will shout, 'Look what I found, two half-crowns.' Pop is half blind and calls Lar over and asks 'Is that a ten bob note or am I imaging it? Lar will say, 'Jaysus, Har, you're right that's a ten bob note alright.' They'll count out the money in front of me at the end of each day and say, how much they've collected.

I won't have a brass farthing. I'll go home asking myself what is it about me that always gets the wrong end of the stick?

The next day they're at it again. We have two wheelbarrows. I'll get the job of digging the earth and putting it into each one. Pop and Lar will bring them outside to the lane because Pop says that the awful rise in the last part of the floor has to go and that means two feet of earth will have to be taken out the back. It will take an entire day. I'm there with the shovel, slowly turning the handle, making sure the earth falls gently into the barrow. If there's any money in it, surely I'll see it. I'm at it all morning and not a penny to be seen. It's raining outside all the time. Pop and Lar are wearing raincoats and hats. Lar is running in with something in his hand, saying 'Look what I found you fupping eejit. It's a pound note!'

'Where did you get that?' I ask. It couldn't have been in the dirt that I slowly shovelled into the barrow. 'It was' he says 'look its fupping ringing wet from the rain'.

'I found it in the fupping dirt you put into the barrow, just a few minutes ago'.

'You couldn't have', I'm saying, 'sure I watched every bit of it as I shovelled it into the barrow'.

'All I did', said Lar 'was to lift the barrow up and let the dirt slide out of it, like I've been doing all morning. And there it was right under my nose. And you were the one that put it in the fupping barrow'.

He's showing it to me, it's wet and full of dirt. I'm like a bloody lunatic. 'How the hell could I have missed that? I never took my eyes off every bit of dirt that went into the barrow all morning. But of course it never dawns on me that they're winding me up. It's their own money they're using all the time. There isn't a genuine coin of any value to be found and won't be either.

The four lads with the strong Dublin accents are taking up the old seats all the way across the full width of the cinema floor. The seats are flying off the floor in rows, the lads are not using hammers or crowbars but whatever they're using it's really fast. Their elbows are up and down like yo-yos. They're working so fast, it's hard to see what sort of tool they're using. One second it's long and then it gets shorter. After two yanks a screw is out. We've never seen anything like it, so Lar will ask, 'what the fupp is that kind of a yoke at all?' The voice with a Dublin accent answers and says 'A Yankee screwdriver'. He puts it into Lar's hand and says, 'Here, have a go'. Lar is holding it while trying to take a screw out from one of the legs of the seats, but it's slipping off the screw. He's told that it takes a bit of getting used to and after another few minutes he has the hang of it.

'Jaysus, Har, we'll have to get ourselves one of these things' and out he goes to McMahon's next door. He's back in a few minutes later looking for a loan of the Yankee screwdriver because the lads in McMahon's haven't a fupping clue what he's talking about. It's another hour before he's back again because he says the lads in there, as well as the customers on the other side of the counter who are builders and carpenters, wanted to hold it and have a go. They were yanking it up and down and making comments like, 'Jesus what will they think of next, the Yanks?' and how it will never catch on over here. The manager rang his suppliers in Dublin and they didn't know what he was talking about either. He's asking the lad who gave it to him to know where he could get one of them. 'America', comes the answer, 'the boss got twelve of them last year when he was on holidays. He says it will be another few years before they arrive in Ireland. Lar is muttering under his breath 'Well why the fupp didn't you say that when I borrowed it to see if I could get one of them in McMahon's?'

Lar is very disappointed because he wants to have everything the modern contractor should have at his disposal, like the new Wolfe drill they bought last month and haven't stopped using since, because it has all the latest attachments. 'The circular attachment' as he calls it, is great for sanding. It's great for making holes too, holes in the new timber flush doors that only have the egg cartons inside to keep it in shape. 'Sand that door', said Lar to me two days after they bought the drill. Before he could tell me how to use it, I had it in my hand, applied it to the door and saw it going through to the other side in less than a second. Boys! Did I get a mouthful! I thought, 'there goes a week's wages'. I was right. The dirty rotten louser! He won't be asking me to use that thing again, and if he does I'll tell him what to do with it.

My sister Jet has been going out with a lad from across the road for the past two years. It looks like they'll be getting married as soon as they have enough money to put a deposit on a house. But with the kind of money they're making, it's going to be a good few years; unless they want to go and live like others all over the City, in hell-holes with no toilets and bawling kids on every floor. They could go to the Corporation for a house but the Corporation won't entertain them unless they're married with a couple of kids, and living in a fla, with rats for companions, awful smells, and in five or six years might get a house. So no one knows when their getting married.

I'm going to find out soon enough, because Lar wants to go for a walk with me along the Quays after we finish work at 6.00 o'clock. I haven't a clue what it's about. He's never done this before. I'm imagining all kinds of things. We're half way down the Dock Road and he's talking about work, what we'll be doing tomorrow. He seems a bit nervous. He's making me nervous too. Is he going to tell me that I'll have no work soon? Sure it's the middle of the summer. They were only talking the other day about a job in Foynes and how it will keep us going for a good month, six weeks at the most. Then without any warning at all he says, 'Your sister Jetta is getting married soon'. I'm looking at him wondering what the big deal is all about. Sure we all know that. Then he says, 'Your father asked me to tell you'. I haven't said a word to Lar yet, but I'm wondering why Pop couldn't tell me himself. 'She has to get married', says Lar. 'I'm sure you know what I mean.' I tell him that I don't. I'm asking him why does she have to get married 'Surely to God you know what it means when a girl has to get married!' Then it hits me, it's going to be a shotgun wedding. Now I understand why Mam has been so upset over the last few days; sniffing all the time, hardly ever saying a word, staring into the fire and no knitting being done either. She'll be thinking of the neighbours and what they'll say, how hard it will be for her to go to town and meet them on the way, when they'll want to stop and congratulate her. They'll be saying things like, 'Jesus, Mrs. Taylor, aren't they getting married very soon' knowing bloody well it's a shotgun wedding, especially since they haven't even got engaged yet. I'm asking Lar why Pop couldn't tell me himself. Lar says that he was too embarrassed and I can't understand it at all.

I'll be even more surprised when I go home and told two extra humans will be living in No. 36 Claughaun Court, Garryowen in a month's time. Mam say's it will only be for six months that it will help them to put a few pounds together to find some place to live. When Nan comes in on a Saturda as she does every week, she'll be bringing down the Holy Family again, calling Jetta a 'dirty bitch' and says that she won't be coming into Garryowen anymore, when the dirty article across the road comes to live here and off she goes again about how things were in her day; no one ever did that until after they got married and there isn't a day goes by when she hears a girl has to go to the altar and not wear a white dress because she isn't a virgin anymore. And that's the second time I heard that word 'virgin'.

The other time was last week when I went to a dance at the Royal George and stood by the wall admiring a gorgeous looking girl, when another fellow, much older than myself, stood longside me and asked 'Are you looking at the one I'm looking at?' I'm asking him which one is he looking at. He says the one in the purple dress and black hair. I say 'Yeah, that's the one I'm looking at alright'. Then he starts to tell me what he would love to be doing to her. 'Would you say she's a virgin?' I'm giving him a look on my face that shows I'm thinking about it, that I know what a virgin is, but I haven't a bloody clue. Is it a religion or a country? Maybe she's from America and lives in that place they call Virginia. But I'm going to have to bluff my way out of this, like I do with everything I don't know. So I answer and say, 'Yeah, I think she is'. I hope to God he doesn't ask me anymore questions because he'll surely find out that I haven't a bloody clue what I'm talking about. So he just says, 'Yeah, I think so', and carries on with the dirty talk.

And there's Nan using that word again, and I think it has something to do with sex. But I can't ask anyone here what a virgin is because I'll get a box in the ear and a mouthful to go with it. I don't want to cause Mam any more grief as she's not in the best of form. I'm thinking too about, that one from Carey's road and the trouble I could be in if I got her in the club. I'm looking at the state Mam is in over Jet and I couldn't bear to be the cause of upsetting her like that.

Lar and I are off to Foynes on Monday to a small hotel that Lar says was bought only a couple of months ago by a man who used to own a petrol station at Punches Cross; a man named Dan Ryan, my old boss with the impediment. He'll be moving out from the Bremen Motors in Thomas Street soon. The man that worked behind the counter in Lipton's as a messenger boy is going to be a millionaire. Pop won't go down with us because Mam found out about the drinking in Killaloe. Mr. Murphy will bring us down to Foynes in a great big Ford Zeypher with our ladders on top of his roof rack. We'll stay down here for the next four weeks and come home on Friday evening or Saturday morning for the weekend. Mr. and Mrs. Murphy's house is a big house with a pub to the side, more like a Bed and Breakfast than a hotel. They have lots of children of all ages. Lar says that Mr. and Mrs. Murphy must be two of the randiest people in Limerick. I won't be doing any overtime down here because there'll be plenty to do once 6.00 o'clock comes. I'll be knocking around with some of the Murphy kids that are my own age. I thought this was a one horse town like Killaloe, it has only one street, but by the time I'll leave here I'll realise that there's more to do here for a sixteen year old than there is in Limerick. Like the day we went over to the island and chased the hares who were stone blind because of a disease called myxomatosis and nearly drowned on the way back because there's fifteen of us in a boat that was only meant for six. The community hall where we went on a Thursday night with most of the gang, and won money over the four weeks I'm down here, except me when we played bingo. The dances to live bands, they were held every Friday night that kept me down here, and missed the lift back with Lar and the Murphy's that night. But was worth every minute, even though I had to thumb a lift back to Limerick on Saturday morning. The set dancing that I learned on the timber floors that gave me a new experience of the culchie and opened my eyes. That made the summer of 1964 one of the best I ever had.

It was down here that I saw more of Lar's meanness when he asked me how much money I give Mam out of my four pound a week. I should have told him to mind his own bloody business but instead I told him that I always give my mother half of everything I earn. I asked him why and he says that he docks his mother half of what he normally gives her. I can't understand why he would do that, so I ask him why. He says 'because she's not feeding me for the five days that I'm down here. You should do the same'. I can't believe it, what a rotten thing to do. I'm telling him, 'what about the years your mother spent money on you while you were growing up?'. 'That's what they're supposed to do for Fupp's sake'.

Mr. Murphy says he's going to Limerick on Wednesday night and asks if Lar and myself want to go home that they can pick us up again on the way back around eleven. I think I'll go. It will break the week as there isn't much happening tonight. So we arrive outside Cruise's Hotel at seven o'clock and I'll head home. Mam is in the kitchen ironing away watching Tom Jones on our black and white TV. She is surprised and delighted to see me. She'll make me tea and get out the spotted dick while singing away to Tom. When the ads come on she wants to know everything about Foynes and the people we're working for and is the food good? I'm telling her that it's all right. We have roast potatoes and beef three days a week, steak another day, nearly an inch thick, with chips and gravy. I never had a steak before, not like the one I got down there. It's completely different to the stuff Mam calls steak that's a quarter of an inch thick and you'd need the teeth of a shark to get through it. She has the mincer for Pop because he hasn't got the teeth, and is the only way she can get it into his stomach. I'll tell her it's alright but that I can't wait to come back home at the weekends to get real food. She smiles, looking pleased. It's a pack of lies of course, but I'm not going to tell her the truth and hurt her. Sure she's only just getting over the hurt and shock of Jetta's situation. When ten o'clock comes I'll say goodbye to her, with no show of emotion by either of us. She just says 'Goodbye Pa'.

I'm making my way up Catherine Street to meet Mr. Murphy and his wife outside the Limerick Leader office in O'Connell Street at 11.00. It's a lovely dark summer's night and I'm about to find out at long last what a 'queer' is. Mr. X who was thrown off St. Joseph's Scouts years ago is cleaning out his car outside his door in Catherine Street. I say, 'Hello Sir. You won't remember me but I used to be in St. Joseph's Scouts, 10th Troop. You were there'. He's all smiles and handshakes. We'll talk for a few minutes. He seems nice and really interested in me. 'Would you like to go for a spin in my car?' he says. I tell him that I have to be at the Limerick Leader by 11.00. 'Sure, it's only ten twenty now; we'll have you back in no time at all.' So I'm thinking, 'what the hell, sure it will pass the time.' We're driving out the Dock Road, he's got his hand on my knee and I'm wondering, 'what's going on here?' And before I can think anymore, he's got his hand inside the fly of my pants fondling my penis. I'm in total shock. He's talking away like nothing is wrong. I want to tell him to stop but the words won't come out of my mouth. I can't even move away. 'Do you like that?' he asks. What the hell is wrong with me, I can't do a thing or get anything out of my mouth. I'm just sitting there looking at him with my hands by my side. Can this be the scout master who used to be in charge of young boys? Now I understand why he was thrown out. And out come the words, 'If you don't take your hand out of my fly, I'll jump out of this car while it's moving'. Stop the car, or I'll go to the nearest Garda station.' It worked. I can't believe I said that. 'Ah come on now', he says, 'there's no need for that. Sure there's no harm in what I'm doing'. What I've said and his reaction gives me more encouragement. 'I want you to turn this car around and take me back to the Limerick Leader right now!' He's doing it and there's not a word said by either of us. I'll give the door a good bang showing my disgust, after I step out on the path just outside the Limerick Leader office, and then wait for Mr. and Mrs. Murphy.

I should be talking to someone at this moment, someone I can confide in. I want to know why a grown up man would put his hand into my fly and fondle my penis. I'm pacing up and down outside the Limerick Leader and can't figure it out at all. Then there's the sound of a horn. It's Mr. and Mrs. Murphy. He's thirty minutes late. I never noticed the time. All the way back to Foynes I'm bursting to tell somebody, anybody, about what happened. But how can I tell them? I'll go to bed that night and won't get a minutes sleep. I tell Lar about it the next day. He starts laughing, then realises that I'm upset because I'm not laughing at all. He'll tell me that 'Queers' are men who want sex with other men. I'm asking him why. He says that he could never figure it out either, that it's unnatural. I'm asking him 'where do they have sex?' He answers 'In their bedrooms I suppose'. He's laughing again. 'You know what I mean?' 'Up their backside', he says laughing. But I'm not falling for that, no way! 'OK' he said, 'ask someone else'. 'I will' I answer.

I'll go home at the weekend. I'm asking Mam the next day what a queer is? And off goes Nan with the 'Oh Jesus, Mary and holy St. Joseph. Where did you hear that kind of talk? Ask your father' says Mam. 'I will when he comes home, but sure can't you tell me? Lar told me a queer puts his thing up another man's backside. That's not true is it Mam?' Now the two of them are putting the sign of the cross on their foreheads saying, 'Jesus, Mary and holy St. Joseph'. It's no wonder I grew up thinking that St. Joseph was holier than Jesus and Mary because of the emphasis they put on the word 'holy' just before they say 'Joseph'. I can't get an answer out of any of them and it's Jett to the rescue. She says 'Lar is right'. I'm asking her why men would do that to each other. She says that she doesn't know and leaves me scratching my head in disbelief.

After we finish in Foynes, I've asked Mam if she would like me to paint the outside of the house. She smiles and says that would be great, and makes me promise to start the back first. But I'll have to make sure that Pop and Lar won't need the wooden double extension ladder that will get me to the upstairs windows on Saturday morning, Mam is gone to the market like she does every week. Nan has arrived in from Cappamore and is sitting by the fireplace knitting away until Mam gets back. I have the ladder at the front ready to start. By 11.00 o'clock, I have the three top windows undercoated and I'm starting on the bottom two. Mam comes in the gate and says, 'Gee Pa but your flying through it. Have you the three back windows done?' I'll laugh and say, 'Don't worry Mam; I'll start out there as soon as I have all the front windows done'. She shakes her head from side to side and says, 'I knew it, I knew it. What did I say, would you start the back first?' But after I have the door and the frame done, the lads are over in the Green playing soccer and I want to be there in the thick of it. So I take the ladder around the side entrance, put the paint and brushes away and five minutes later I'm tearing all over the Green having a great time.

When seven o'clock comes I'm in for the supper. Mam says, 'You made a great job of the back Pa. Well done'. 'Oh I'm sorry Mam, I'll do it tomorrow after Mass.' 'Do you promise?' she asks. 'I do Mam. If I said I'll do it, it will be done.' I'm up in the toilet firing away, Mam shouts, 'Come on Pa, your supper is getting cold'. So I catch the zip of the fly on my pants and give it a good yank and let an unmerciful scream that echoes down the stairs and into the sitting room. Mam is out in the hall, roaring up the stairs, 'What's wrong Paddy? Are you alright?' 'No I'm not Mam.' She's up at the door of the bathroom. I'm roaring like a hyena. Now I'm the one with the 'Jesus, Mary and Holy St. Joseph'. 'Tell me what's wrong', she's shouting back. 'I've caught my flute in the zip of my pants.' And Mam wants to know if I'm bleeding. I'm telling her that I don't think so, because it's still caught in the zip. 'Let me have a look at it', she shouts. I'm shouting 'Jesus, Mary and Holy St. Joseph, are you serious?' 'Of course I am', she says. 'Sure once you've seen a sausage and a pound of mince meat you've seen them all.' Dad is out in the hall roaring with laughter, saying 'Once you've seen a sausage and a pound of mince meat you've seen them all.' I'm shouting back at Mam saying, 'If you think that I'm going to open this door and let you walk in here to look at my sausage, you can think again'. 'Ah for God's sake', she says, 'wasn't I sick of looking at that thing for years when you were a baby'. 'Well it's a lot older now and a lot bigger too, so you're not coming in to look at it or handle it either.' 'Is it still stuck in the zip?' she asks. 'Yes', I'm shouting, 'so will you buzz off and let me get on with it?' I can hear Nan and herself laughing as she walks down the stairs.

After half an hour I'm walking down the stairs with great difficulty. When I walk in, Pop is there with his shoulders doing their usual when he's laughing. Nan is at it too, saying, 'Jesus, Mary and Holy St. Joseph, will you look at the way he's walking?' Mam comes in with a cup of tea for me, and says 'Well Pa love are you OK?' I'm trying to sit down with a straight face because one minute I'm suffering in agony and the other I'm laughing because I can see the funny side. At any minute now, Pop will have the funny comments and when he does, Mam and Nan will be at it too and sure enough, off he goes. 'You know,' he says 'you're very lucky that all your vitals weren't hanging out when that happened?' 'Why?' I ask. 'Because your voice would be a lot higher now and you'd be wearing a bra for the rest of your life. And off goes Nan with, "Jesus, Mary and Holy St. Joseph, he'll be wearing a bra for the rest of his life.' Twenty minutes later he'll ask if the top is still on it. Off goes Nan again. I can see his brain working away for the next comment. I don't have to wait too long. 'Why don't you bring it down to the nurse with the thick glasses in St. John's Hospital and ask her to have a look at it and tell her that you'll call back for it tomorrow,' and off goes Nan and Mam again. I won't be able to climb a ladder tomorrow to start the back of the house for Mam. She'll understand and says that I can finish it when I'm able to walk properly again.

Pop and Lar are at it Monday morning. I knew it would happen. I knew they couldn't leave an opportunity like this pass. Lar is giving me work that I have to stretch a lot. I'm holding my pack all the time because the bandage I have is falling off every time I move. I think it's because of all the Sudocream I have on it. In another four or five days I'll be able to walk properly again, when I'm back on the ladder, as I promised Mam. Mam is back from the market and says 'I thought you promised to do the back first'. I said that I will, as soon as the sun leaves the back because the white paint will blind the eyes out of me. She says, 'OK'. But by the time I have the five windows glossed at the front along with the gutters, the boys are over in the Green again kicking the ball around. Sure. I can do the back tomorrow after Mass. I'll have to do what I did last Saturday, sneak around the back with the ladder, put it away quietly with the brushes and take off over the front wall and on to the field.

I'm getting better at the soccer now and it's great to be more involved. When I'm finished I'm over sweating like a pig from all the running in the beautiful sunshine. Mam says with a smile on her face, 'God, but you're a great one for the promises alright'. I'll smile and say 'after all my hard work you never said the front was nice, not even a word of thanks'. 'Never mind that now', she says. 'Are you going to do the back for me or not?' 'I will Mam; I'll start it after I come back from Mass tomorrow'. But they'll be too interested in the front door and the colour I have for it because Mam says I can put on any colour I like. I want to do what Lar does when he paints the front of a house. We'll be there painting away, minding our own business, when women will pass by with their shopping bags. They'll lay their bags on the ground and gawk at what we're doing. Others will join them and before long a chorus of voices will be shouting up at Lar on the ladder saying 'Oh Jesus, Mary and holy St. Joseph but that's a great job you're doing there. What's the name of that colour on the front door?' Lar will shout down that he made it up himself and that he has no more left. The voices will go, 'Oh God that's an awful pity. I wanted the name of it for my fellow to go down and get it.' Lar is lying through his teeth he says, if he lets them know, every house on the fupping road will have it, on the doors, chutes, downpipes, around the fupping windows, on the sills, the gate and God knows what else. They'll be standing on chairs with a big fupping lump of 2x2 wood in a fupping pint tin to stir the paint and then they'll try to get the corner of a fupping four inch brush into the tin and get a drop of paint on it. The wood is two foot long and it would never dawn on them to take the fupping 2x2 out of the tin first. It won't dawn on them either that the reason the house we're doing looks so well is fupping the colour is only on the door and no place else.

I have left the front door 'til last for that reason. I have it all ready for the final coat of sage green that's going to have every neighbour on the road talking; Mam is standing longside me looking curious at the colour, saying that it's very nice. Then she says, 'I thought you said that you'd start the back today after Mass'. She'll walk away saying, 'I knew it, it won't be done at all. Wait and see!' She's right. The same will happen again next year and the year after, in fact it will never get done at all. I'll promise her and she'll believe me. Lar will have a new colour for all our customers who tell him to choose the colour himself because they trust his taste, and I'll want to have the door at 36 Claughaun Court changed every year too.

Mrs. Houlihan who lives across the road is one of many neighbours talking to Mam, saying 'what a good job your son Paddy made of the house, especially the front door'. She wonders if I would be any good at the papering because she has all the furniture of the sitting room in the middle of the floor with space around it to paper the walls after she and her husband have took the old stuff off. She asks Mam if I could call over tonight and give her a price. I'm no sooner in the door that evening when Mam tells me Mrs. Houlihan wants to have some work done. I'm gone out the door before Mam can say another word. Mrs. Houlihan says that she was talking to Mam, blah, blah, blah, and how I made a great job of our house and wants to know would I be able to paper her room. 'Of course, absolutely! No problem at all! I'll have that done by Saturday.' She wants to know how much it will cost. I tell her, 'four pounds'. She shows me the very expensive paper that she bought at Newsom's and says how much she's looking forward to seeing it up on the wall next Saturday, when I'll be over to do it. I'm walking back home asking myself how I'm going to do it. I never hung a sheet of wallpaper in my life. Ok, I've been working with Pop and Lar a year and a half now; I'll work with them and watch them carefully week-in week-out, at the papering, ceilings and walls with all kinds of materials. I've hung a couple of half sheets now and then. Sure I can double check with Pop tomorrow, just to make sure. I can look forward to having an extra two pound in my pocket for Sunday after I giving Mam her half.

When Saturday morning comes I can hardly wait to get over and start the papering. I should be nervous. I'm not, because this is a challenge. I have all the gear borrowed from Pop and I'm ready to start. Mrs. Houlihan says that I'm to give her a shout whenever I want a cup of tea and that she's going to leave me undisturbed. First I'm going to mix the paste and while I'm waiting for it to settle I'll write my name and date on the wall, like Pop and Lar do every time we paper a room in Limerick, to join all those that are already on the wall. But I want to put something besides my name and date; so it's 'this is my first time ever wallpapering a room followed by my name and date. Then it's out with two rolls of paper to see if it has a stepped pattern. It has, and that's going to make things a small bit complicated, no matter. Next I'll measure the height of the wall and add a few inches over and above for trimming. I need sixteen full sheets,' they'll have to be cut first. I'm not cutting one, then pasting it to the wall and when that's done, measuring and cutting another, the way most women who'll paper their own rooms. If I do that I'll be here for two days. But if I cut sixteen lengths like Pop and Lar, eight with the one step and another eight to match, I can put X on the back of one lot and 0 on the back of the other, put them on the table with an X on top of an 0 and that way every second sheet will match the one I put on before it. I can paste four at a time and I'll have them up just like Pop and Lar in no time at all. It means that I'll be an hour preparing before a sheet is on the wall, but once I start it will just take off. I'm on my knees rolling out three rolls at a time, measuring and cutting, marking the sheets, rolling them up again and putting them to one side when I'll need them shortly.

Mrs. Houlihan has her head in the door; asking 'how is it going?' It's grand Mr. Houlihan. She looks around to see how the paper she bought four weeks ago is looking on the walls, sees nothing at all closes the door rushes over to my mother, knocks on the door several times like there's a fire in the house. When Mam comes out with a worried look on her face, like most mothers do worrying, that her son might have fallen off a ladder or something worse, she says, 'Mrs. Houlihan what's wrong?' 'Oh Jesus, Mary and holy St. Joseph, Mrs. Taylor, come over quick! I thought you said Paddy knows how to wallpaper.' 'Why Mrs. Houlihan, what's happened?' 'He hasn't a sheet of paper on any wall, and there's loads of it all over the place. Jesus, Mrs. Taylor, I don't think that he's able to measure at all. I don't think he has any paper left over'. Mrs. Houlihan and Mam have the arms folded walking across the road.

Mam is trying to reassure her that I wouldn't have started the job if I couldn't do it. 'OK', says Mrs. Houlihan, 'wait 'til you see all his mistakes, they're everywhere'. There's another knock on the door. Again Mrs. Houlihan sticks her head in and says, 'Your mother is dying to see how the paper is looking'. Mrs. Houlihan has a surprised look on her face because I'm putting the last sheet of eight on one wall. Mam sticks her head in too and says, 'Oh that's lovely Mrs. Houlihan, won't it be lovely now when it's all finished, God bless it'. There's more expressions coming from Mrs. Houlihan; how lovely the job is looking. Of course I know nothing of this until I come home later that evening when Mam tells me everything; how Mrs. Houlihan was worried sick about buying another ten rolls of that paper again.

Aunt Kathleen with the blue hair lives on her own with her son Tom who came home from England a couple of days ago. He has no work and Aunt Kathleen wants to know if Pop and Lar need an extra pair of hands and would they keep her son Tom in mind. He's working with us now. I remember Pop bringing him to our house in Upper Carey's Road at Easter with three huge Bugs Bunny Easter Eggs. He's a great worker, handsome too, and he's going to steal Lar's girlfriend any day now. Lar has been going out with her for six years. She wants to get married and Lar doesn't. They'll fall out every month and when they do, Lar will take his watch, the one he paid a hundred pounds for, from J. J. KenNelly and hop it off the wall. The following morning when he's sober, he'll bring it back to J. J. in Wickham Street and ask him to fix it. J. J. will tell Lar that he's one of his best customers. Lar will give him the watch in eight or ten bits and pieces and get it back in one piece four days later. Tom will see nothing wrong with asking the gorgeous Marian out and Marian is delighted because Marian wants to get married and Marian wants to make Lar jealous too. She wants to put a fire under his arse and poor ol' Lar is in an awful state because the man that was looking for a dig out, and was given one, has now stuck a knife in Lar's back. It won't last long because it has the desired effect. Two weeks later when Lar can't take anymore, his girl puts him out of his misery, but only on the condition that they get married soon.

Now Lar is taking all the jobs that would have have been mine. I'll have to find my own from now on, because Lar is working all the hours God sends. He has a lot of money to get together because he is on a six month deadline, or else. Monday mornings are a dream now because Lar isn't going to 'The Bedford' or 'The Chinese Restaurant' anymore, on the Sunday nights. Hence no bad gas on the plank, well not until after he gets married; when the new wife will be throwing all kinds of experiments into his stomach and God help us on the Monday mornings, because it will be worse than ever.

CHAPTER 8

Jacky Glenn has a music shop on William Street under the store that Pop and Lar never got paid for. He's a relative of Uncle Dave in America. Jack's wife is looking for me to paint and paper the small bedroom in their house in Caherdavin. She is expecting a new baby, her first. She says that I can work away any night of the week I like. I'll be out there Monday to Friday every night, but won't manage to finish the job. She says that if I want to I can come out on the Saturday morning to finish it that it won't be any problem at all. When I arrive out on the Saturday morning she says that I can work away, that Jack is in bed and that I'm not to worry because he's a heavy sleeper and noise will not be a problem. But it's hard working in someone's house when one of them is in bed asleep. I'll do my best to keep the noise down. I'll keep the door of the bedroom I'm working in closed. After one hour I need to mix some Polyfilla. I need to get to the bathroom for some water. So I spread some filling powder into a biscuit tin cover and bring it with me to the bathroom. Its door is slightly open. When I walk in, the wash hand basin is opposite the door. I'm working away nice and quite gently mixing the water and powder together when out from the corner of my right eye, I'm aware of a shadow or a presence. My heart misses a beat. I don't look but, Jesus, I think someone is sitting on the Jacks. I mix away pretending I haven't noticed. What the hell am I going to do? I can't stand here forever mixing Polyfilla. I'm here so long now it's starting to go off and I'm sure whoever is sitting on the toilet, is wondering when I'm going to get out so that he can wipe his backside. So I look over and sure enough it is Jack. He's got his arms folded and his jocks are down around his ankles. I can see the cheeks of his backside resting on the seat. He's looking up at the ceiling with a big red head on him. I say, 'Good morning Jack'. He grunts in response. 'Not a bad morning', I say. He grunts again. I'd better get out of here fast. I don't think he's in a good mood.

I'm back in the small room wondering why the hell he didn't close the bloody door of the toilet. Maybe he didn't know I was in there. I think if it happened to me at home, how I'd feel, if someone else came into the bathroom while I was sitting on the jacks, with my jocks around my ankles. I wouldn't be a bit happy. Jack's wife is bringing me up a cup of tea. I'm telling her how I walked in on top of her husband while he was on the jacks. 'Oh I forgot to tell him that you were coming out this morning, that's why he never closed the door. Ah sure, don't mind. He'll get over it', she says. I'm thinking if the roles were reversed and 'twas you sitting on the jacks when I walked in, it would be a different story'. She says that she wants two bedrooms done next week and would I give her a price, which I do. She said that she'd talk to Jack about it tomorrow and if I call into his shop on Monday, he'll let me know if they want to go ahead with it. I'll call into Jack on the way home for lunch that Monday. He shakes his head from side to side and says that they won't be doing the rooms for another while. But I know that Jack doesn't want me out in his house again because he's too embarrassed with my presence. He can't even look me in the eye while he's telling me.

Goodwin's, the people who have a large shop close to Todd's, are opening showrooms for the trade overhead the shops in Bedford Row opposite James McMahon. It's a big area. They want it divided into six separate rooms. We have the job of doing the whole lot. Partitions, ceilings, toilets, painting, we'll be here for the bones of three months. It will be like a regular job in a regular building; like the other three jobs I had before I came to work with Pop and Lar. It will also be my first time using the saw, hammer and other tools since I started working with them. Lar is impressed and says that he never realised that I was so good with the tools. 'Sure haven't I been telling you that for the past twelve months, and all you say is that there's too much painting to be done.' I'll be in my element here for the first month, making partitions, hanging doors too and able to keep up with the two of them, and only getting half the amount they're taking home. But I don't mind. I just love working with wood.

We have to make our own tea here in the mornings. That means lighting a small portable heater fuelled by paraffin oil. The stories will start. Lar might say, 'Jaysus Har, do you remember the days when we would fall down and worship someone if they gave us a job, when we'd do any kind of fupping job at all?' Pop starts laughing. Lar looks at him and says, 'He's after thinking of something'. Pop says, 'Tell him about the job we did for Newenham the architect out in his holiday hut'. Lar says, 'Ah Jaysus, what about that Har?' I'm all ears.

'We were given the keys of a holiday home three miles outside Ballina, near Killaloe. They had no fupping toilet and we were told that we could sleep there until the job was finished. We had to go to the railway station on our bikes with our tool bags on the carriers. I got an ol' fupping bag from my mother to put a few things in, like a toothbrush, towels, some soap. We put the fupping bikes into the luggage wagon at the station and when we got to Killaloe at twelve that day, and left our bikes outside the first fupping pub we saw. We stayed there all fupping day except when I went out to the nearest shop to buy an fupping loaf of bread, some tea, sugar and milk because we had fupp all to eat. There was a butcher's shop close to the pub, so we went in and bought a huge fupping steak which the butcher wrapped in brown paper, and tied some string around it. I brought the whole lot back to the pub, where we drank until all our fupping money was gone. We put the few groceries on the back of the bike, and I hung the fupping steak on the handlebars, got on the bikes and cycled the fupping three miles out to the holiday home, drunk as fupping skunks. After about two miles I looked down to see if the fupping steak was alright and the fupping thing was gone. The fupping brown paper got damp and the fupping steak fell out. 'Jesus Har', I shouted 'our fupping dinner is gone'. We stopped our bikes, got off, walked back down the road looking for the fupping steak and there it was a hundred yards from where we stopped, lying there on the road. So I picked it up and shoved it down inside my shirt where it stuck to all the fupping sweat that was pouring out of me from all the fupping cycling that we were doing. When we got to the holiday home what was it only a fupping single Decker bus? Can you believe it, a fupping bus out in the middle of a field, thirty feet away from the fupping River Shannon'.

Pop's shoulders are at it all the time. Lar has to stop every now and then from all the laughing. I'm getting a pain in my stomach. 'We got into the bus', says Lar 'and there were two bunk beds. So we said we'd make ourselves some tea with bread and butter before we went to bed. While your father made the tea I went down to the river to try and wash all the small fupping stones that stuck to the fupping steak when it fell off the bike for our dinner tomorrow There I was at one o'clock in the morning down by the fupping river, drunk out of my skull in the fupping dark I cant fupping swim and if I fall into the river your father will never hear me because he has the transistor radio on trying to get the news. Anyway, there I am on the edge of the fupping Shannon, in the dark, washing an fupping T-bone steak in the river. I'm feeling the steak with my hands to see if I got all the stones out, along with the sweat from my chest. When I get back in the bus with the fupping steak your father says, 'Give me that thing, I'm going to fry it up now'. So I tell him 'You can't do that Har,' and he wants to know why. 'Because it's Friday and you can't eat a fupping steak on a Friday'. So your father says, 'What time is it?' 'ten thirty' I answer. 'Well it'll be Saturday in another hour and a half or so,' he says. And I tell your father that I'm not going to have a sin on my soul because of eating a steak on a fupping Friday. So your father says, 'Give me the fupping steak'. 'But Harry if you eat the fupping steak now, we'll have nothing for the dinner tomorrow'. And then a big argument starts. Your father says one thing and then I say another. Now insults are flying all over the place. I call him outside because we didn't want to wreck the bus. Now we're outside trying to give one another a fupping dig. Sure I don't know where he is, and he doesn't know where I am, its so fupping dark. All we can hear is each other's voice. I say, I'm going fupping home, and go back into the bus to get my few bits and pieces.

I grab my bike and cycle a couple of miles up the road in the dark. The country is an awful place to be on your own in the blackness when you're not used to it. So I stop the bike, reminding myself that I have no fupping money. I've no fupping job either. In fact, I have fupp all. So back I go to the bus and your father is inside in one of the bunk beds shaking. 'Who is that,' he asks?' 'It's me Harry, I'm back'. Your father looks at me and says, 'Sorry about that Chief, I was hoping you'd come back. I'm scared out of my mind because the fupping bus is moving all over the place'. 'It's the cattle Harry, they're scratching themselves against it.' Anyway we ate the fupping steak an hour later and it was the best fupping steak we ever had in our life!'

While I'm heading home for dinner, there's a lot of commotion going on in O'Connell Street. People are shouting and running down towards Patrick Street. When I turn out of Bedford Row onto O'Connell Street, there's hundreds of people looking at smoke coming from a building that's across the road from Cannock's four-sided clock, the clock that keeps most of Limerick City on its toes every day. Without realising it, I'm joining the groups that want to investigate. I have my bike with me. I could have hopped on it and cycled the two hundred yards but I just forgot with the excitement. I just managed to get myself in to the hoards of bodies that have gathered outside Cannock's. That's where the best view is because it's straight across the road from the fire. The Fire Brigade are here and the smoke coming from the back of the roof of Cruises' Hotel is black and getting heavier. This is very exciting. There's people opening windows on the top floor and shouting down, but nobody can hear what they are saying. They seem to be in a right state because there's smoke coming out of each window that they're talking from. I think they're saying 'We're trapped' and God help them if they are. Everybody here is shouting, 'Don't jump, don't jump.' Now there are three people sitting out on the sills of the windows, with the windows closed behind them. They are sales assistants from Cannock's who are asking us to get out of the way so that they can get every new mattress that's in the shop across the road fast, because these people look like they're getting ready to fall or jump any minute. There are rows of steel railings, four foot out from the walls of the bottom of both sides of the front entrance to Cruises' Hotel. Firemen and ordinary Joe Soaps in the crowd are helping to put twenty or more mattresses between the railings and the wall at the bottom. Everybody around me is asking what the hell the Fire Brigade are doing about getting the three people down from the window sills. They're just looking up and shouting at them. The crowd around me is getting angry. One man shouts, 'Why don't you do something instead of talking? What the fupping hell are ye being paid for?

Will ye get them down before they jump for fupps sake?' That's followed by more comments from the crowd at both sides of me until we're all shouting at the Firemen, but they're just there standing looking up at the people on the windowsills. The three misfortunes are just sitting there wondering like the rest of us what the hell the Fire Brigade are doing about getting them down, with the smoke bellowing out of each window they're sitting on. I've got this horrible feeling that this whole thing is going to go pear-shaped any minute.

I haven't taken notice of the hunger I should have for the dinner I was going to eat at quarter past one, because the hunger has now turned into a knot that's in my stomach worrying about the poor folk on the windows. My mind is going back to the time in Upper Carey's Road in 1957 when Dinny, Phonsie, Noelie and myself saw the black smoke heading into the sky and when we saw it, took ourselves off at lightening speed into town to see which building was on fire. We could not believe it was Todd's. The fire was blazing away in O'Connell Street, William Street and the bottom of Thomas Street. We never saw anything like it before with explosions and flames rising high into the sky. The heat was so great that shops on the opposite side of the road had their paint work scorched, and how it lasted for days before a helicopter was engaged to help pull it down. But as bad as that fire was then, no one was killed.

A helicopter tearing down the old walls of Todds after the fire in 1957

If the heat breaks the glass on any of the three windows these people are sitting on, then they're going to jump. At long last the Fire Brigade have their long ladder against the wall, extending it up to the window that most of the smoke is coming out from. But it's four feet short. Everybody is in shock. They are asking how is it possible that Limerick Fire Brigade have a ladder for the whole of the city, including all the Georgian buildings that have been here for the past one hundred and fifty years and don't have a ladder to reach the top of any of them. Sure the ladder that Pop and Lar have is bigger than that. Well the crowd are going mad, throwing every kind of abuse at every Fire Officer nearest to them. There are three firemen standing at the bottom of the ladder shouting at the women to try and reach the ladder with their legs even though it's four feet short of the window sill their sitting on.

Out of nowhere a man, who looks like he might be working on a building site by the way he's dressed, runs over to the ladder, pushes the firemen aside, climbs to the top to the cheers from the crowds. He gets to the top of the ladder as far as he

175

can. His head is just above the window sill. He's got his left hand holding the ladder, which is at his waist level. There's complete silence. All that can be heard in the background is the crackling sound of wood and other inflammable material burning away. We can see he's talking to the three girls, gesturing with his right hand for one of them to climb down and he'll catch her. It takes a while. She hesitates but the crashing of glass behind her causes her to move down towards him. Nobody is moving as everybody's eyes are on the two of them including the other two who surely must be hoping that they're turn is next if this man is successful. We're all willing the chap on the ladder to succeed. The woman is making her way down. We can hear the guy shouting to her. She slips. Everybody gasps. He grabs hold of her, comes down the ladder to thunderous applause and cheers as they both reach the ground. He repeats the same thing with the other two to more cheers.

I'm back at work with an empty stomach because the whole episode robbed me of the dinner I would have had If I went home. Pop and Lar are hungry too for the same reason and send me up to the Savoy Café in Roches Street for three bags of chips and six sausages while they put the kettle on. Of course the conversation centres on the fire at Cruises' and the disgraceful equipment that's at the Fire Brigade's disposal. They'll be the talk of the town for days. The Limerick Leader will ask questions of the City Council and by the end of the year Limerick City Fire Brigade will have a state of the art fire engine with a ladder that can reach the highest building.

In the days and weeks to come working in Bedford Row, Pop will be telling more stories and yarns; like the time the sweet salesman from Dublin would call and stay overnight at The Bedford Hotel. 'A nice quiet man', says Pop 'and would always pay for his accommodation.' Two nights, the minute he walked in the door, plus his breakfast and dinner too, the man never wanted to be in debt, not for a minute. After staying the night, he would take Pop on his journey around Munster, stopping at shops all over the place, asking Pop to bring whatever sweets and chocolates were required from the large van that travelled everywhere. After spending several nights in different parts of Munster, it's back to The Bedford for the dinner, more Guinness and a night's sleep before he paid Pop, but the travelling salesman whose name was Mr. Cassidy fell asleep at his table half way through his dinner with the knife and fork still in his hands that are resting on the table.

It will be another half an hour before it dawns on someone that there's no sound coming from Mr. Cassidy's nose or mouth. It's left to Pop to investigate. After sticking his ear to Mr. Cassidy's mouth, Pop moves away from his presence and shouts, 'He's dead'. There's a gasp from everyone present. Someone should feel his pulse. 'Where are they?' asks Pop as he slowly makes his way back and places his fingers on the wrist of Mr. Cassidy's right hand. Pop waits a minute and says that he can't feel a bloody thing, then adds he's cold so he must be dead. Mrs. Dennehy comes up from the kitchen and into the bar, takes charge of the situation, puts her hand to Mr. Cassidy's neck and says, 'he's dead alright'. She puts the sign of the cross on her forehead and adds, 'May the Lord have mercy on his soul'. She tells her daughter Maureen to phone for the Guards and a Doctor too, and tells everyone present to get down on their knees and say the rosary for the repose of the poor man's soul. There's Our Fathers', Hail Mary's, Glory Be's coming from the Bedford Bar, just like it does from the Franciscan Church across the road. Mrs. Dennehy's customers are totally confused when they arrive into the bar and have to fall onto the floor on their knees and join in the chorus of Hail Mary, etc. They haven't a bloody clue what's going on because the corpse is around the corner in the other room where they can't see it. They might have had plans to go the pictures across the road in the Savoy after a pint or two, but these plans are scuppered now because what's going on here is more interesting than what's going on across the road at the Savoy.

By now word has gone into the streets of Henry Street and Bedford Row. Customers in other pubs will finish their pints and find themselves in the packed bar at the Bedford Hotel now that the rosary is over and the cold Mr. Cassidy is still in his chair with his hands still holding the utensils while the Guards ask for a bit of room for the Doctor to investigate before the ambulance comes and takes the body away. Mrs. Dennehy can be heard muttering under her breath, while helping to fill the mouths that are dry from talking and saying the rosary. She say's that it was just as well that he paid his bill before departing and wouldn't it be good for business if somebody was to die in her pub every week. Someone overheard her and said, 'Sure if that was to happen, wouldn't all your customers be afraid to walk in the door in case it might be one of them that might die on her.'

Now word has come through that the only ambulance in Limerick has gone twenty miles out the road to a farming accident and won't be available for another four hours at least and there's poor Mr. Cassidy sitting on the chair getting stiffer and colder every minute, while the on-lookers have a good stare and are making comments like, 'God, but isn't it a grand way to go, sitting at a table in a hotel, having your dinner'. Others will say 'His next of kin should be notified', and 'won't someone have to put their hands in his pockets to see if there might be some kind of ID with an address'. Pop is telling Lar and myself that he volunteered straight away because Mrs. Dennehy got her money before him laying his head on a bed a few nights before, and sure he didn't get a fupping penny. It would be a good excuse to have Mr. Cassidy's wallet in his hand and take what's due to him in front of many witnesses. But there's nothing except ten, ten pound notes, an Irish Hospital Sweeps Stake Ticket and two receipts for ten gallons of petrol. Denis and Tadhg Dennehy are there too. One of them says, 'What about his sweet truck? There may be something there'. Pop has to root around Mr. Cassidy's pockets, searching for the key and when he finds it, himself and the Dennehy boys are out in the truck rooting through every nook and cranny and come up empty handed.

The Guards who are here say that he can't be buried until his next of kin are informed and if he has no next of kin it could be weeks before he'll go into the ground. After another two hours, Mrs. Dennehy takes a phone call from an Operator informing her that the ambulance which was on its way to bring Mr. Cassidy to Barrington's Hospital has broken down and that he will ring in the morning to give a time when they will collect the deceased, and poor ol' Mr. Cassidy has to stay in the chair for the night. Mrs. Dennehy says that she'd better get a few candles and put them around Mr. Cassidy out of respect and have the wake just in case the poor man has no one belonging to him and wouldn't now be as good a time as any to have it, seeing there's so many here in the pub. Pop, Denis and Tadhg decide that seeing that the man has no one belonging to him, well not that they know of anyway, wouldn't it be a good idea to drink to the man's future happiness in heaven and spend one of the man's ten pound notes. When that was gone, they said 'Sure we might as well have another few glasses,' and on it went, with a song from everyone present as it was expected. Then there was only sixty pounds left and 'Sure wasn't I entitled to some of it?' said Pop seeing as he never got paid.

When twelve o'clock comes and the front doors of The Bedford Bar are closed, the place is still packed and Mrs. Dennehy has a smile on her face that hasn't been there for a good few years, ever since the Munster Hurling Final came to The Gaelic Grounds. There's only thirty pounds of Mr. Cassidy's money left and Pop, Denis and Tadgh are legless and shouting how great a man Mr. Cassidy was; a regular visitor to the Bedford Bar every three weeks, very religious, never a cross word or curse came out of his mouth, and won't heaven be a better place, now that he's there. When all of Mr. Cassidy's money is gone along with most of the crowd that helped drink it, it's time for bed.

When the following morning arrives, with the sun bursting in through the bedroom window on top of myself, Denis and Tadhg snoring our brains out, until the door of the bedroom opened to the sound of the local Gardaí entering the bedroom to get the three of us up and wanting to know why Mr. Cassidy wasn't in the place he was supposed to be downstairs on the chair at the table and asking how he came to be in the bed with them on his back and legs still in the sitting position. Lar and myself can't stop laughing. We're asking how the hell did

Mr. Cassidy find his way into their bed. Pop says that he hadn't a clue and neither did the two Dennehy boys, but guessed they must have carried him upstairs because they probably didn't want to leave him on his own.

Mr. McMahon or Dentist McMahon as he's known, has a practice at the back of the first floor on one of the Georgian houses in O'Connell Avenue, a few doors down from Mr. Newman the Architect, who is a father-in-law to Mr. Ferris, number 75, that we'll work in over the coming years. Dentist McMahon is related to the McMahon's, the builder suppliers in Bedford Row and also the Dock Road. Lar says that he's going to pay him a visit because his teeth are in an awful state and he'd better get them seen to before they all fall out. After all he's a businessman and a businessman should look the part. It would be no good being well dressed, calling to a potential customers, residence to quote for a job while talking out through a mouthful of bad teeth. He says that it's going to cost him fifty-five pounds to get the job done properly. I'm thinking sure that's a bloody fortune. It would take me fourteen weeks to earn that much. When it's all done, six weeks later, Lar walks around everywhere with a big smile on his face showing off the gold fillings. People will gasp and say, 'Jesus Lar, you're gold teeth are gorgeous. They must have cost you a fortune.' Lar is keeping an eye on the price of gold every day and if the price goes up, so will the price of the teeth when he's asked. Next week he'll walk into work with a pair of black trimmed glasses because he says that his eyesight is going. He needs them for the good finish he has with everything he does or puts his hands to and we have to listen to him every Monday morning with the list of things he has and wears, it gets longer and longer, and so does the speech. He is very generous to himself and miserably mean to everybody else and I'm about to find out just how much.

Rick McCarthy, another one of the skin and hide merchants, and also a great committee member of St. Joseph's Scouts, has a house two doors up from Mrs. Mills Bed and Breakfast in O'Connell Avenue. He wants all the downstairs redecorated. When Monday morning comes, the usual routine starts again.

I'm up on the plank with Lar holding the ceiling paper and he's dropping one every few minutes. Mr. McCarthy will be wondering what the awful smell is, like others. The same lies will be told about where the smell is coming from. I'll get a bit of peace because he has to keep the cheeks of his arse closed and when Friday morning comes I've got the flu. I can't come to work. When Pop comes home for his dinner, he says 'Lar needs you up at Mr. McCarthy's to finish the gloss work because Mr. McCarthy has a special event coming up on Saturday night and he needs the room finished'. I don't know what it is about me, but I can't say no when someone needs me or depends on me.

So out I get from the bed coughing and choking. I'll exaggerate it more when I walk into Mr. McCarthy's downstairs rooms. 'Good man', says Lar and then ask, 'Is there any way you could finish all the woodwork this afternoon?' The work that would have taken me the whole day to do! I'll answer and say that I'll do my best. By the time six o'clock arrives I have the whole lot done. All I want is go home and fall into the bed and have Mam fuss over me. She is great at that. I won't be even interested in spending the extra few bob I'm sure I'll get for getting out of the sick bed and the awful exaggerated cough I have all afternoon. Well am I in for a shock. When Lar hands me my wages it's less a half day. I can hardly speak; I'm in so much shock. I got the same amount of work done in half that time and the dirty rotten louser docks me a half-day. But there will be other days too and more to come and I'll still be just as surprised.

The local FCA, or the Free Clothing Association as they were known above in the soldiers barracks are looking for recruits and I'm all ears because there's money involved: Sixteen pounds for two weeks training, square bashing, marching and firing a 303 rifle at the shooting range, making bombs and disarming them too. I'll be down at the front gate an hour before the once weekly meeting starts to sign up. When I get there, they ask me how old I am and I'm lying through my teeth telling them that I'm seventeen, because if I tell them I was sixteen they'd send me home. I'm nearly seventeen, I will be next, July but I can't tell them that or they will send me home. There are eight others here wanting to join as well, lying through their teeth about their age. The sergeant has the forms and the pens here on the table for us to sign, he knows we're lying. Some of us here don't even look ten, never mind seventeen. We're told that if we miss any meetings it will affect the money we get, come the end of the two weeks in July at Fort Campton, down in Crosshaven, Co. Cork, one of the four forts the British Army built before the First World War. They'll take us out to Knocknasheen to shoot the 303 rifle that some say are as old as the First World War, left over after the Black and Tans left the country around the 1920s. I'll stand behind the regular soldiers when they show us how to lie on the ground holding the rifle properly and watch their shoulders try to break out of their backs each time they fire the gun, because the force of the explosion is so strong every time they fire it.

I'm asking myself what the hell I am doing here at all. I want to quietly sneak away and forget the whole thing, but the reward of the sixteen pounds in July won't let my legs go anywhere. When my turn comes the heart that had such good practice at the beating is at it again. Five will walk over to take their turn. Each will have an instructor by his side making sure that he doesn't point the rifle anywhere except at the target that's in front of him. I'll lie on my stomach with the rifle that weighs a ton, hold it tight into my right shoulder. I'll listen to my instructor and won't take a blind bit of notice of what he's saying because I'm terrified. I'll point the bloody thing at the target, close my eyes and do the complete opposite to what I'm told. After pressing the trigger I think I've been pucked in the head by a mule. Mother of Jesus, I have to do this another four times to empty the cartridge of five. I'll pull the bolt back, allowing the second bullet to go up from the cartridge and into the chamber, and shove it with the bolt and fire again. My heart is beating faster now because it knows what's coming, but when the last bullet is gone I'm pumping blood from my nose, because I've got my right hand so close to my face it's like I've digged myself in the nose five times. I have soldiers all around me, telling me to lie down, stand up, hold my head back and God knows what

182

else. Some are saying that all in their years in the army they've never seen anything like that before. There I am getting the kind of attention I never want, the kind that makes me look like a right gob-shite, weak and stupid and not able to take what everybody else can.

There's worse to come too. Each instructor will go and collect each paper target that's pinned to a post twenty five yards away to see how their man is doing. I wish they would do it privately because mine won't have any bullet holes close to the target, but its worse, I didn't hit the bloody target at all. I just want to dig a bloody hole and go into it and cover myself over. But I'm getting used to it now, it's happening so much. I'll make sure that I'm at every meeting and that my name is on the attendance book. They'll take us out to the yard and march us around with hob-nail boots that has the great sound with the hundreds of nails from the boots when they all hit the ground at the same time. The heavy rifles from the First World War will tear into our shoulders. We'll be asking ourselves what the hell we are doing here at all when we could be at home watching the TV or chasing a few girls. But that's the power of sixteen pounds and the fun we'll have spending it, that will bring us back here every week.

When July comes I'll have the two pounds I normally get from Mam out of my week's wages and no holiday money because Pop and Lar say that they never had a holiday in their life and if they don't take a holiday with pay, simply because they can't afford it, I won't be getting one either. They'll say 'Sure aren't you getting a free holiday from the Irish Government, sure won't that do you?' The four green army trucks takes us, the Third Field Engineers, to Crosshaven on the old pot-holed road, has us hopping off the timber benches into the air and will also have us sick from stomachs that can't settle in one place, and have most of us dying when we get there. But the sight of Fort Camdon with its towers rising out of the sea up the steep mountainside where it commands a great view, and was used to protect the bay, has the lot of us enthralled. We'll stay here for the next two weeks, sleep on three wooden planks six inches off the ground, in one of the many stone buildings and love every minute of it. They'll show us how to make pipe-bombs, take a machine gun asunder and put it back together again. And if you want to get out of square bashing and drill that we'll have to do every day, we can join the long list of names who'll want to walk around the Fort in the dark on their own at all hours of the morning with a heavy 303 rifle resting on a sore shoulder that might have a towel under a tunic to ease the pain. We'll be given five rounds of live bullets and told to put them in the rifle and keep the safety catch on, and be very close to soiling our pants' when we walk into the dark passages that takes us around the Fort that will take us a good thirty minutes to walk. We'll imagine we're hearing all kinds of things in the night, only to hear a shuffle of feet or laughter. Because it's a gang of lads from one of the stone houses out to scare the bloody daylights out of us. But we'll have the next day off to avoid the square bashing that we're all getting to hate and the sore shoulders that go with it. But when the evenings come, well that's a different story.

It's back to the billet and into the only set of good clothes we have and down the long hill that has holiday homes of all shapes and sizes on both sides belonging to the wealthy. Most of us here will drool our way past everything and wonder how can there be so many rich people in this part of Ireland. The few bob we bring with us will be stretched until Friday when our first eight pounds comes our way. Crosshaven is a hive of activity. We'll walk there every evening to the carnival because that's where all the girls will be, and throwing the shapes to do our level best to catch their eye and impress. It will be just like Dunmore East when the Scouts were there, with too many guys and not enough women. So it's a case of first down, first served.

We'll be starving with the hunger because of the awful food the army gives us; lumpy porridge first thing in the morning with a quarter loaf of bread and a lump of butter that's as hard as ice on top of it and no bigger than an oxo cube and we're wondering how the hell we're going to cut this quarter of a loaf into slices with the awful blunt knifes they've given us. Sure what's the point of cutting it into pieces when the piece of butter they've given us won't even cover one slice? So it's a question of having one slice with a decent bit of butter, or three slices without any butter at all. After the first one, I'm missing the spotted dick already. The bloody dinners are lousy too; beef that's as tough as leather, spuds that need another ten minutes in the pot, peas that are like bullets, turnips that are so pale they're like potatoes. When supper time comes we won't even bother to turn up because that's going to be lousy too. All the takeaways and chippers in Crosshaven know it. They'll be ready for us and the few bob we're trying to hold onto. The few bob that we need to impress a girl; a girl that we think might like us. We'll ask her if she would like a bag of chips, a fish too and pray she'll say no, and politely take one or two of ours. After the first week we'll get sick of it and complain. It won't do us any good because it falls on deaf ears.

General McKeon is coming next week to inspect the Free Clothing Association of Limerick. When he comes we're fed like Kings; four or five slices of bread, more if we want it with lots of butter. A fry too! We can't believe it! We wonder what's going on and ask ourselves why we can't have this every day? He'll walk into the big dining room. We're told to stand to attention and sit down while he tells the lot of us how proud Ireland and Limerick should be of every one of us, young men willing to give up their two weeks and learn to defend their country. We're all having a right laugh later on, saying 'Sure we wouldn't last ten minutes in a battlefield, and if it wasn't for the sixteen pounds we wouldn't be here at all'. He's talking about the great Irishmen who died for Ireland, men who didn't know one end of a gun from the other, but in spite of that were able to run the Black and Tans back to where they came from. When he's finished all that rubbish he'll ask us are we happy with the food; but all the mouths that were giving out last week are now nodding their heads saying, 'Grand Sir'. Not me though. I'm on my feet saying, 'Permission to speak Sir.'

'Go ahead young man, what's on your mind?'

'Well Sir, since we arrived here last Saturday, all of us are getting our energy from the takeaways in Crosshaven, because what we're getting here Sir, is only fit for the pigsty. I'll take a quarter of a loaf of bread I got yesterday morning with the lump of butter still on top that I kept in a brown paper bag in my locker and show it to him. 'This is what we get Sir, every morning along with the porridge that's musty and nothing like the porridge we get at home Sir. We're all wondering Sir where the loaf of bread and the lump of butter is this morning Sir. We're looking at the great spread laid in front of us too Sir, and wonder is it because you're here Sir. Well if it is Sir, you need to know about it Sir.' He's looking at all the tables while I'm addressing him. Then the Captain in charge along with the Sergeant Major, they're both red-faced and only look at the ground. I'm still standing waiting for a response. You could hear a pin drop. 'Is that all young man?' he said. 'Yes Sir, thank you Sir'. 'Good day then', he says as he walks out the door red-faced too. I don't know what that man said or who he said it to, but for the rest of that week the Takeaways in town are wondering why the boys from Limerick aren't frequenting their premises so much. I have become the most popular guy in this place but not with the Captain or Sergeant Major.

Sergeant Browne owns a pub in Fox's Bow and gives us a loan of a few bob and cigarettes on Wednesday and Thursday of the first week because our money will be gone. And if we don't have a smoke, someone will be killed. We'll be bored out of our skulls too if we can't get to the town and chat up the few girls who will have the pick of the best of us every Saturday night. It will be no good going down there without the few bob. Sure what girl would want to hang around any of us if we couldn't buy her a bag of chips or a bottle of Fanta? So Sergeant Browne is our hero on Wednesday and Thursday and a bloody nuisance on Friday, because he's is waiting outside the back door of the hut we'll walk into to get our first weeks money he'll have a list of every name in the place, what we got and when we got it. There'll be a few bob interest too and the small fortune we thought we had is nearly halved. But we have to pay because we'll be looking for more come next Tuesday, as most will be gone after the weekend.

Paddy O'Keeffe is in St. Joseph's Scouts as well. He's the one that told me about the FCA, a nice, tall, handsome lad; a brother of Timmy. I'll knock around with Paddy and Gerry Kennedy and strike it rich with the girls because of their good looks. I'm up a lane with a drop-dead-gorgeous blonde, shifting away, when I get the cramps, or the gallops as Pop calls it, and ruin the whole bloody evening for the other two lads. It's the same anytime I go away and eat different foods. I'll always get the scutters. I'm on my knees rolling in agony from the cramps and trying to keep the cheeks of my backside closed so there won't be an avalanche of waste into the only pair of good pants I have. And there's the poor blonde looking on at me asking am I alright, and all I want to do is get into a field and drop the pants and get some relief. So I take off down the road like Ronnie Delaney, holding the seat of my pants with the two hands, looking for a place, any place to ease the pain. And when I get back to the Barracks that night, Paddy and Gerry won't talk to me because I ruined their night. They said I was the one who wanted to go back to the barrack's and they couldn't concentrate on the shifting with the blonde looking on at them all the time. I'll be thrown out of the FCA with a dishonourable discharge by the end of the second week and after I get the second eight pounds, I'll be discharged for telling the Captain to go and fupp himself. He'll take me before a committee of two other Captains and ask me apologise. I tell him and the other two what to do with themselves, and I'm on my way back to Limerick on my own. Next week I'll be looking to join something else that might give me an extra few bob for my troubles.

Mam says she missed me while I was gone. She's two spotted dicks on the kitchen table waiting for my mouth and stomach, and while I'm stuffing myself I'm telling her how much I missed the spotted dick. She'll smile while I answer her questions and say, 'Did you miss your poor mother at all?' I'll answer and say, 'Of course Mam, sure no one looks after me the way you do'. I'll give her a wink. She'll smile again, walk into the room saying, 'Oh in another couple of years you'll be gone, you'll find yourself a girl and be gone out of here and I wonder will she look after you the way your mother does?' 'I doubt it Mam', I'll answer. 'Will you teach her how to make the spotted dicks, because I nearly died below in Cork for the want of the spotted dick?' She'll smile again and say, 'Is that all you'll miss, the bloody spotted dicks?' It's great to see her smile. I know she's pleased I'm home. She'll fuss and fustier over me for the next few days and puts extra portions of everything on the plate, until she thinks I'm back to the way I was when I left for Cork. I'll tell herself, Pop and Nan about the blonde I was shifting, and that I had to run because of the dose I got from the army food and they can't stop laughing.

It starts Pop talking about the Emergency when he was in the army as a cook, how he had no experience of cooking anything at all, not even how to boil an egg. 'And there I was under-cooking and over-cooking everything they put in my hand'; how he had his life threatened every day. And I'm asking him 'What was the Emergency?' He said, 'When Hitler started invading every bloody country in Europe. The Irish Government thought he was going to take over our country so he could be next door to England, every man in Ireland had to have some kind of military training. So every gob-shite in the country that could stand or had a pulse was given a uniform and sent to a camp out in Knocklesheen. He'll tell me about fellows he served with, like Grumpy Malone who spent all his time complaining about everything and anything; Itchy Hogan because he was always scratching his arse', Nosey Deegan who never stopped picking his nose. He'll tell us about the things he put in the food, the pots and pans that fed the multitudes and if they knew what he was putting into them, he'd have to get out of town. We're asking what kind of things, but Mam says she doesn't want to know and that puts an end to that.

CHAPTER 9

Jetta is getting married next week and has adjusted to the idea of living in the back bedroom in Garryowen. It has to be painted. Pop and Mam will use the small bedroom, while Harry who's four now, James, twelve, and myself, will share the biggest room. Jetta will get married in St. John's Cathedral and have the reception in the small Cecil Hotel in the same street. It's a burden on Pop and Mam, mostly Mam because of the limited time she had to prepare for it. Mam works wonders with money; always has, ever since her days in London working as a housekeeper, and coming home just before the Second World War. The early days in Bedford Row and Upper Carey's Road, scrimping and scraping, especially in the winter months when Pop didn't have the work. There's always a couple of pound in her purse for any who needs a loan, like her brother, Uncle James, who does the painting too and lives out in Cappamore and has to borrow the small Baby Austin from his mother, Nan, who always looked after the payments for the family car. Uncle Peter has it most of the time because he's living out in Tower Hill with Nan living in the village now because she got the small cottage years ago.

James will hand Mam back the few pound he got a week or two before when he gets paid and it won't be long more before he'll be looking for it again. He says Mam is like his personal bank and wonders what he would do without her. When Jet and her husband move in they'll be short a few bob too, trying to get the few things she'll need for the baby that's coming soon. There'll be money in Mam's purse for that too. She'll never moan or complain and do it all with a lovely smile she has most of the time, especially now that Pop is heading into his best ever time off the drink at home.

She smokes ten cigarettes at home every day. She'll never smoke in the streets because she says it's not lady-like. 'I'm giving them up', she says. 'I wish I never started the bloody things, they're a curse'. When she starts she gets no support from any of us, not even an enquiry of 'How are you doing Mam? Aren't you great?' Pop will come home every day, smoke like he always does, and be oblivious to her cravings. And I can't understand why he doesn't give them up too. Sure he doesn't smoke proper at all? When he takes a drag he lets the whole lot out at the side of his mouth and won't take any of it down to the lungs like Mam does. So I can't understand how he can be addicted. But in spite of all that, Mam will succeed and then worries about putting on weight. She's obsessed about that and won't eat properly. A cup of tea with brown bread for breakfast; then it's more tea and brown bread with a rasher for the dinner and the same again at supper time. She'll make it last for ages, getting up each time to fend to all of us like we're totally incapable of standing or walking and reaching out across the table for anything.

She's a dainty little woman, always in her slippers and nylon housecoat. And when there isn't any fetching or running for her family to do, she has the small finger of her right hand folded in a half-circle gathering the crumbs of her brown bread to the edge of the table, into the palm of her other hand and then into the fire. She'll ask Pop and myself about the jobs we're working on. And when we're finished, she'll sigh and say, 'Isn't it great to have the work these days and not like the time in Upper Carey's Road?' And add, 'God weren't they hard all the same?' She'll look in the mirror over the mantelpiece while she stands on her toes, brush a few curls if she has to go to town. I'll grab her by her leg, just above her knees and say, 'Jesus, Mam you're putting on weight'. She'll come down off her toes, turn around and say, 'Jesus, Mary and holy Saint Joseph, am I really Paddy?' She'll have a worried look on her face as she says it. I'll tell her 'I was only joking' and I'll have to tell her over and over again, till I reassure her and try to remember not to say that again.

Jetta is expecting her baby today, any minute now. There's great excitement in the house, especially with Mam. She's been helping Jet buy all the things she needs for the big day. I'm trying to finish the crib Jetta saw in a women's magazine that's very unusual and it will turn into a family heirloom. I'll need another week and a half to finish it. Jetta says that I haven't got a week and a half. She says she can feel the pains coming already. Everyone is panicking, mostly Mam. We all want to get Jet out the door as soon as possible. We don't want her dropping the child anywhere in the house causing more panic and confusion. Pop is gone across the road to the neighbour with the phone, the one Mam said that she'd never go next or near because of all the pestering the poor woman gets, but this is different. This is an emergency. Its only minutes when a taxi from the rank at the bottom of Thomas Street that has the public phone on the pole comes to our door. When Jet walks out the door with what Pop calls a belly like a bill-poster's bucket, the poor taxi driver has a face on him that says, 'Jesus I hope she won't have the brat in my bloody car!'

She's gone now, the husband and Mam too, along with the suitcase that's full of all the things that were bought by Mam. She'll be looking for the Mrs. Cullen's Powder any minute now because the headaches will be on their way and won't stop till the child arrives and has two legs, two hands and all the fingers and toes it's supposed to have. And when the child does arrive, she'll be on her knees thanking the saints she's been praying to since the day she got the news about Jet expecting. It's a girl. Everyone it thrilled. And I've only four days to finish the cradle that everyone who puts their eyes on will say, 'It'll be grand when it's finished please God'. Mam is all excited and can't wait for the baby to come home. And when it does, she wants to take it everywhere, showing it to everyone. She's washing it, scrubbing it, goggling over it, and we're all wondering who had the bloody baby because the dinners aren't on time anymore. And when we're watching a programme on the black and white TV with the one TV channel that we had to wait a bloody hour and a half for before it started, we're told to turn it down in case we wake the child. Pots and pans that normally have the dinner in them, now have the shit stained nappies that have to be boiled for hours to find their way back again to the arse for more of the same stuff. I don't think 36 Claughaun Court will ever be the same again. Its like we never left 82 Upper Carey's Road, when we all slept in the damp-ridden room.

The day I bought the present for Olwyen

After two months Mam is depressed because Jetta and her husband are moving to a house in Shannon. Pop, James and myself will be delighted because things will be back to normal, only better, apart from looking at Mam sniffling all the time. And the four helpless males who live in 36 Claughaun Court, Garryowen who don't know their hands from their mouths are back being fed again every day and things are back to normal. Jet will be here the weekends with Mam cooing and gooing over the child. We're all taking turns holding the baby, talking to it, and wanting to be the first to get it to smile. Mam and Pop are back in their own room now and Harry in the small room. I suppose its hard getting used to my pal Jetta not being in the house anymore; when we could talk about anything, anytime. I can still do it, but it's hard for her to find the time with all she has on board.

It's coming up to another Christmas, I'm heading towards my seventeenth birthday. Phonsie and myself, along with Tommy Deegan, Niall Carey, his brother Seán, Paddy and Billy Madigan will be out 'on the Wren' when Stephen's Day comes and make a small fortune for St. Joseph's Scouts. Billy will have the accordion that's making all the music. Phonsie will have two bits of wood in each hand pretending it's a violin. Niall and Sean Carey, along with Paddy Madigan, will be roaring their heads off and when four o'clock comes there's nearly a fiver in the tin can that has 'Please help St. Joseph's Scouts' on a sticker around it. We're well and truly hoarse from the singing we did the night before at Billy and Paddy's mother's house up in Prospect. Billy will be at the piano belting out every song we can think of until three o'clock in the morning. We'll go home to our beds for the four hours sleep and have to get out of them again in no time at all to do the 'Wren'.

Back in early November, Jack Brosnan, who owns a record shop in Upper William Street, the shop that Jet and I bought our first single record by Del Shannon called 'Multiplication', . will have most of the senior scouts down in the main hall, arms resting on collapsible tables, writing addresses on envelopes, folding sheets of hard cream paper with twenty lines on each side and putting them into envelopes that will be sent all over the country to places we never heard of. He'll give us two bob for every hundred envelopes we'll address. He says if only quarter of the people who they send them to would send them back again, with the pound they'll get for filling in the twenty spaces, at a shilling a line, with three prizes, that St. Joseph's Scouts will be able to keep going for another year.

Gerry Costello who plays the guitar in our group says, 'Mary O'Connell is having her sixteenth birthday around the corner from where we live', and says that she said he's to bring me along. I'm all questions like, 'Where does she live, what does she look like and why did she ask me when I've never met the girl before?' Gerry is telling me I do know her, he describes her to me, even brings me down to the house where she lives, and how she works with him at The Limerick Shoe Factory. But it's no use. I haven't a clue who he's talking about. I'm thinking all kinds of things, like 'she must really fancy me. I'd better look my best when I go to the party and be on my best behaviour too, take my time and not rush things'. We're on our way down to her house from Gerry's. He lives in one of the small old cottages on Garryowen Road. I have him pestered still about who she is. He's getting annoyed with me. 'Look', he says, 'the girl is with a bunch of other girls, when we're down in The Roma's basement where we practice. We talk to them every time we come up for a break. They're always together, six or seven of them sitting in the one seat, the whole lot of them sharing a glass of Fanta and a plate of chips. Mary is always stuck in the corner. She's the quiet one of the whole lot. You must have noticed her in all the nights we've been there'. But it's no good; I can't recall the girl at all. 'Is she good looking?' I'm asking. 'She's only gorgeous', answers Gerry. 'I'm hoping to shift her tonight'.

We're at the door of her house. There's a great buzz of laughter, talking and music coming from the two downstairs windows that are open. When we walk into the small hallway a beautiful girl in a white dress that has black lines and a row of black buttons on the left and right side of the front of her dress says, 'Hi Gerry, I see you brought Paddy, come on in'. I'm asking myself how the hell didn't I notice this girl every week at the Roma Café. Maybe it was because of all the bloody talking I do. I'm saying to Gerry, 'You'll shift this one tonight, over my dead body'. But Gerry is a fast mover, faster than me, because in ten minutes he has her on the couch and he's eating the face off her. I'm looking at the two of them and wondering is this the woman who said to be sure and bring Paddy to the party. And I'm miserable for the next half hour until I spot another gorgeous girl with long black hair. I'll ask her to dance. She looks down at the ground while saying yes. And I'm thinking, not only is she gorgeous looking but she's shy as well, just what I like in a female, that won't have much to say, and will listen to me all night, a perfect combination! We'll dance away for the next two hours and I'll forget all about Mary O'Connell and her white dress with the black stripes and eight buttons down the front.

I'll do all the talking while waiting for a record to be changed with the shy girl I'm dancing with, and when it's twelve o'clock, she's gone home and I haven't asked her out. Everyone is gone home and I'm down at the gate of 12 Claughaun Court talking to Mary O'Connell because her parents are home and I've only to walk around the corner and I'm home. I'm asking her to fix me up with the shy girl that I spent most of the night dancing with because I couldn't get a word out of her all night. Mary says she knows her well and will talk to her on Monday and let me know. I'm taking it for granted that Gerry will be going out with Mary now, that they were mouth swapping on the couch for half the night. Mary and myself are talking for the next hour in the dark warm summer night, about everything and anything, until her father calls her to go to bed.

I'll be back again the following day,which is Sunday, to Mary with a stupid excuse like has she seen the shy girl with the long black hair, knowing full well that she won't be seeing her until tomorrow. But I just want to continue where I left off the night before. I'll sit on the wall of her house with my legs dangling away on the outside. She'll sit on it too, with hers resting on the inside. She'll make the tea that has too much milk and not enough sugar and ask me if it's OK. It's bloody awful but I'll drink it, every last drop, and tell her 'it's lovely'. I'll smoke two fags in that time and drink another three cups. I don't want to be anywhere else. We talk. I'll ask her if she's going out with Gerry. She laughs and says no. I'll ask her why, seeing as she was eating the face off of him the night before. She gets red-faced and says she doesn't know,and now I'm gone off the shy girl with the lovely black hair. I'll ask if she's going out tonight. She says that she's going to the Pictures with some of the girls that were at the party to the Grand Central in Bedford Row. And that's where I'll be going too. I don't know what's on there and I don't care either. I just want to be around this gorgeous woman as much as I can. I say goodbye and tell her I might see her tonight, after I check and see what's on the other cinemas first.

I'll walk the short distance around the corner and home to the spotted dick and mug of tea and wonder should I ask her to go out with me, seeing as she's unattached. She seems to like me. I'm sitting at the table staring at the wall and Mam wants to know why I'm not eating the spotted dick she's buttered and left on the table, like she does every evening. She'll call me several times and Pop will ask what's wrong with him at all. Pop says, 'Maybe he's in love, and if he is he'll have to talk to Lar about it, because if he is, he'll be going back to two pounds a week again because we'll get no bloody work done out of him at all'. Mam smiles and says, 'Well Pa, are you in love? Will you be leaving your mother's nest for another woman and there I was thinking you'd never leave your poor mother, the woman, that cleaned your backside for the first three years of your life, wiped every snot off your nose, fed you and found you, worried about you all those years when you caught every germ that was flying around Limerick, and what was it all for, only to hand you over to another woman who won't have a clue about the worry and stress you put me through.' She has me rattled because I know she's trying to wind me up. Nan is over in the corner laughing away too, adding her bit like 'she does' every time. 'Jesus, leave him off, why shouldn't he learn from his mistakes like the rest of us did'. Pop wants to know who she is and when I tell him he'll be off again like he does every time I'll bring a girl home and say to them 'Who's father are you?' He'll have them totally confused and upset because he'll ask them if their father is around the dump looking for copper and scrap down the Dock Road called Corcanree. They'll sit up straight and answer in a snotty way that their father would never go near such a place, that he has a very respectable job, that he works for so-and-so or that he works in such a place. And the crystal shining snot that's always hanging off Pop's nose will be there. I'll be told they won't want to see me again when I walk them home that night. I'll have to tell Mam, Pop and Nan that I'm not going out with the girl yet because I haven't asked her. Pop wants to know where she's working. I know once I tell him he'll be off and I'll be loving it. 'The Limerick Shoe Factory,' I answer. 'Do you mean the bloody boot factory?' he goes with the slagging and another story.

'I remember the time I worked for the boot factory. I was only seventeen. We had a foreman, a right grumpy old article, who never had a kind word for anybody, was hated by everyone who worked in the place except of course the owners, because he licked their backsides all the time. I remember the time he spent the odd hour every day making himself a special pair of shoes, that had double everything on them, the best pair of shoes that were made in the place, and if the owners found out, he would be in right trouble, but I was keeping an eye on the shoes he thought nobody knew he was making. I wanted to wait until they were finished and, finally, when they were, I took out the two six inch nails that I kept in my pocket and waited until he was well out of sight, then walked into his office, took the shoes from one of the drawers were he had them hidden, put them on the wooden floor were his feet would rest when he was in his chair at the desk, and drove a nail into the heel of each shoe, and down into the floor, left them there and waited. Pop says there were over a hundred workers in the place. Word went around about the shoes and all waited to see what would happen when he sat in the chair and could see through the glass door of his office, and there he is walking in the door, leaving it open and over to the chair with two hundred eyes looking at him from the factory floor. He's looking down under his desk and then he's on his knees and when his head comes up over the desk his face is red. We can see his mouth shouting out the 'F' word now his pacing around his desk, then he's tearing out the door and the eyes and bodies that are lurking behind all the machines that were working only five minutes ago and producing nothing because the human hands that were feeding them had been idle for the last few minutes, are scattering back to their places, the red head is tearing around the factory looking for something and after five minutes, he's shouting if anybody knows were he can get a crow bar and every worker in the place has to turn away because they don't want him to see them laughing. After an hour of turning the place upside down, he finally walks into the office with a lump hammer and a crow bar and after finishing laughing, we're asking Pop did he get the sack, he says, 'sure

197

how could I get the sack, if he did find out he would have to tell the boss what he was doing, but I did get the sack a month later for something entirely different', and Mam says, 'you never told me that,' Pop says, one of the lads he worked with needed to get away at five thirt, because he was playing in the final of a football match at six o'clock outside in Landsdowne Park. And that it takes a good fifteen minutes to get there by bike and another ten minutes to tog off, he said he would give me a pound if I went into the foreman's office and blew the factory hooter that normally goes off at one o'clock and six o'clock everyday, I hadn't a penny nor a fag in my pocket. So in I went at five thirty, blew the hooter, and out the door went over a hundred workers who thought the factory clock and their own watches were on the blink. I was the most popular guy in the place the following day when word went around that I was the one responsible and the most unpopular the day after because everybody had to work an extra half hour. One of them got sour and told the foreman and I was out on my ear with no job at all.

I'll go to the Grand Central that night and see Mary in the queue with her friends outside the door and join it, a yard or two behind them. I'll look for them in the dark when I get in, and sit a row or two behind and when the support film is over I'll go to the shop, while the ads are on, and spend my last few bob on two bottles of Fanta and two tubs of ice-cream and go down to the row that Mary is sitting in, reach over, and ask one of her friends to give her the bottle and tub of ice-cream. She'll look back smiling and thank me and I can hear her friends go 'ahhhhhhh, Mary's got a new fellow'. When the main feature is over I'll pretend to walk into their path by accident because she'll be going home with her friends the same way as myself and sure it just might happen. It does and there we are the two of us walking up William Street, talking a couple of yards behind her friends. And the more I'm with her the more I want to be with her. I don't understand how I can't remember meeting this girl before. All the years I played on the same road. Surely the days I played down the hill and fell on my arse every year since we lived here, starting in 1959, she must have been there too, but now I have a big problem, I told this girl the difficulty I've had with other girls before, how after two or three nights I'd lose interest and bring then down home to meet Pop. So they'd drop me like a hot brick. Like Rose, the girl with the big lips and the big bust who used to walk around with her left hand in her groin to keep her overcoat closed and the cold out in the winter time, even though the same coat had six or seven buttons. She's doing it because half of the youths, male and female in Limerick are doing it. It's the latest craze. She'll wear white high heeled shoes every day with the dark brown nylons and a fag in the right hand and the lads in Garryowen will tease me saying Paddy wakes every morning feeling Rosie.

Then there was the girl who I thought was the quietest in Limerick until the first night that I went out with her and couldn't get a word in and the only sentence I got was would you like to come and meet my parents' She did and Pop did the rest. He did what I hadn't the guts to do.

I'll never forget Betty who kept winking at me all the time because I thought she fancied me every time I went to the hop in St. Patrick's scout hall and found out, after I asked her out, that she had a twitch in her eye and realised that she couldn't put two words together. I mean this girl was shy. She wasn't speechless either. I didn't bother bringing her home to meet Mam and Pop, I just said goodnight after I walked her home on the first date. And Diana whose head was only up to my shoulder and lost the rag with me and went home because I went and got a big rock for her to stand on to avoid getting another pain in the back of my neck from the shifting we did the night before.

And now I've notions about asking this girl out, a girl I've never felt this way about before and I'm wondering what will I do if she says no. So I'll wait and say to myself I'll do it in a minute, and the minute becomes an hour and the hour, three, until I'm walking home at one o'clock in the morning and the mouth that never stops talking couldn't find the words or the courage to ask the girl out, and I'm totally confused. Never before has my mouth encountered a problem like this. I'll try again tomorrow night because she asked me to bring over my guitar and play a few songs for her father and when tomorrow evening comes its into the good clothes and not even bothering with the five or six slices of spotted dick that Mam has on the table like she has every evening. She's asking what has me in such a rush and not bothering with the spotted dick and have I gone off it like Jetta and James did years ago, and that's enough to stop me in my tracks and say 'Janey no Mam don't ever stop making the spotted dicks, I'll eat it when I come home tonight', and there's questions from Mam and Pop when they see me tearing out the door and asking were am I going with the guitar, but I'm not answering because the slagging will start and I wont be here to enjoy it. I'm asking myself what's the hurry, sure there's plenty of time, but I know its the excitement of being with her again and answering the questions she'll ask me all night about myself, work and Mam, what's she like. I'll spend most of the time talking about Mam because Mary is really interested in her, maybe it's because I love talking about Mam too, and when I've told her everything there is to know about Mam. Mary says 'your mother sounds like a lovely woman', and I'm thinking if this girl ever finds out that I'm bloody useless she'll drop me like a hot potato. Sure Mam has me spoilt rotten, I'm just about able to wipe my arse, yes I'm a hard worker, I'll work all the hours God sends, work at anything, but the minute I'll walk in the door of 36 Claughan Court, Garryowen I'll become bloody useless because the Irish mother I have will do everything for me. What am l saying, she'll do it for the whole lot of us and love every minute of it. I don't realise it but I'm looking for a woman just like my mother. A woman I heard say on many occasion that' your father never saw a dirty nappie in his life,' not in her house. I've grown up with the same attitude that the home and everything in it is the woman's reasonability and everything outside is the man's. I'm still trying to get the courage to ask Mary out, sure there's plenty of time, three or four hours if I play my cards right.

Mary brings me in to meet her dad, his a small thin man, has lots of black hair. Mary has me warned that he's shy, fusses a lot when he's in company or has nothing to talk about. She says if he doesn't do that he will be 'diddle idle doing' instead, and sure enough after being introduced he's talking about the weather, how good the day was and how tomorrow will be as good, and off he goes whistling away, looks at the ground singing 'diggley idle doodle dom', whistles again and then talks about the weather that we had the day before yesterday, and I'd better put this poor man out of his misery and start talking to him. Mary calls her mother in and introduces me, and says I am a neighbour from around the corner. There's comments from the two of them how they never heard of the Taylors around the corner in spite of the fact that we're living there for years. Mrs. O' is the same height as Mr. O' but four times his width and weight.

And there in front of me is the evidence of the years Mary told me about of her dad and the time he spent in the sanatorium with TB out at St. Camillus' Hospital. He'll cough every now and then and I'll wonder why a man with a chest that's so bad and a history of TB would be sucking smoke into his lungs and finding it hard enough to handle the air he's getting every few seconds. Mrs. O'Connell says she's very glad to meet me and did Mary offer me a cup of tea at all, while Mr. O' whistles away two verses of the Black Velvet Band, tapping his shoes on the floor to the tune he's whistling at the same time. Over the coming weeks Mary will tell me of the times her father walked the country roads with the cattle for farmers who used to abuse him, how he walked for miles until the blisters on his feet would turn into sores, and then blood, and had to leave Ireland with his new bride Mrs. O' and work crazy hours in factories for small money in Birmingham. But still a lot more then he would get here. And then had to come home when her mother got pregnant on herself and found a house just like the one we had in upper Careys Road . Her house was right across from Crosses the funeral undertakers, and after only a few months back in Ireland her father contracted'TB, and spent four years on his back in St. Camillus' and came out of the place alive, unlike thousands of others.

I'll look at Mrs. O'Connell, scrubbing the family clothes on the ribbed timber frame that she has in the big galvanised bath out in the small kitchen, the kitchen that she had built last year, with the eighty pound she borrowed from the Credit Union for the first time since she started saving there. I'll think about her physical and emotional strength, how she was able to look after her family, keep a part-time job, washing up in a restaurant after six o' clock every evening, and think how lucky all of us are in 36 around the corner.

And I can hear Mary telling her father I brought a guitar over to play a few songs. 'Will you play the Black Velvet Band please Paddy. 'I will' I said 'If you sing it,' and off I go strumming away, and off he goes singing completely out of tune with every word. I never heard the Black Velvet Band sung like that before. Now I can't play that good but I can do a damn sight better than this because Mrs. O' is at it outside in the kitchen and she's out of key too. When I come in with the bad voice in the right key along with the only few words I know, her eyes they shone like the diamonds, you would think she was the queen of the land with her hair swung over her shoulder tied up with a black velvet band, so I'll leave them at it now that they're singing in the right key, but I'll stop because I don't know any more words. There's no one singing now because they don't know the words either, and off goes Mr. O' with the diddedly idle doo and after a few more he'll stop and start whistling again before I put a stop to the agony.

Mary is smiling away and that's all I care about. Mrs. O' shouts in 'can you play the Blackbird of My Heart' and before I can answer, she starts and she's all over the place again in and out of three or four different keys, I've never heard that song before, well not the way she's singing it. Now Mary's brother David and two sisters Kathlyn and Chrissy are in wondering what's going on because they heard the singing on the road and want me to play all kinds of songs, they can't sing either and between the whole lot of us there's a right din going on. And before I know it Mary has to go to bed because she has to get up early in the morning and I still haven't asked her out yet I'll leave my guitar in the room on purpose so I can come back again tomorrow evening and finally get the chance and the courage to ask her out. I'll go to bed thinking about her and dream about her several times during the night .

When Sunday comes she'll want me to bring the guitar over again. I will. We'll be in the room on our own, I'll ask her would she like to know what it feels like to put a guitar in her hands, she says, 'yes', and when I give it to her I'll stand behind her while she sits in the chair, I'll hold her right hand and tell her what to do with it while doing the same with her left hand. The scent off her neck and hair is making me weak, I'll keep saying 'no, no not this way, do it this way', and there she is pretending that she can't do it and there I am hoping she still can't pretend and loving every minute of it.

But Mary has to get up early in the morning and I still haven't asked her out yet, so I'll leave my guitar in the room on purpose so I can come back again tomorrow evening and I get the chance and the courage to ask her out. I'll go to bed thinking about her again and can't stop dreaming about her several times in the night, and work away on my own with Pop and Lar the next day, and think about nothing else before I am back home again in the evening gulping down the tea and leaving most of the spotted dick on the plate again. I'll tear out the door to the sound of Pop saying 'there he's off to meet the one with the six inch nail holding up her stocking', Over I'll go knocking on the door, Mary answers it, gets all embarrassed because she is in her blue nylon coat with her hair tied back in a small pony tail with an elastic band. She is fiddling away at her hair, fixing this and that while saying 'you left your guitar after you last night', she seems pleased to see me, and says her mother and father are talking all the time about how much they enjoyed last night. And there it is my opportunity to strike I am just about to open my mouth when out comes Mrs. O'Connell and asks me in for a cup of tea but I am determined now. I can't go on wondering if this girl that has got in to every bit of me will go out with me. So I say 'I would love to have a cup Mrs. O'Connell, but I just want to ask Mary something first', Mrs. O'Connell winks at me and closes the door, leaving the two of us alone, I think she knows what's going on and I am wondering have I made it that obvious, so for the first time in my life I can't get the bloody words out in the order that I want them, so I say, 'Mary I was wondering well, if, well, you know, I mean the last few days I've been thinking a lot about, well I don't know if you remember or not, I mean I won't mind if you don't.' Mary is there with her hands folded and a look on her face that kind of says, 'What the hell is he talking about, or for the love of God will you get on with it'. Her look is making me worse, I mean all the signs are good. We've talked for hours, over the last week and she always has to be called in by her parents to go to bed so she must be interested, I mean I've never had so much trouble asking a girl out before. I'll die if she says no but I have started now and I can't just stop, I'm kind of hoping she'll understand what I am trying to ask her and put me out of my misery and please God say yes. I suppose she would if she knew what I was talking about, so when I go with the, 'well so you know ahem, I was telling you about the other girls I went out with,' and the heart that has had plenty of exercise down through the years beating away at all kinds of speeds, is belting away now with the worry of rejection. I'm getting awful used to it, she says, 'yes I remember', with a puzzled look on her face and on I go. 'Do you remember me saying how I get browned off them after one night and wondered if there was something wrong with me because I just can't seem to find a girl I really like. 'Yes' she says puzzled, 'Well I think I found a girl that I like, I mean I met her a good few times and every time I talk to her I can't get enough. Mary smiles and says, 'that's great what's her name?', Jesus this is hard, I thought she'd get it by now, I mean I couldn't have made it any clearer so I'll try again with the heart pounding away. 'Mary, her name is Mary', I think she is getting it at long last; well she's starting to get a bit red around the face. I am looking for a face that might recoil at the thoughts of going out me, there isn't any sign at all 'and were she is living?' asks Mary, getting a little bit mischievous. I think she's on to me but is not making it any easier. 'Garryowen', I answer smiling, now her face is on fire, and she knows it, because she's covering her cheeks with both hands. I'm still smiling because I know she knows and the Taylor confidence is on its way back because things are looking good and so are the signs, and with her hands still over her cheeks she asks smiling 'What part of Garryowen?', I smile back, look at the ground while fidgeting with my right leg moving it forward and backwards I look at her again and say ' 12 Claughan Court, Garryowen', Mrs. O'Connell opens the door again and asks 'will you have that cup of tea now Paddy?'. 'Yes, please Mrs. O'Connell', 'Come on in so', and I walk behind Mary with my heart pounding away with the beat of excitement even though Mary hasn't said yes or no. Mrs. O' will ask me to play the guitar again, we'll sing the same songs, I'll look at Mary every now and then looking for a look that might convey a positive sign that says, I'd love to go out with you, and I think I'm getting it every time I look at her.

I want to get back out into the hall and be with her on my own and get her to translate that look into words that I am dying to hear that 'I'll go out with you', or just seal it with a nod but Mr and Mrs. O'Connell are still at it with 'play this Paddy and play that'. They'll sing out of tune again and my poor bloody fingers are killing me my throat as well. I don't care the woman of my dreams is only feet away in her working gear and I am loving every minute of it because I'm telling myself if she didn't want to go out with me, I'd be gone a long time ago because the family are mad about me. When 12 o'clock comes Mary says she has to go to bed for the same reason she went last night and with the guitar in my hand, I say 'goodnight' to every one they'll be thanking me over and over again, saying goodnight. Mary closes the door on the goodnights that's coming from everybody. I'll look at Mary, she's looking at the ground with the nail of her small bent finger in her mouth. I wait a few minutes and say 'well' she lifts her eye lids and look at me for a second, looks at the floor again and says 'well what?', ' Will you go with me tomorrow night?', she's still looking at the ground with the small finger and the nail in the mouth and the woman who talked for hours and hours has died on me and won't even look at me, she's still looking at the ground and says, ' I don't mind'. And there it is again that expression, 'I don't mind', and

I'm thinking of the last time I heard that it was from the one I took up the lane of the rugby grounds in Carey's Road and I'm wondering do all women use that expression when they really want something. I'm laughing and saying, 'don't get too excited about it now', she laughs back still looking at the ground with the little finger in the mouth, 'well that's it so' I say, she nods her head. I say 'goodnight so and I'll call over tomorrow night then ok', 'ok', she says giving me the odd look with the big gorgeous eyes. 'I'll be off then', I never felt so bloody awkward in my life I'm on top of the world so why do I feel like this. I open the door walk out and say 'I'll be off then', 'ok', she says, 'goodnight', I'll walk out the long footpath I'm half way down and decide to look back. She's still there with the finger in her mouth looking down at me. I run back and say, 'can I kiss you'? she takes her finger away and nods, so I move in and give her a quick kiss on the lips and taste in a very small way what Gerry Costelloe tasted in a big way last week. I'm running all the way around the corner, I want to tell all at home that the girl just said yes, but they've all gone to bed and I have to wait until tomorrow. I'll go to bed and dream about her again only this time the dreams are better.

The next day I'll work with Pop and Lar and think about her too, I'll go home at lunch time and talk about her to Mam for forty five minutes, work the afternoon, come home, go upstairs wash myself like never before, put on the only good clothes and shoes I have, comb the hair, brush the teeth, rush downstairs, gulp the tea again leaving most of the spotted dick on the table, look in the mirror over the fire place and listen to Pop saying, every time he looks in the mirror he sees my face in it. I'm heading around the corner when I suddenly realise I've no money. I've asked a girl out for the night and I've no money. What will she think of me? So I' m back home again looking for the new camera I bought a couple of weeks ago and in no time at all I'm over at her house, knocking on the door. Mary answers looking like a million dollars so I'll ask her, 'Is Mary O'Connell her please?', she smiles and says, 'No, she's gone, you'll have to come back tomorrow', I'll ask would she mind going for a walk because I am broke. She says a walk would be lovely.

There I am with the hands in the pockets of the only good pair of trousers I have. Mary has a pink cardigan and before the evening is out we'll be sweating like pigs because it's a long balmy summer's night. She'll ask me about the band, how it got started, when did I start playing the guitar. I'll tell her about the melodeon Pop brought home in Upper Carey's Road and how I started playing the thing even though it was full of holes, and the day I walked into the bedroom and saw the lovely pearl accordion that cost Pop and Mam fifty five pounds. I have to give her a handchief because she's crying. She says that's the nicest story 'I've ever heard', I'll tell her about Billy Madigan in St. Joesph's scouts, how good he is on the accordion and the difference between the one he had and the one I had, and how I thought the button piano accordion was for the country culchies and that I had to learn all over again because the piano accordion plays the same note whether you're pushing or shoving the thing in or out, but the button accordion had a different note pushing it in and another one pulling it out. Now Mary wants to know if I play the guitar and the accordion as well and I have to tell her that I got tired of the accordion after four or five years and traded it in for the guitar. I'll ask her to stand against the whitewash wall to have her photograph taken and when I have taken hers, she offers to take mine.

Our first date

I wanted to have a memory of our first date because I hoped it would be the first of many. We've walked and talked all the way from her house to the top of St. Patrick's scout hall up by Rhegbogue and back by the bottom of St. Patrick's Road, and I've never walked so slow in all my life. By the time we get to her house we're down at the wall talking away. Its dark and Mr. O'Connell shouts down that the kettle is on and that I'm to come in for a cup of tea. I'm delighted because I'm gasping for a fag and if Mr. O'Connell is there he might offer me one and put me out of my misery. Ever since I started working with Pop and Lar, fumes from the paint leave me with a terrible taste in my mouth after I've take a drag from a cigarette, but if I have a sweet or a drink I'm able to enjoy the smoking much better, there's nothing like a fag with a cup of tea. I have the cuppa in my hand and I'm wondering when Mr. O'Connell is going to light up, because he has a cup in his hand too. I'm there watching him whistling a few bars of nothing, then a diddly idle do, followed by the tapping of the feet, a comment about the weather and no sign of the hands that are folded together going in any direction to his pockets. Mrs.O'Connell, Chris, Kathleen and David are here as well, but nobody is talking, its uncomfortable and I cant stand it when I'm in the company of people that aren't talking. I could be in a doctors waiting room with a group of people all waiting to see him, and I'll have to break the silence cause I can't bear it. I'll just open my mouth and say something and its usually something stupid, so without thinking, I'll say 'would you like a cigarette, Mr. O'Connell', and what the hell did I say that for, sure aren't I waiting for him to ask me, but he says, 'Jesus, Paddy I'd love one, I'm gasping all day for a fag, good man yourself', what the hell am I going to do now'. I pretend to look for them in the left pocket of my jacket with my left hand, the right pocket with my right hand, I'm saying 'now where the hell did I leave my packet of fags?,' Mary is looking at me knowing I didn't smoke one, with all the talking and walking we did all night, and I think she's on to me.

I'm on my feet putting both hands into every pocket I have again, and again trying to have a confused look on my face, and there's poor Mr. O'Connell with a face on him that's getting more and more disappointed with every second that passes, 'Ah, for goodness sake', shouts Mrs. O'Connell, 'why the hell don't you give those things up, sure your only out of the Sanatorium a few years, and still coughing and choking every night' and I have to say I'm sorry Mr. O'Connell, 'I don't have any', 'not to worry Paddy' he says,' and off he goes again whistling away, diddly idle doing and the tapping of the feet. I'll say goodnight to every one and listen to the repeated voices of the family saying the same thing back to me and I'm out in the porch again. I'd forgotten about the longing for the nicotine because I want to get my mouth around those gorgeous lips of Mary, but I'm feeling very awkward. I cant understand why, sure I've done this loads of times on the first date with all the other girls, real cool and couldn't care less if I made a wrong move at the wrong time. They could tell me to get lost and it wouldn't cast me a thought, sure I only went out with some of them for the shift but I don't want to mess it up with Mary. So I'll stay clear of the gorgeous lips tonight, and remember the golden rule about courting, never kiss a girl on the first date, so I say, can we go for a walk again tomorrow night Mary?. The finger is back in the mouth again, she's looking at the ground and says that crazy answer, 'I don't mind', So I say goodnight walk down the long foot path, turn around to see if she's still there, she is, I'll run back and get another quick taste of her gorgeous lips again. They're all in bed at home and there's six slices of spotted dick on the table with another plate over them to keep the flies away. But I can only eat the one and the following morning when I come down for the breakfast Mam is asking me if I'm alright, and I'm asking her why she's asking me if I'm alright. Because there's still three quarters of the spotted dick in the bread bin, it should be all gone by now, and you should be pestering me to have another one baked before the weekend. 'You're only eating half the dinners I'm putting on the table every day, you didn't even finish the pound of your favourite sausages on Wednesday', she's feeling my forehead with the back of her hand while asking, am I feeling ok. I'm telling her that I never felt better in my life, and ask her to stop fussing but its no good. I know if it was ten years ago she'd have me down at the dispensary, sitting on the wooden benches to see Dr. Crowe to find out what's wrong with me, but I can tell her now that she wouldn't have a hope of getting me down to have him stick that wooden yoke down my throat again. She'll ask me again when I come home for dinner at one o'clock and leave half of the dinner after me again, but I'll her that I'm fine and that I haven't a clue why my appetite is gone.

She'll be at it when I come home at six o'clock, when I will rush up the stairs and put the same clothes on, the ones that I had last night, sure they are the only ones I have. Pop will answer and say, 'if there was anything wrong with him, I don't think he could tear up the stairs four or five steps at a time and get dressed and washed in five minutes and be back down again in two leaps', Nan is over in the corner laughing away saying, 'I think he's found himself a girl, maybe he's in love', Pop says, 'well if he is Bid, you'd better get ready to lose another of your four children'. Mam smiles and asks, 'have you got a new girl, Pa?,' I'll smile anyway and answer, while gulping down the tea, and doing my level best to choke myself, stuffing one of the buttered slices of spotted dick that had gone a bit hard even though Mam had them covered all day. 'Well if he has got a new girl I hope she is nothing like the other ones he brought down here', and off Pop goes again. I'll hang on because I won't want to miss what's going to come out of his mouth, and I need to get a loan of two bob from Mam for a few fags. Pop looks at Nan and says. 'Jesus, you should have seen the things he brought in the door to meet us Nan, ones with three or four coats of paint on their faces, lips like English post office boxes, earrings you could swing out of, high heels that they must have borrowed off their mothers and wobbled all over the place while they walked in them, arses like turnips you'd buy at the market', then he stands up and genuflects while putting on a female voice, 'hello, Mrs. Taylor,' hello, 'Mr. Taylor, and that's all you'll get out of them for the night', And then its, 'yes, 'Mrs.Taylor' or no 'Mrs. Taylor', I don't think any of them knew what a conversation was, so I hope the one you're going out with now isn't like any of that lot'.

Mam and Nan are laughing away. I'll ask Mam for the loan of two bob that I know I'll get and I'm gone out the door listening to more of Pop's comments about 'how big is the ones backside your going out with,' and Mam laughing away at his every comment. I'll call into Mac's shop and buy the ten Carrolls that will keep me going for tonight and most of tomorrow, and take off walking the same route with Mary, that we took the night before. And I just can't get enough of this girl, she'll talk about her job at the Limerick Shoe Factory, how she got it, her friends who work there. I'll tell her the stories that Pop told me about his working days there, she'll laugh and say she'll tell her friends tomorrow, and it will be all over the factory in no time at all.

Mrs. O'Connell will call me in again for the cup of tea. Mr. O' is there again doing the very same thing he did over the last two nights with the whistling and the diddley idle doing, talking about the weather and still as shy and uncomfortable as he was the other nights. I'll take out my packet of fags and offer him one, he'll say 'its alright Paddy I have my own, thank you', the two of us will smoke away in the company of the whole family and every one with a cup of tea in their hand, and no one saying a word. So I'll start again talking about the first thing that comes into my head like. 'That's a grand cup of tea Mrs. O'Connell', it's bloody awful, too much milk not enough sugar and as strong as Author Guinness, 'your welcome Paddy', she'll answer. That's followed by another five minutes of listening to the clock on the wall before one of the kids says, 'is there anything on the telly?' and Mrs. O'Connell says 'there'll be no television while there's a guest in the house'. Now I am asking David and Chrissie how old they are? What would they like to do when they grow up and any bloody thing else I can think off. I don't think I can take any more of this so I'll say I'd better get going its getting late and one of the kids say, 'sure, its only nine o'clock.' 'Is that all?' I'll answer, acting the eejit and sit down again. And on it goes, and on goes Mr. O' again, diddley idle doing and whistling. Mrs. O'Connell starts wiping things with a cloth which breaks the silence and asks me, 'where does your father work Paddy?' So I'll give her a good long answer and tell her about Granddad Taylor, Taylor by trade, and lived in Taylor Street, and straight away everyone in the room is listening to every word that is coming out of my mouth. The atmosphere changes and Paddy is on his tod because Paddy likes nothing better than an audience.

I'll tell them some the stories Pop told me,' how he got started in the painting and decorating business, our time in Upper Carey's Road and how we came to live there, there's questions coming from everyone, mostly from Mrs. O' about how much would it cost to do up her front room, hall, stairs and landing. I'll answer and say, 'not a penny, Mrs. O', and I'm thinking to myself, I could be here every night with Mary working away sure why would I want to be paid for that. Mary looks pleased but Mrs. O' insists and says she'll get the paper and paint at the weekend and asks if I could start on Monday night, and by the time the talking is over its nearly twelve o'clock and Mary and myself are down at the gate at the end of the long footpath. She's thanking me for offering to do the hall for nothing and says her mother would always want to pay her way, I'll tell her I only want to do it because I can be with her every night. And up goes the hand with the little finger in the mouth again, and her looking at the ground. 'Will you come to the pictures on Friday night and please don't say, I don't mind', 'I'd love to' she says, I'll say goodnight, get another quick taste of the luscious lips before I head around the corner to number 36.

When Friday night comes I'm all decked out and Mary looks great when I call over, we'll get the bus that takes us to Roche's Street. I'm asking her what picture would she like to go and see, and out it comes again, that bloody phrase, 'I don't mind', so I suggest we go and see what's on in the Carlton first, seeing that its only down the road at Shannon Street. I'll say to her it's about time I held your hand, and she'll go all shy on me again. So we're there looking at the few colour photographs in the two glass cases that gives everyone an idea of what's on tonight, I'm asking her. 'Will we go in?', and again she says, she doesn't mind, I don't know what I'm asking her for because I have no intention of looking at anything. I'm going to be stuck to her mouth all night. In we go and get the two tickets for the balcony, no girlfriend of mine is going to sit in the back stalls.

I'll ask her would she like something in the shop and out it comes again, 'I don't mind', so I buy two bottles of Fanta, two packets of crisps and there we are up in the back row in at the corner the best place in the Carlton for a good ole shift with no one bothering you saying, 'excuse me', and have to leave your partner's mouth and stand up only to do it again five minutes later when they have finished peeing in the toilet or gone to the kiosk for rations. I'm watching Mary to see when the orange and crisps I bought her are gone, so I can get on with the tasting of those beautiful lips. I'm not a bit interested in my grub or the black and white film that's showing on the screen, so I lift my right hand, throw it over her shoulder and pull her in towards me and up goes her hand to her mouth again with the little finger in her mouth.

I'll watch and wait until she's finished eating a mouthful and in I go for the long kiss I've being waiting for. The kiss that she can do like she did with Jerry Costelloe and, boys oh boys, I'm in heaven. My nose is taking in all her smells of creams, perfumes, hairsprays, deodorants the fresh breath from her nose and I don't want to stop, after about a minute I'll pull away just a few inches look at her, smile, she'll smile back and back I'll go for more and on it'll go all night and we wont have a bloody clue what the two films were about, and wont care either, and its into the café Capri in Patrick's Street, for a plate of chips and a glass of orange and make it last until they want to close or throw us out.

We'll walk home, I'll hold her hand again, and when we get to her house spend another half an hour taking off the lipstick she put on after coming out of the Carlton and before I go around the corner to number 36 I'll ask her to come to the Jetland the following night. Her eyes light up she says she'd love to go, that she's never been to the Jetland before, I've only being there once myself, and spent the whole night up on the balcony near the stage watching and listening to Eileen Reed and the Cadets, and never asked a girl to dance because they blew me away with the music they played. Jetta, my dancing partner, is gone from the dance floor now, and rarely gets a chance to go out. I miss her and the rhythm we had. But Mary O'Connell from Claughan Court is about to fill her shoes, it's only a matter of minutes before we're dancing the Jive like we were at it all our lives.

Brendan Boyer and the Royal Showband are beating out all the latest songs and Mary and myself are sweating like pigs. The slow waltz will give us a chance to get our breaths before Brendan and his band have us at it again. We'll get a bus home at one in the morning and Mary cant stop talking about how great a time she's had. I'm asking her will come again next, week she's nodding her head up and down saying, ' how she would love to'. I'm telling her I'd love to take her to the pictures tomorrow night but I am flat broke because it is nine and six a head for the Jetland. She said she'd like to take me out to the Savoy Cinema, and I'm thinking great, another two hours of mouth to mouth, before whe're back again to number twelve, were we'll talk for ages. I'm asking her will she do me a special favour tomorrow, she won't say yes until I tell what the favour is. 'Will you go back to work at lunch time a different way tomorrow please,' she wants to know why. 'I've being telling my parents about you and if you went past our front door they would get a good look at you'.

She says 'but, I'll look a holy show, I'll be in my working smock, I wont even have my hair done.' 'Ah go on', I'm asking.

She'll keep saying no in a half hearted kind of way, but I'll keep at her and then she says 'I'll see.'

The following day I'm telling Mam and Pop that the new girlfriend will be passing the house around half one today and they can get a good look at her. I'm telling them that she is doing it for me, that she doesn't normally go to work that way at all. Nan isn't there, thanks be to God, and I know Pop will be at with the funny comments again. I'm sitting at the table and only half concentrating on my dinner, I'm sticking my head up out of my shoulders every few minutes, even though it's only one fifteen. Pop says that if I stick my head up any more out of my shoulders I won't be able to breath. Mrs. Egan is an elderly lady living up in one of the bungalows at the hill. She has a walking stick because she is getting old. She's walking past our house on the opposite side of the road and Pop says, 'is that her, Jesus she's a fine looking bird, you did very well there Pa, well done', Mam and myself are laughing away I'm still at it up and down with the head. Mam is giving out to me about my dinner, or what I'll eat of it, that's its getting cold.

I'm checking the watch on my wrist and there bang on one thirty, is Mary walking past Leahy's house with the finger in her mouth and the head looking at the ground. She's dying of embarrassment. 'There she is' I'm shouting 'that's her, well, what do you think?' I'm looking into their faces and back over at Mary every few seconds. I'm making myself dizzy. 'Well' I'm asking, 'What do you think?' She's going past Jackson's house now, and heading for the corner to turn up towards the markets field. 'Will ye tell me what ye think before she's gone out of sight?' I can see Mam has her x-ray eyes on taking everything in and says. 'well she looks like a grand clean girl,' and Pop says. 'well the right side of her looks grand', and as Mary rounds the corner, Pop says, 'her backside looks good too',

'Is that all your going to say about the girl, that she looks clean, and that her right side and her backside looks great'. 'What do you want us to say sure, we only got to look at her for a couple of seconds. Why don't you bring her over to met us so we can have a good look at her even talk to her', says Mam, 'I will', I'm answering,

I'm over at Mary's to thank her and tell her the reaction from my parents, 'my mother says you're a grand clean looking girl. I told her there was a smell off you all the time but that it was a nice smell.' I told her about what Pop said about her right side and her big backside, she looks worried and says, 'he didn't, did he, I haven't, have I?',

'No you haven't', he's always messing, they want to met you, 'now?', she answers really startled. 'no next weekend, we can come in after the pictures on Sunday night.

I'm working away on Mrs. O'Connell's hall pulling whatever paper will come off easy. Mary is longside me helping too, I'll spend more time talking and loving every minute of it and the following morning at breakfast Mam wants to know if I'll ever be seen again at number 36 between the hours of six thirty and twelve midnight between Monday evening and Friday. I'm telling her I have a job to do for Mrs. O'Connell. 'I hope you are getting paid for it', she says, I tell her I offered to do it for nothing but Mrs. O'Connell insisted that I get paid. 'I should hope so' said Mam. But today I'm going to have a big argument with Lar, I'm sick and tired of being told for the last two years the same bloody thing over and over again, being told what to eat, how to speak, what to wear, how to conduct myself, its like I'm back at school, back home as a child listening to Mam telling me not to speak with my mouth full. And serving as an apprentice at the same time, so I explode in temper and tell him what to do with himself. Pop isn't there because he's gone to McMahon's in Bedford Row for something. I'm telling Lar that I'm sick and tired of hearing the same things over and over again. That I can paint and decorate as good as him, that I'm seventeen years old now and should be getting more money. He's losing the cool telling me that that's no way to be talking to an employer and before I know it I'm heading back home on my bike in a right state, because I've told Lar what to do with his job. By the time I get to 36 Claughan Court on a Tuesday morning at eleven o'clock, I'll realise that I've just closed the door on four pounds a week, that Mam will be down half of that and the new girl around the corner will have the legs walked off her because the Jetland Ballroom on the Ennis Road and the Savoy Cinema will be minus our presence for the foreseeable future.

I'll have no fags either, and I'm coming down to earth real quick and I'm asking myself what the hell am I after doing and how my actions are going to reflect on others. Mam wants to know what I'm doing back home so early and when I tell her she wants me to go back and tell Lar I'm sorry, and he'll give me my job back, but when I tell her the way he's being treating me over the last two years she's starting to get upset. 'Does your father know about this? I'm telling her 'sure he must, isn't he there most of the time', she says she'll have to talk with him when he comes home at one o'clock for dinner.

But in the mean time I'm over at Mrs. O'Connell's telling her I have a few days off and can have her hall, stairs and landing finished by the end of the week, she's thrilled and says 'you wont have Mary stuck to you every minute holding you up', and when twelve forty five comes Mary walks in the door to number twelve, she's standing in the kitchen with her mouth opened and wants to know what I'm doing in her house drinking tea, and eating a few sausages that her mother threw on the pan for me. After telling her about Lar and the row she says, 'you have no job, so what will you do', 'I'll have to go looking for one, at least I have your mums hall, stairs and landing to come back too, and Mrs. O'Connell's says 'when you've finished I want you to do the bedrooms upstairs,' 'no better man, Mrs. O'Connell, thank you very much Mrs. O'Connell', and that's Mam looked after and the Jetland Ballroom, along with the Savoy Cinema for the next two weeks and things aint looking so bad after all.

I'm late home again that night because I'll work until eight o'clock and spend the rest of the night talking to Mary outside at the front wall. I won't see Pop until the morning, he's giving out to me saying I was too cheeky to Lar. After all he says, 'he's paying your wages too. I know he can be a pain in the arse, but at the end of the day he is your boss.' I'm stuck to the chair I thought Pop would be on my side. Mam isn't saying a word, 'are you going to go down to the man and apologise?' 'No, Pop I'm not', 'well that's the only way you'll get your job back,' I don't know what your going to do when every Friday comes and your looking for money to take the one around the corner out, with no money in your pocket.' I'm telling myself I'll be ok, sure, I have work the next two weeks and something else is bound to turn up. But by the time the first week is gone.

CHAPTER 10

I'm looking at the Sunday Press I brought home, there's an add in it, the Royal Airforce in England are looking for recruits and that you can apply in writing or ring a phone number in the North of Ireland, and that all travelling expenses will be reimbursed.

I'm down at the Bedford bar using the public phone, asking the operator to book a call to the Royal Airforce in Belfast. After half an hour of waiting the phone in the bar rings and the operator says she's going to put me through. There's a English accent at the end of the phone. I'm telling him I would love to come up and join the Royal Airforce, particularly the aircraft mechanic section, He says he'd love to have me join the Airforce but I'll have to come and do some tests first before I can be accepted. I'm asking what kind of tests, hoping he's not going to say a written test if he does I'm goosed because of the problems I had at school. And if it is I might as well forget it. Sure, any time I sat at school and did a test of any kind I failed and the only thing I ever passed in school was what I did when I went to the toilet. 'Oh. Don't worry', he says, 'its only a simple eye que test', and I'm saying to myself, thanks be to God, I'll pass that no problem at all sure, my eye sight is great, but why the hell do I have to stand in a que?. He asks me when would I like to come up and I'm asking him could I come up the week after next on a Wednesday, he says, 'fine', and asks me for my address so he can send me on the address I'll have to travel to for the eye que test and accommodation too, And adds, keep all your receipts of your travels so we can reimburse you. I don't know what reimburse means but I think it means I'll be getting my money back. Two days later there's a letter in the post with an English stamp on the cover I'm glad I got it before Mam saw it otherwise she'll be full of questions, if she finds out her son is looking to join the British Forces she'll be very hurt and worried too.

I'm telling no one about this except Mary, and when I tell her she seems to be a bit surprised. I think she's disappointed too, but I'm too excited, and when Tuesday comes I'm on my way to Dublin from Limerick's railway station. With the ticket I got from the British rail office in O'Connell's Street a couple of doors down from the Five Star supermarket.

It's a beautiful sunny day, I'm sitting at the right side by the window that has the brilliant sunshine coming through, and my mind is in overdrive. I'm overseas in the lovely sunshine with my head in a aircraft, where the engines are, and the world is my oyster, I'm thinking how well I'll look in the blue uniform, and best of all, when I leave the British Forces after a few years, I can leave and get a job in Aer Lingus at Shannon, and live happily ever after. But its time to get off the train and wait the hour for the train that will take me to Belfast, and I'm on my way sitting again in the sunny side and when I get to Belfast, I'll have spent a total of six hours in the sun. I don't know it yet, but I'll be rattling later on tonight, I won't have a clue why, or what's wrong with me.

Belfast is a big place, some of the people here seem to be speaking in a foreign language because I can't understand a word they're saying. Police here are walking about with guns on their sides. I'm thinking of the things I heard about Sean South, how the police up here shot and riddled him to death. Ian Paisley is causing a right racket up here, making public speeches and saying 'no surrender'. Every street has blue, white and red buntings hanging from one side to the other. It's a bit scary, I had to ask several people to help me find the hotel for ex-soldiers so I can get a bed for the night, and be ready for the eye que test tomorrow. When I find it, they say that I am expected, it's a very big clean place and full of soldiers in uniform, ex-soldiers too. My room is small but very clean, its nine o'clock I should be taking a walk around just to see a bit of the place. But I'm tired; maybe it's all the excitement. But I'm gone a few minutes after my head hits the pillow and sometime later in the dark of night I'm awake because I'm shivering. I'm not cold and can't stop shaking I haven't a bloody clue what's wrong with me. I'm wondering all kinds of things, have I been poisoned, or maybe I picked up something in a public toilet I used at the railway station. I'm really worried I'm asking myself am I seriously ill and if I am who will I call, what will I do, Jesus, I could be found dead here in the morning and my poor mother would be wondering what the hell I was doing in the North of Ireland with all the unrest up here. She might even think I've joined the I.R.A. and was here on a spying mission, she'll blame herself too. I manage to turn on the light it's four o'clock in the morning and after another hour of rattling in the bed and trying to figure out what the hell is wrong with me, it hits me that I had this last year when Pop, Lar and myself were on top of the roof of Savin's in O'Connell Street, pointing the slates with that new red powder that had to be mixed with sand and oil and had a smell that made me sick. And the three of us having a great laugh because Lar and Pop were on the dangerous side of the roof, the side above a lane that has a seventy foot drop by the Royal George Hotel and a rope tied around the top of one of the ladders to an old chimney stack and Pop holding onto Lar's long legs because the ladder was too short and there's Lar's head hanging out over the gutters as he tries to clean them. And Pop having to pull him up every time the ladder had to be moved a couple of feet for Lar to go back down again, I don't know what we were all laughing at, sure the two of them could be killed and if they fall I'll follow them because I'm on top of the ladder holding on to the rope as well. They wont let me anywhere near the bottom of the ladder, because Pops says if anything happens to me he might as well move out of the house, the two of them are making all kinds of comments in the lovely sunshine about making out a will, and Lar says, if he falls off and breaks his fupping neck that I can have his part of the business. The two of them are there with a knot on each end of the four corners of the handchief and telling me I should do the same or I'll get sunstroke, I'm telling them I haven't got one and that I'll be fine, but of course I spend the whole night and all of the next day rattling away in the bed like I am now, with a great mother to look after me, and telling me I'll be ok, and that it should only last a day and that I'll be grand in the morning. Pop will be giving out how himself and Lar warned me what would happen but I wouldn't listen and here I am up in the top half of the country shaking like Elvis Presley and no mother to tell me I'll be ok or bring me the drinks and the aspirins, and I wish to God I never set foot in this part of Ireland.

When nine o'clock comes I'm in a coma because I had fallen into a deep sleep from exhaustion and when my eyes open the rattling is back and its twelve o'clock in the day. It won't stop until ten o'clock that night. And I've missed my eye que test, but I don't give a monkeys. Eight o'clock the following morning and I'm up in great form and eat a good breakfast. I'd better get down to the place were the tests are and tell them what happened. If they tell me I'm too late or I'll have to come back next week at least I'll get my expenses back, it will be all I have, and if I don't get it I'll have nowhere to go back to. So I'm down at the place were I should have been yesterday making my excuses in my best manners. It seems to be working because they're asking me would I take the eye test with 46 women because Wednesday is for the men and Thursday is for the females, otherwise I'll have to come back again next week. I'm asking him will I have to stand in a que for the eye test half naked and women at all sides of me, he laughs and says the medical is after the eye que test, and if I don't pass the eye que test there'll be no medical because I'll be on my way home. So I'm escorted along with 46 women to a large room that looks just like a classroom except there's a chair in front of a small desk for one person only. There's a pencil on every desk and I'm wondering were the chart that has the big black letters on the top followed by more rows underneath with each row getting smaller for the eye que test, maybe they're going to bring one out any minute. But after ten minutes there is no sign of it at all, only a woman dressed in a blue uniform telling us she's going to hand out the eye que test forms that we will have thirty minutes to answer thirty questions, and we are to stop the minute the bell rings, and I'm thinking this is the funniest eye que test I have ever done in my life. Maybe its different up here or maybe its for the pilots that might need eyes in the back of their heads when flying around, but I'm horrified when she places two sheets of paper on my desk that has questions that I don't have a bloody clue how to answer, and I'm back in school again feeling like a right clown. I've got a minute to answer each question I'm looking at the first one I haven't got a bloody clue what the question is never mind the answer. How the hell did I think an eye que test was a test for the eyes, this is more like a test for the brain, why the hell are they calling it an eye que test, I'm goosed. I can forget about going into the R.A.F but each question has four possible answers I'll just guess one for every question, it will be better then handing back the flipping two sheets empty after the thirty minutes.

I'm finished. I'm thinking to myself I surely get at least a quarter of them right, even though I couldn't understand one bloody question. I mean talking about asking a question in such a stupid manner, so I'm sitting back in my chair with my arms folded I have to pretend a smile on my face like I'm a real swot and this was a doodle. I can see other girls looking at me, I'm sure they're saying to themselves, 'Janey, your man is right swot,' and that it was a piece of cake for me. I wish I was as intelligent as them, the lady in uniform that gave us the sheets is sitting at the top of the room, arms folded, with radar eyes wondering all over the room making sure that everyone has the eyes on their paper and not trying to get to cog off anyone next to them. She's looking at me, gives me a smile and a small nod of the head letting me know she knows I'm finished, all this pretending I'm doing is making me feel good like I'm intelligent. I wish I was. I would enjoy feeling like this all the time. When the bell rings we're told to wait for one hour, but I'm called in after ten minutes and I'm wondering why. I'm brought in to an office and introduced to another man wearing the same Royal Airforce uniform as the lady. He introduces himself, he's a Lieutenant something, but I'm looking at all his decorations and straight away I think he might be the top brass around here. He has his hand out wanting to shake mine. I respond, it's a good hold as he shakes it twice and I'm remembering what Pop always said about a handshake, that your hand should be dry and not damp or sweaty and that you should hold the other person's hand firmly and smile at the same time. And that there's nothing worse than a limp, sweaty hand that can put the other person off in seconds. I'm asked to sit down, then the Lieutenant asks with a puzzled look on his face, are you really Patrick Taylor from Garryowen in Limerick. 'Yes sir,' I reply, I'm puzzled. 'My goodness' he says, but you're a very smart well dressed young man. Do you know you have us all amazed in here, 'really', I answered. 'Yes', he said, we have being going through your answers in the on the IQ test and it's amazing. This has never happened before', And I'm thinking 'Janey mack I got the whole bloody lot right every one of them', how can I have been that lucky?. I mean there were thirty questions and four possible answers to each question, that meant a hundred and twenty possible answers, I picked thirty and got the whole lot right. Talk about luck.

The Lieutenant asks, 'did you really go to the Christian Brothers school in Sexton Street, Limerick?',Janey they must have a terrible reputation up here. I'm sitting up in the chair with my head held high, chest out. I can see myself over there in England, working on the jets they have in the Royal Airforce. Maybe I'll be working on an aircraft carrier overseas and my thoughts are interrupted when the Lieutenant says, 'you didn't get one of the questions right Patrick', I have a puzzled look on my face because I'm asking him what did he say, 'I'm saying you didn't get one of the questions right', and while my bubble is slowly reducing in size he says that based on the answers I put on the two sheets, he was expecting to see a rough character, that wouldn't be able to put two words together and never before has an Irish man come up here to do this exam from any of the Christian Brothers schools in Ireland and done so bad. And that he is sorry he can't offer me a place in the Royal Airforce. I'm stuck to the chair my body position gone from being upright and cocky to a bent and limp figure. Would there be another position I could take in the Royal Airforce, one that wouldn't require an eye que test? He says, the only position available for someone of my limited schooling was in the kitchen pealing potatoes or washing up, and I don't think you'd find that suitable. I agreed, thanked him for his trouble, got my four pound travel expenses and made my way back to the military hotel, where I'll meet three lads from Longford who are up to join the Royal Irish Fusiliers at three o'clock. I'm telling them how difficult it is to join the Royal Airforce and that I'll be heading home tomorrow.

They're at me to come with them and join up, they're telling me that all I need is a pulse and that I'll have nothing else to do. I'm browned off and before I know it I am inside the recruiting office of the Royal Irish Fusiliers in Belfast, on the main street. There are three or four men in smart brown uniforms looking after the three lads from Longford, they're gone into another room and one of the uniformed men wants to know my name. After telling him, he says I should fill out a form just like my three friends did, and I'm telling him I'm only here waiting for the lads because I am going back to Limerick tomorrow. He sits down beside me and wants to know what brought me to Belfast all the way from Limerick and I'm telling him about my disappointment of not being able to join the Royal Airforce. 'Ah you should join a man's army', he says, ' like the Royal Irish Fusiliers, just imagine after your six weeks training period in England, you'll be over in Aiden, serving in that lovely warm climate with hundreds of other Irishmen. Who knows, you may even have Limerick men you know serving longside you. There's many a young man out there that would give there eye teeth to travel the world free and be paid for it too.' I'm asking, 'if I signed up could I go home for a week or two just to get a few things organised first', he says 'Ah no young man, when you sign on the bottom line you become the property of Her Majesty the Queen, you'll be in England first thing tomorrow morning', he has me talked into going, but hang on a minute it would break Mam's heart if I take off and never give her time to get used to it. Then there's the spotted dick, I mean I spent two weeks with the FCA and nearly died of starvation, sure I'd never get used to living without the spotted dick. Then there's Mary. I really like her and I am just getting to get to know her. And I don't know which or who I'll miss more, and you're man has the form all ready to be filed in and starts to ask for my details. I'll ask him to give me a few minutes, that I'll take a walk and think about it. He says 'fine, I'll see you shortly', and I'm gone out the door, I don't need to think about anything, I am already half way back to Limerick, to Mam, Mary and the spotted dicks, because I don't think I could live without any of them.

I'm keeping well out of the lovely sunshine that got me into so much trouble on my journey up here. I don't know whether I'm depressed or relieved, I have only four pounds in my pocket. Mam will have to get half, the Jetland Ballroom, and the Savoy will get the rest of it and come Monday I'll be flat broke with no work in sight. Mary seems pleased to see me back in Limerick, and wants to know why I didn't join, I'm telling her about the so called IQ test and what I thought it was, she's killing herself laughing, she says, 'you're an awful man Paddy I never heard of that one before,'. She thinks I'm joking, and I am not going to tell her otherwise because if she realises I'm a gobshite she'll drop me like a hot potato. I'm not going to tell her I got thirty questions wrong, just that the exam was too hard.

She says her mother was talking to Mr. Noonan at the end of the road, 'he wants you to call down and give him a price to paper all the rooms,' and things are looking good. When I go over home Mam says Aunt Eileen is back from the States and will be calling down tonight, and when she does I'm asking her about Tom and how is he doing. She says that if I ever want to come to the States that all I have to do is get my fare together, that I will have a roof over my head and that there is plenty of work over there. And now would be the right time to go because I'm a young man. I'm looking at Mam and she's not one bit happy about it, and I know I made the right choice in coming back to Limerick, and now I have a dilemma, I can go to the States and Aunt Eileen is going to be here for the next two or three weeks and every time I'll see her, she'll keep talking about the States and how well I would do over there with my hands and my ability. She says I can come over anytime with a small bit of notice and now I'm back were I started before I went to the North with a head and mind that's all over the place. I know Mr. Noonan very well, sure didn't I play football with his sons Alec, Billy and Michael for years, over in the green patch that divides Garryowen in two. He's a fireman in Thomas Street and works with Paddy Bremen. I'm telling Mary of the time I worked at the Standard garage just across the road from the fire station and used to talk to himself and Paddy when they walked pass the front entrance of the Standard garage to keep themselves occupied.

And Mary and myself will talk for ages about Mr. Noonan's wife dying so young and leaving so many children behind her, and the way Mr. Noonan is looking after the lot of them on his own and holding down a job at the same time. Mam wants to know how I got on in Dublin and had I any luck with a job. I'm giving her the two pound out of the four I got in Belfast while telling her I couldn't stick it up there how there's no place like home, especially a home that has the spotted dick on the table everyday. Nan is there and starts to sing the Bridie Gallagher song it's her latest hit called 'you'll never miss a mothers, love until she's buried beneath the clay', and then starts laughing. Mam says she won't take the two pound off me because I have no work and I'm telling her that I do, that Mr. Noonan around the corner wants a few bedrooms papered and that I'll be alright for another week. And sure don't I still have a mouth and wouldn't my mouth still need the same amount of food whether I was working or not. She laughs, takes the money puts it in her purse and asks if I am taking the girl around the corner out to the Jetland at the weekend and if I am going to the Savoy, will I bring her in for a cup of tea on the way back.

The Jetland Ballroom

The Savoy Cinema

I am down at Mr. Noonan's house that's full of kids running wild all over the place, and I'm wondering how long will it be before I'm back here again, ripping paper off the walls in the three bedrooms I'm going to be doing this week at two pounds a room. Mary wants me to go into town with her on Saturday at one o'clock. She wants to buy a dress and says she'd love my opinion. We'll get the bus from outside Mr. O'Dwyer's house at ten to one and wind up in Roches Street and its straight across the road to Eve's smart wear, one of Pop and Lar's good customers. Mary will take the bones of an hour going through every frock and dress in the place, she'll hold each one in front of her just under her chin and ask my opinion. I'll tell her 'no, no that's too dark' or 'that's too bright', and ages later I'm telling her to try on the one she's got under her chin. She'll go to the dressing room, put it on, come out looking absolutely gorgeous. I'll have my chin dropped as far as I can get it in amazement. 'Wow, that's the bizz', she's looking back at me, saying 'really, you're just not saying that now are you, 'no, no' I am saying 'that really suits you, honest to God it's beautiful, buy it, buy it' she saying 'no, tell me the truth, what do you really think?' I'm there in disbelief, I mean is this girl feeling ok, she's turning around in front of the mirror trying to look at how it hangs on her back then on the left side slowly turning to see how it looks on the right side. She'll do it a hundred times and ask me every time she does it. She'll come over next to me and ask me if her bottom is very big in it. I'll tell her for goodness sake you can,t see your backside at all and now she's asking me, what do I mean 'you cant see my backside at all?' is it just hanging there straight with no shape, 'no, no its hanging great on you, lovely curves and your shape it,s great'. She's in front of the mirror again saying,

'Do you really think it's nice, what should I do?'
'Buy it, buy it, go on buy it, it looks great.
'I don't know' she says.
'What do you mean you don't know, I'm not sure', she says,
'Why aren't you sure?'
'I don't know'.

'Is it too small?'

'I don't know'.

There's an assistant standing by her side, she taking clothes from hangers and putting them back again for the last hour. She's telling Mary how lovely the dress is, Mary has a look on her face like someone belonging to her has died, and I think she is going to start crying any minute. She is over again asking me my opinion,

'Do you really like it?'

'I do, honestly its lovely, tell the woman you'll take it',

'I don't know',

She'll walk back again to the mirror turning left and right, walk back to me and ask me again,

'What do you think?'

So I'll try a bit of logic I mean surely if I present the facts in a simple logical arrangement it will take her brain out of the mess its in.

'Look' I say, 'do you like the colour?'

'Yes',

'Do you like the design?'

'Yes' she says.

'Are you comfortable in it?'

'Yes.'

'Is it making you feel good, is it making you feel confident?'

'Yes'.

'Does the size feel right?'

'Yes'.

'If you buy it will it be the best item in your wardrobe?',

'Yes'.

'How much is it?'

'Five pound', she answers.

'Have you got five pound?'

'No, but I can put a pound deposit on it now and a pound every week until I have it'.

'Can you change your mind and get your money back in four weeks time?',

'Yes,

'Then go over to the assistant and tell her you'll have it, give her the pound and we'll go and have a cup of tea'.

'Will I?' she says.

'Yes, go on, do it now'.

'Is it really nice' she says.

'Yes its gorgeous now go over and buy it'.

'I don't know'.

This is exhausting, I'm knackered I could be digging a hole in the ground and not feel as tired. I've never seen anything like this before, how can a person like something so much and not be able to make their minds up. When I go shopping I'll look in the front window if I see something I like I'll go and ask if they've got it in my size. I'll try it on and if it fits I'm gone out the door in minutes. So I'll ask Mary, 'Well what are you going to do then?'

'I don't know'.

There's a fella over by another mirror his with his wife or girlfriend, she's going back and forward asking him the same bloody questions. He's just nodding away, saying 'Ya, your lovely', he looks over at me, throws his eyes up to the ceiling, walks away like he can't wait to be gone out of the place. Mary comes over to me again and says, 'what do you think?' so I say 'look come away, we'll have a cup of tea and I can have a smoke, you can think about it and you can come back and tell the assistant what you have decided', 'I don't know,' And I'm thinking what am I going to do with this woman. She is back at the mirror again and I am beginning to feel like the your man across on the other side. Mary is back in the changing room, comes out and says 'I'll think about it' and I'm saying 'great'.

But it isn't great, because now she is heading down to Roches Stores. She wants to see if they have anything nice and I am wondering have I got to do this all over again. She's off again going through every dress in her size, giving every single one a good look, making the odd face of approval. She'll take one out show it to me for an opinion and I am asking myself what bloody difference is it going to make what I say. But I say it anyway 'that's lovely Mary try it on'.

'Will I?'

'Ya go on.'

She'll look at it, make a face put it back, carry on looking at more, then goes back to it again takes it out, makes the same face again, carries on drawing each hanger out as far as she can, away from the others, puts it under her chin asks me what I think. I'll tell her, but it won't make any difference. Then she'll ask 'Will I try it on' I'm telling her go on, she does and comes out looking gorgeous and asking me what do I really think. Then it's is 'my bottom very big' I'll tell her 'no it's fine',

'Really now, tell me the truth how does it really look from the back,' and I'm ready for the bed. On it will go for another half an hour with the same questions and I'll give the same answers, until she decides she wants to go to Todds. We'll be over there for the bones of an hour, I'll be answering the same bloody questions all over again about her arse, her chest, her hips, her hands, and her legs, until I am blue in the face. Then it's up to Lower Cecil Street to Ame's to do it all again and I am wondering where is this woman getting all her energy, because mine is gone and we have to go dancing tonight and were the hell am I going to get the energy to dance. She tells the sales assistants here that she will think about a dress she's looked at. And when we come out it is five forty five and she says we have ten minutes to get back to the first shop we looked at, to try the same dress that she tried when we started our pilgrimage at one o'clock and will ask me the same bloody questions all over again. And as the door is about to be locked she'll put the pound note on the counter, get a receipt, walk out the door turn and say to me,

'I hope I've done the right thing, what do you think, tell me the truth now, I won't mind if you don't like it'

I'll tell her anything, anything at all and it's a good thing the bloody shops are all closed otherwise we'd still be here.

We'll call into the Talk of the Town Restaurant at the Savoy for a cup of tea were her mother works from six o'clock to midnight every night of the week. I'll fall into the chair and feel I'll never be able to get out of it and think this has been the worst afternoon of my life. Mary's mother will come out, ask what did we do, and Mary will say she put a deposit on a dress and tell her mother that I said 'it was lovely'. We'll will sit at the table for half an hour, go home on the bus and she'll keep asking me about the bloody dress that she's put the deposit on. I want to tell her that if she doesn't shut up about the bloody thing I'll strangle her. I'm back home with Mam sitting at the table eating the spotted dick for my supper and asking her how long would it take for her to buy something like a dress, a coat or anything else. She wants to know why I'm asking her and I am telling her I have just spent the worst five hours of my life in every bloody woman's shop in town with Mary, and how she couldn't make up her bloody mind about anything and when she did she kept asking me did she do the right thing.

Mam is laughing and says 'your asking the wrong woman in me, sure I haven't bought myself a hat since I got married, and anyway most women are like that.' By the time we're on our way to the Jetland my strength has returned and Mary is still on about the dress, but I'll keep changing the subject otherwise I'll go barmy. Dicky and the Miami showband are playing tonight and the legs that dragged me around every bloody shop in Limerick all afternoon, are now taking me all over the Jetland ballroom at a hundred miles an hour because the Miami are brilliant.

We're on our way home in one of the ten buses that's waiting outside the Jetland every Saturday night, to bring the hundreds back to Limerick city and county. With our clothes stuck to us from the sweat that Dicky and Co put on us over the last few hours, and Mary is still talking about the bloody dress, she'll be at it again tomorrow after mass, until I ask her to relax and stop worrying about it.

She does, because I think I might have shown in my voice a small bit of annoyance. Then its down to the Savoy on Sunday night to see Sean Connery in his latest James Bond movie 'Goldfinger', and then to the Savoia Café to spend my last few bob on a glass of orange and a plate of chips. Mary will have the glass of orange and pick at the chips because she says she's watching her figure. Now its up Mulgrave Street and down the hill of Garryowen and I'm telling Mary, that Mam said I was to be sure and ask her on our way home to come in for a cup of tea and off goes Mary, with the 'I'll do it next week' routine, because she says she's too shy, but I'm telling her Mam will have gone to a lot of trouble putting out the best set of ware, the ones that are only on show most of the time, and only come out of the press that was bought in Cavendish's a year ago, and how disappointed she'll be if she doesn't come in. And after a lot of persuading we are on our way in the hall after knocking on the door and then turning the key. I'm shouting, 'We're home', so Mam will be able to put on the airs and graces, she'll have for the new face that comes to 36 Claughan Court. Pop won,t be there for another twenty minutes because he'll be at bingo up at St. John's Pavilion, and when he does come home Mary will get what every fella Jetta brought home before she got married, along with the girls I wanted to get rid of, and the contrast of Mam tripping over herself and never taking the smile off her face with Pop doing his best to worry and upset the girl I'll bring home, will be well worth waiting for. Mary has asked me to go in to the room first , I'll look at Mam, wink at her, hold Mary back behind the door that's halve open, raise my voice and say Mrs. Taylor I'd like you to meet the one and only gorgeous Mary O'Connell from around the corner, and lead Mary in through the door. 'Don't mind that eejit Mary love, come over here and sit down', says Mam, as she gives me a thump on the shoulder and says 'will you don't be embarrassing the poor girl, can't you see that walking into a strange house and meeting a strange person for the first time is difficult enough, so sit down and shut up. Take no notice of him love. Now would you like a cup of tea Mary'? Mary nods her head real polite and says she'd love one. Mam has six slices of the spotted dick cut, and left on one of her best plates along with all the other bits that she got last year on the green shield stamps. Sure half the bloody things in the house came from the green shield stamps; like the kettle, two hot water bottles, an electric iron, a bread bin, a set of knives and forks, and God knows what else. I'll start on Mam and say how come you never put any of the good delve out when I brought other girls down for a cup of tea, and Mam says, mind your own bloody business' and says to Mary, 'oh Mary O'Connell love, I'd be careful if I were you going out with that fellow, will you not have a bit of sense and keep well away from him'? Mary is tearing into the spotted dick. She has three slices gone already and asking Mam about the recipe. How long has she been making it, and Mam is filling her in on the history of the spotted dick, and how Nan, her mother, out at Tower Hill, used to make it for them when they were kids. Then she started making it herself after she got married, and used to only make the one for Jetta, James and myself, and when Jetta and James went off it, I got more fond of it, and she had to make two instead of the one, and that if she didn't make the two every week they'd be no living with me and tells Mary that it's a simple recipe; self raising flour, sultanas, a pinch of salt, plenty of sour milk, four eggs, put it in the oven, keep an eye on it and Mary is going into her fourth slice and she's the first person I never minded eating my spotted dick.

Mam looks at the clock and says Pop will be here any minute, and then says, she better put the kettle on. No sooner has she said it when the front door opens. He'll take a minute to hang his coat on the baniste then walk in, see Mary and say is that the one living around the corner? Now the fun is going to start! I haven't told Mary anything about Pop and his antics. I want to see if she will react like the other girls I brought home and get their knickers in a twist. Pop, I'd like you to meet Mary O'Connell from just around the corner. Pop puts the forefinger of his right hand under his chin, looks at Mary, genuflects and says, I'm very pleased to meet you young lady. Mam gives him a dig on the shoulder and tells him to shut up and sit down. She says you'll have the poor girl gone off my son the way you're carrying on. She's laughing away while saying it,and loving every minute of having the girl from around the corner at 36 Cloughan Court, and off goes Pop with the usual. 'O'Connell hmm, O'Connell, what's your father's first name,? David answers Mary. 'Jesus, that's right, David O'Connell. Is that the fellow who has the disease they can't find a cure for,'? That's right says Mary. 'How did you know that,'? Did Paddy tell you,'? and Pop is taken completely back. I'm behind Mary doing my very best not to laugh. Mam starts cutting a extra slice or two of spotted dick because Mary has just downed the six slices. Mam has a look of astonishment on her face. What's the matter with your father love,'? and Mary says he had TB over in the sanatorium in St. Camillius Hospital' and is only out a few years. Mam gives Pop another thump on the shoulder and says 'Jesus, Mary and Holy Saint Joseph, now look at what you've done', and Pop is all apologies and says he was only joking.' Mary says 'it's okay, don't worry about it we're all hoping he's going to be okay', and Mam is asking all kinds of questions about Mr. O'Connell; how did Mary's mother manage rearing the four of ye and Mary is talking so much I don't think she has any idea of how much spotted dick she's eaten and Pop is the quietest I've ever seen him, but he's going to put his big foot in it again any minute now before Mary goes home, and that will put a stop to his taking the mickey out of Mary and it'll be an awful pity.

For the next thirty minutes it's just Mam and Mary talking away about everything and anything, their relations, friends and neighbours, mostly about the hard years for Mary's parents. They're getting on like a house on fire. It's great and there's Pop sitting on the chair quiet as a mouse and doing his level best to keep the watery drop off his nose with the odd sniff, and a wipe with one of the sleeves of his jacket. He's starting to relax again and I can see the mischievous look is back on his face. Any minute now he's going to have another go at Mary and out it comes.

He's only been half listening to the conversation Mam and Mary have been having for the last half an hour, with one eye and ear tuned into the black and white TV that's stuck in the corner; 'is that your mother who works down at the Savoy cinema in the restaurant washing up all the dirty dishes, and looking for the leftovers to take home because there's never any food in the house,'? and Mary says, 'that's right Mr. Taylor, when my father went into the sanatorium my mother needed a job where she could be home during the day to look after us, so they gave her a job doing the washing up after six o'clock until midnight seven nights a week. How did you know that',? and Pop is in shock again and can't get a word out. Mam gives him another thump and follows it with the usual 'Jesus, Mary and Holy Saint Joseph, and says wasn't the first time you put your big foot in it a sign to keep your big mouth shut, and it's time you met your match'. She turns to Mary and says 'you're to take no notice of him Mary love'. 'Every girl Paddy brought into this house he gave them an awful time, and you're the first one to put him in his place'. She turns to Pop and says, 'now let that be a lesson to you'. Pop stands up, puts the same forefinger under his chin, and says 'evening all' and takes off upstairs to bed.

Mam reaches out, touches Mary on the hand and asks her would she like another cup of tea, and on goes the kettle again. Its one o'clock by the time Mam is washing up. Mary and my,self are saying goodbye to Mam at the front door. Mam tells Mary she is to be sure and call again next Sunday night on her way home from the Savoy, and all Mary wants to talk about is Mam and her spotted dick, and how lovely she is, and that she never expected her to be so nice. I'm very pleased and it just seems to dawn on me how much closer to Mary I'm getting and the thoughts of my girlfriend and my mother being close was too much to hope for. We're over at Mary's front door for the twenty minutes shifting away. Mr. O'Connell will be shouting down for Mary to go to bed because she has to get up early for work in the morning, and in between the kisses all Mary wants to talk about is Mam's spotted dick and I have to tell her about the history and the recipe again, and Mary wants to know would Mam mind giving her the recipe so that she could try and make it herself, and I'm telling her sure all she has to do is ask her next Sunday night.

The following morning Mam is all talk about Mary at break-fast. She has her forefinger right in front of my nose telling me to look after the girl and that I'm not to blaggard her, and says how much she's looking forward to seeing her again next

Sunday night. When I come home on Monday at dinner time, Mam is still talking about Mary, then looks at Pop with a cross face followed by a thump saying, 'you're to leave that girl alone when she comes here again on Sunday night. Do you hear me talking to you', and Pop is sitting in his special chair, the one he got from Paddy McCarthy out in Clarina, the one that Mr. McCarthy said still has the original horse hair in the seat, that has Pop so high off the ground, Mam is able to eyeball him when she's standing longside him. Pop makes a grunt in response and then adds I won't be putting my foot in it with that one from around the corner again. Mam says 'you bloody well better not and her name is Mary not that one', and when six o'clock comes Mam is very excited because her new Electrolux washer come spin dryer, has arrived from Power & Hogan in Patrick Street, the same place she got the stereogram with the opera records that still has Pop screaming his head off every Sunday afternoon, and keeps Mam free from the headaches because Pop is staying away from the Bedford bar and Arthur Guinness. She has us out in the kitchen showing us how the thing works. It has two compartments; one big one and the other smaller. She says the bigger one does the washing and when that's done all she has to do is take it out and put it into the smaller one that's called the spin dryer, switch it on, and out comes the water. The old one is out the back waiting for Uncle Peter to come with his truck and take it away. She says, 'she won't know herself not having to take each item out and put it through the wringer that has her arms the size of Charles Atlas'. Pop says, 'Im to call down to Sarsfield Street and give the owner of the *Echo* office a price, to put a suspended ceiling in the downstairs room'. I've only one more night to do at Mr. Noonan's house and only two pounds to collect because he gave me four last Friday, and if I get the job at the *Weekly Echo* office I might have a bit more for myself and Mam come Friday.

I'm knocking at the door of the office in Sarsfield Street the next morning waiting for an answer, and when the door opens there's a man with a camera in his hand waiting for me to tell him why I'm at his door and when I tell him I'm Harry Taylor's son he smiles and says 'you've come to look at the ceiling, come on in and I'll show you. 'Jesus, but you're only a young fellow, will you have someone to give you a hand'? I'm shaking my head sideways saying, 'no, I won't need anyone'. 'Are you sure'? 'I mean that's a big ceiling'. 'How will you manage it'? 'I have my two hands out in front of him saying with these sir'. He laughs and says, 'well if you're Harry Taylor's son, you must know what you are talking about'. So he asks me what it will cost, how long it will take, because this is where he does all his work. I'm asking him to give me an hour or two and I'll be back. I'll need to cycle down to the Dock Road to James McMahons and get a price for the wood I'll need. It's going to have to be a suspended ceiling, made of three by two wood, and the new aeroboard tiles, and if the man with the camera thinks two men are needed, then I'll be able to charge the price of two and this could turn out to be a good week. After coming back from the timber yard and giving the whole matter a lot of thought, I'm telling the man with the camera that the job will cost thirty-five pounds and if I get it, I'll make twenty for five nights work, and I'm beginning to like working for myself. The man with the camera has a look on his face that isn't showing any sign of shock. He's just mulling away and then says, 'when can you start'? I'm so excited I can hardly answer. When I do, I'm saying the day after tomorrow sir. He says I'm not to be calling him sir, that his name is John. I'm on my way out the door when John asks will I need a few bob to buy the materials, and in all my excitement I forgot about that. So he hands me fifteen pounds and says if I need anymore to ask him. I'm back home for the dinner at twelve forty-five telling Mam I'll have ten pounds for her in two days and asking her will she buy herself something nice to wear, like a new pair of shoes,a handbag, or even a new dress. She smiles and says, 'what would I be doing with a new coat or a new dress,? Sure where would I be going with a new dress'? I know I'm wasting my time but it would be great to see her all decked out and looking the business when she goes to town at the weekend. But Mam will have other uses for the money. Like she might buy a sleeveless cardigan for Pop in Bulger's stores,or Cannocks, or it might be a pair of shoes or something for James, or Harry, at school. Pop is on his way in the hall and when he comes into the room I'm telling him I got the job, and how much I'm getting for it, and how much I'll make, and can I have the loan of his hand cart with the iron wheels that will rattle and clang all the way down the Dock Road. He says I can take it for two hours, that I'd better have it back by four o'clock as himself and Lar will need it later,' so I'm gone out the door and off up the hill in Garryowen on my bike heading down to Bedford Row to the back of the Grand Central cinema where the hand cart is kept most of the time. I still have the key for the store, so I'm leaving my bike there and heading down the Dock Road running behind the hand cart that has my ears going deaf listening to the awful racket coming from the iron wheels. I'm outside the entrance of the main gate of James McMahon, and just in time to be first in the queue after the hour lunch break, and when three thirty comes I'm back behind the Grand Central cinema putting the cart back and heading home feeling really happy with myself, now that I have everything over in John's office ready to start at nine o'clock in the morning. I haven't a bloody clue how I'm going to do a suspended ceiling that's twelve foot, by ten foot, on my own, but I have plenty of time to think about it. When Pop comes home I'll have him pestered with questions about how I'll go about it and all he'll say is 'Jesus, Mary and Holy Saint Joseph, I got you the job, gave you the loan of the hand cart and now you want me to tell you how to do it? Next thing you'll want me to go down and do the bloody job for you'. Mam is eyeballing him as he sits in his chair, gives him a thump and says, 'Jesus is it too much trouble for you to give him a bit of advice, Pop answers back and says, 'can't he do what I did when I got my first carpentry job' 'and what was that says Mam'? 'Figure it out for myself', and off goes the shoulders up and down. He'll be out of control in a minute. I'm laughing too but Mam isn't. She's outside in the kitchen giving out to him and it's only making him worse so I'm saying to Pop, 'okay then, I will figure it out myself', and I'm off over to Mary's and as I walk out the hall and stop at the mirror to comb my hair I can hear Mam giving Pop a piece of her mind and it's only making Pop laugh more.

I'm over at Mary's telling her the good news, that I have work that's going to pay well and we'll be able to head out to see Brendan Boyer, and the Royal Show Band at the Jetland at the weekend. She's pleased and wants to know if I will come down town with her again on Saturday, that she wants to put ten bob on the dress she put away last week, and that she's still not sure if she made the right decision,and that she wants to buy a pair of shoes and a handbag to match it, and I'm saying 'yeah, no problem,' sure last Saturday was only a one off. I mean she couldn't be like that every Saturday could she?, Next morning I'm down in Sarsfield Street in the office of the *Weekly Echo* scratching my head as to how I'm going to get ten twelve foot lengths, of three by two timber from one wall over to the other on my own. First, I'll get my spirit level, climb the ladder and make a pencil line all the way round each wall six inches below the old ceiling. Then measure from the line down to the floor and cut two pieces of wood to that measurement and put one in each corner against the wall. I measure the distance from one wall to the other, cut another length of wood to that size, drive four steel nails into it, climb the ladder again and rest it on the two pieces that are against the wall at both ends, drive the nails home and repeat the exercise for the other three walls and after one hour, I'm now ready to cut and nail the other lengths and when six o'clock arrives, I'm all ready for the aeroboard tiles in the morning and by six o'clock tomorrow evening I'll be finished with my hand out looking for the balance and can't wait for the weekend.

'Did you finish that job in Sarsfield Street asks Pop'? 'I did'. 'I made twenty pounds from it. Ten pounds a day thanks for the recommendation'. 'Well are you going to tell me how you got out of the problem you had'. 'No, I'm not'. 'Why not' he says. 'Because you told me to figure it out for myself and I did'. Mam gives Pop a dig and says, 'good on you Pa', and Pop will say, 'oh you'll be looking for advice again and who will you be coming to only your father', and Mam says, 'sure when he came looking to you for it you told him to figure it out for himself'. I'm off over to Mary's after listening to Mam and Pop slagging one another. I'll comb my hair in front of the mirror in the hall and when I get over to Mary's we'll talk for an hour or two at the front wall. Mary will remind me of my promise to go to town tomorrow and look at more clothes. Mrs. O'Connell will be calling me in for the cup of tea. Mr. O' will be singing and diddly idle doing and when Saturday comes, I'm down in Eve's Smartwear with Mary and she's looking at the dress she took ages to decide on last week. She's asking me again what do I really think, and I'm not going through all that again, so I walk over to the assistant and give her the four pounds while asking her to wrap it up, and there's Mary with the mouth wide open asking why I'm doing that. I'm telling her I couldn't put up with another afternoon of 'is it nice and do you really like it, and no now tell me the truth, and is my arse too big in this, and is my arse too big in that'?, She laughs looks very pleased, gives me a squeeze on the hand and whispers a 'big thank you in my ear', but God love me and my innocence, I'm in for another four hours of what I got last week, and thought because I paid the four pounds for the dress that I wouldn't have to put up with it today. Because Mary has an extra pound in her pocket to spend and the five bob that was going on the pair of shoes and a handbag is now going to be fifteen and we're heading down to Leavy's Shoes on the corner of O'Connell Street, and 'it's what do you think, tell me the truth, are they too big or too small? Are my legs very fat in them'? She'll have every bloody pair of shoes in the place tried on before she'll leave the place and not buy anything and then for the rest of the day, try every shoe, in every shop in Limerick that has a shoe, or a handbag to sell, and then before the day is out, go back to Leavy's at ten to six to buy a pair she tried on hours ago, and I'd better find something to do on Saturday afternoons because I can't do this every Saturday, week in week out. I love being with the girl but this is ridiculous.

Mary has the new dress and shoes on for the Jetland tonight. She looks great and keeps thanking me all the time. After Sunday night at the Savoy it's the walk home and into Mam's for the chat, the cuppa, and the spotted dick. Mary turns to me before we go to the front door and says would there be any chance that I might go out into the kitchen, while herself and Mam talk away, and cut a few slices of the spotted dick for her break at the factory tomorrow morning, and I'm saying, 'let me see if I understand you correctly, you're going to keep my mother talking or distracted while I go into the kitchen and steal some of her cake'. Mary interrupts, 'no no, not steal'. 'Oh I see, you want me to borrow some and you'll give it back to-morrow'? 'Will you just get me a couple of slices for the break tomorrow please'? Mam is inside waiting with the good delve on the table along with the seven or eight slices of the spot-ted dick, and off goes Mam with the smile and the lovely talk again. 'Come on in Mary, it's great to see you. God, but you're looking gorgeous'. Mary is doing everything but genuflecting and saying, 'Paddy bought me that yesterday, and I swear to God Mrs. Taylor, I never knew a thing about it, and if I did, I would have gone into town on my own'. 'Well you must be very special Mary. I don't think he ever did that, or anything like it for any of the other girls he went out with before' and I'm saying to Mam, 'would you like to know what that lovely gor-geous girl was asking me to do before we came in the door to-night', and Mary starts, 'oh God, Mrs. Taylor, I never said any such thing I swear to God Mrs. Taylor'. Mam is standing there laughing away and I'm looking at Mary saying, 'why don't you let me finish what I was going to say before you start saying you never said it,' 'but I didn't' she says'. 'You didn't say what, I'm asking?. Then Mary says, 'I didn't say what you're going to say I said'. 'And what am I going to say you said'? 'I don't know she says'. I'm looking at Mam and she's saying, 'will you leave the poor girl alone'!. 'But Mam, she wants to keep you talking while I...........', Mary butts in, and says, 'oh God, Mrs. Taylor that's not true at all'!. and I'm saying, 'will you let me finish!' and Mam is thumping me on the shoulder like she does to Pop and saying , 'didn't I tell you to leave the girl alone'. But Mam!, 'Mary wants me to steal four slices of spotted dick while she keeps you talking'. 'Oh God, Mrs. Taylor I swear on all belong to me, I never said anything like that' and Mam says, 'now don't you be worrying yourself. Mary I wouldn't believe a word out of that fellow's mouth. He's only trying to embarrass you'. Mam hands me a knife and tells me to go out to the kitchen and cut five slices of spotted dick so that she can wrap it up and give it to Mary for her lunch break tomorrow. Mam looks at me and gives me a wink, because I know she knows I'm telling the truth, and she has the look of being very pleased that Mary likes the spotted dick too. 'That fellow is just like his father Mary, trying to wind people up all the time, so don't be taking any notice of him because I'm not'. Mary smiles in relief but I can't leave it go.

I'm saying to Mary, 'Mam will be asking me in the morning, 'did Mary really ask you last night to go out to the kitchen and cut some slices of the spotted dick behind my back', and Mary is off again 'swearing on everything and anything she can think of' and Mam says, 'look Mary, just ignore him'. The hall door closes the same way it does when Pop comes home at night. In he comes, looks at Mary, puts his forefinger under his chin, genuflects and says, 'good evening your royal highness' and as he puts his backside into the chair, Mam has her forefinger in front of his nose wagging it away, telling him to leave Mary alone, that if he can't say anything constructive or nice then he is to say nothing at all. And Pop says, 'oh you needn't worry, I've put my foot in it twice already. I'm not going to do that again. But it's only a matter of time before he has us all in stitches. When it's time to go home we'll go round the corner to Mary's house with the buttered five slices of spotted dick in my hand. Mary is giving out to me with a smile on her face saying, 'why did you tell your mother that I asked you to cut some slices of spotted dick for my lunch tomorrow' and I'm saying, 'because I knew you'd get your knickers in a twist, and you did', she laughs, gives me a thump on the shoulder just like Mam, takes the five slices of spotted dick that Mam gave me out of my hand, puts her finger under my nose and makes me promise that I'll get her another five slices next Sunday night, and warns me that if I tell Mam that she is looking for more spotted dick, she wont go out with me anymore. She wants to know if there's always laughter in my house or was it just a coincidence on the two nights she's been there. I'm telling her that when my Nan, whose over in Northampton for a couple of months visiting her daughter Tess, is around, the laughing is even better and hardly ever stops. And Mary wants to know if Mam would mind if she came over during the week, maybe of a Wednesday night, just to talk and eat more of the spotted dick and I'm thrilled. Mary says she could do with being around that kind of environment more often and Mam is going to have to start making three spotted dicks a week now, because Mary has to share the five slices she brought up to the factory on Monday. Patsy O'Meara and Margaret O'Brien get a bit and wind up having a slice, and now the whole bloody shoe factory wants a piece but they're not getting any. I have four pounds left over for the week and no sign of work but surely something will turn up. I'll go looking and when Wednesday night comes, Mam has the table set again. She's sitting by the fire knitting away like she does every night and if it's not for Harry or James it'll be for Olwen, Jetta's baby. There's a few gentle taps on the door. That'll be Mary she says,'go out and let her in' and when Mary comes into the room she's all apologies to Mam, how she hopes she didn't mind her asking to come over and Mam is beaming saying, 'you can come over here any night you want to, just knock on the door and I'll be here'. Mary wants to know what Mam is knitting and before Mam answers she turns to me and says, 'are you going out?, and I'm answering no. 'Did you not hear me the first time I asked you',? are you going out,? and I get the message', 'Oh, this is a lady's night then,' and I'm out the door not having a clue where I'm going, Mam is saying, 'take your time and don't be in a hurry back'. So I'm out in the green belting a ball around the field with the Leahy's, the Noonan's and all the other lads that I've been knocking around with for years, and feeling really pleased with myself that my girlfriend wants to be in my house with my mother, and when I come back three hours later sweating like a pig, I'm told to clear off and not to bother coming back for another hour, and there's Mary with a pair of knitting needles taking instructions from Mam and the two of them look like they've been friends all their lives, and I have to go out and sit on our wall and talk to whoever passes. I'll look at the watch on my wrist waiting for the hour, that seems like two to pass, and when the hour is up, there's Pop getting off the bus wanting to know what I'm doing sitting on the wall on my own. I'm telling him with a smile on my face that the two women are inside and that his house is out of bounds and if he goes in he might be thrown out on his ear. I'm following him in the hall as he shouts 'permission to enter my own house,' but Mam and Mary are outside in the kitchen. She's showing Mary the new washing come spin dryer machine and telling Mary how it only takes half the time to do the washing now, and that her right arm used to ache from the constant wringing of the clothes with the handle, and Mary is telling Mam how her mother is still using the washing board in the sink and in spite of appeals from everyone won't have anything to do with electric this,or that,and Mam is there in disbelief that someone is still using the stone age system of washing clothes.

When it's time for Mary to go home,Mam is asking her will she be back again next Wednesday night and before long Mary is over in my house as much as I'm in hers. When the weekend comes there's no sign of work. I'm down to three pounds in my pocket. Mam says there's no need to give her any money as the ten pound she got last week will keep her going but I didn't want that. I was hoping more work would come my way and make enough to give her another tenner. Jetta is in on Saturday with bad news. She's pregnant again and is totally depressed because she says Shannon is an awful dive to live, and her husband, whose lucky to have a job, works nights and is in bed all day and I'm wondering if that's the case how the hell did she get pregnant in the first place. Now Mam is depressed because she wants to help and there's a bit of gloom in the house now. And when Mary comes over the following Wednesday and tastes the gloom in the house she says it's unusual because the laughter that's always here is the one thing that brings her over.

CHAPTER 11

Pop says Richard Ferris is opening a barber shop on the floor
above the ladies hair salon and that he wants it decorated fast,
that Lar and himself are too busy so I'm gone the following
morning on my bike tearing down Roches Street and turning
into O'Connell Street and leaving my bike against Whelan's
window, not bothering to lock it, hoping it will be still there
when I come down. I'm rushing up the stairs taking three steps
at a time only to find that Mr. Ferris is with one of his laudy
dawdy ladies and that I've to come back in a half an hour, and
when I do, he takes me upstairs, shows me the large room and
says he wants two sinks fitted, presses under the sinks, mirrors,
here there and everywhere, sockets, painting and wallpapering,
and that the wallpaper is three foot wide and has real straw
stitched on to it, and could be difficult to hang. He wants to
know if I'd be able to do the whole lot fast and before I can
think about it my mouth is saying yes,because my pocket is
going to need money for the next two weeks and Richard Ferris
is going to fill it. He wants to know how long will it take, and
how much will it cost, but he's more interested in the length
of time it will take so I'm telling him four weeks he wants to
know if I can do it in three. I'm saying, 'yes, sure I can work
evenings and weekends, but I need a day or two to price it'. Mr.
Ferris wants me to start now, and think about the price while
I'm working and that suits me fine. So I'm there pulling shelves
and presses apart that were used by the last clients, a car rental
company, thinking how much should I ask for. Would I try for
fifteen pounds a week for four weeks do it in three and Mam
won't know herself with a tenner every week. Sure I'll nearly
be giving her as much as Pop. I'm concentrating so much on
the money I'll make ,I haven't given any thought to what I have
to do. I mean Mr. Ferris thinks I can do all this on my own.
Sure I've never turned a nut on a copper pipe before,but I'll
learn and I'll learn fast. Mr. Ferris says sixty pound is fine and

if I finish it in three weeks he'll make it eighty. Boys, but that puts juice in my tank. I can't believe it. Eighty pounds in three weeks. Boys, but this working for yourself is the business. I'm home for the dinner asking Pop for the loan of everything I'll need. I'm thanking him too for the work. He turns to me and says 'now that you're nearly a building contractor and a millionaire, don't you think it's time you had your own tools.' I'm asking him where and how I'll get those. He says the same place himself and Lar got them, 'McMahons', 'and what will I use for money'? 'Do the same thing we did. Go down and ask for a bit of credit'. I'm back down at McMahons looking for the credit Pop suggested. I'm using his name too and by the next day I'll have every tool I need except the experience to use them, but I'll get that from Pop. Mam says Jetta and her husband have a place got in Catherine Street on the top floor. Mam's much better now because Jetta's husband has a new job as a rent collector down at City Hall for the Corporation, and Jetta won't be as depressed because she'll be able to visit Mam in Garryowen, and her other friends whenever she wants, and the gloom that's been hanging around 36 Cloughan Court for the last week is gone.

Mary and Mam can enjoy the talking, and the eating again every Wednesday night except Mary's coming every Monday night as well, and the three bloody spotted dicks aren't lasting the week anymore, and I think Mary is putting on a bit of weight. Pop will come home on those nights after the bingo, look at the two women with the knitting needles, the mouths and the hands flying in all directions and says, 'Jesus I thought I got rid of a daughter a year ago', and the next thing I know the one from around the corner will be occupying one of the beds upstairs. The girls laugh and when Saturday comes every week, Mary will spend as much time looking at the patterns for Mam and herself, as she does for clothes. The patterns that will keep the two of them going for weeks. Mary's wallet is getting much bigger now because she says that before she met me, it took her four to six weeks to pay for a dress and another two for shoes and a handbag or two months for an overcoat, and then try and have a few bob left over for the dance on a Saturday night or the pictures, and because I'm paying for the entertainment every week along with the chips and the orange juice, she says, 'she's never being so well off before,' and now that I'm nearly finished the job at Mr.Ferris's in the three week period, because Pop kept calling in to see me most days giving me the advice on whatever problem I had, I'll have the extra few bob and so will Mam, and Mary is looking like a million dollars. I can't do the Saturdays with Mary anymore. Well maybe two in a month. I'll go looking for clothes for Mary on my own. It's much easier. I'll just walk into a shop, have a look around and after five minutes I'm asking the assistant has she got such a thing in a certain size. Sure I know the sizes off by heart. Then I'll go and look for a pair of shoes and then just for the craic walk into the lingerie department, pick up a bra, and a pair of knickers, look for the shyest assistant, go over to her and in a loud voice ask her what size these are and watch her die. I'll act the eejit and use my hands to show her the size and shape of my girlfriend and be aware, out through the corner of my eyes, the attention I'm getting from the other assistants and customers too. There's always an assistant who'll come to her rescue and give me as good as I'm giving, and that's when the fun starts with each of us trying to embarrass the other to the laughter of all looking on.

I'll go home with the parcels to Mary. She has a look of surprise on her face as she opens a large carrier bag and takes out a dress I've chosen for her, and watch her try it on and off she'll go again, with the 'do you like it routine', is her arse too big in it, and so on and so forth. Her mother will be called in along with the two sisters and they'll have their mouths wide open saying 'oh God, but that's beautiful.' Then she'll try out the shoes. There's more, oh Gods and they'll say to me aren't you very good Paddy, and then say to Mary that it's great to have a boyfriend like myself, a boyfriend that will go down the town and buy his girlfriend a dress and a new pair of shoes. And I'm thinking yeah, the kind of guy who doesn't want to go to town every Saturday and walk into every bloody shop and handle every garment and be asked a thousand questions every Saturday of every week, and have to answer the same question every time and getting blue in the face from it, and how I wondered why she bothered asking me at all. Mary kisses me a couple of times and tells me with a big smile on her face that I'm not to do that again, then sees the other package, puts her hand out, picks it up and while opening it asks me what it is. When she pulls out the bra she's in disbelief. Mrs. O'Connell and the two sisters are screaming their heads off in laughter. Mary is looking at me in shock with a knickers in one hand and a bra in the other and asks me where did I get them. 'I bought them'. ' Where' she asks? 'In the same shop, I bought the dress and where was that'? 'Todds'. Mrs. O'Connell is roaring out to Mr. O'Connell to come in, and see 'what Paddy Taylor brought your daughter'. Mrs. O' has the two items, one in each hand, high in the air and when Mr. O' walks in the door whistling away puts his two eyes on what Mrs. O'Connell is holding, makes an instant turn back out the door just like he was square bashing in the army out in the square. Mary is giving out to her mother and looks at me with a cross look on her face. The first cross look I've seen since we started going out. You're after making a holy show of me in front of my father. I won't be able to go down town with you again, and I'm thinking mission accomplished. That will be the end of my trips to town every Saturday from now on. I can't stop laughing. Mary's mother wants to know is she not going to try them on in case they're too small or even too big, and won't Paddy have to go back down to Todds and change them for ones that's the right size and Mary says 'Paddy isn't going anywhere', but it hasn't worked at all, because she's asking me to go down again the following Saturday and when I remind her of what she said during the week, she said, 'it's Todds I'm never going into with you again'. 'We can go into all the other shops', and I'm thinking I'll have to try something else to get out of it when the work might dry up in a couple of weeks time.

The following week Mary is over at my house with the needles, filling Mam and myself in on the terrible accident that happened at the shoe factory that afternoon. She's asking me do I know a chap by the name of Mick McCarthy, telling me what he looks like, where he lives and when I realise who she's talking about, she says the machine he was working with cut his left hand completely off at the wrist, and three fingers of the right hand leaving him with only a stump on one hand, and a small finger and a thumb on the other. She said the whole factory came to a standstill, and all watched as Michael was being brought out to the ambulance with a white coat, drenched in blood wrapped around his hands and two of the factory workers following him behind with the hand and three fingers in an empty shoe box, and I'm telling Mary that Michael is a great junior soccer player and used to play with me at Dominic Saviour's Boys Club.

It's coming up to my nineteenth birthday and I'm almost twelve months going out with Mary. It's still the Jetland every Saturday night and the Savoy on Sunday. Jetta's second baby Rory is nearly three months old and if Jetta isn't above in Catherine Street with Olwyen, she's down in Garryowen where Mam can indulge herself with her first granddaughter, and three month old grandson. Nan isn't in Garryowen as much due to old age and bad health and has never met Mary. The Mondays and Wednesday nights are still a regular with the two of them. The work is hit and miss, and Pop asks me would I like to come back working with Lar and himself. He says that they were talking about getting another pair of hands, and Pop told Lar that nobody else was coming on board while his son was at home working two weeks out of every month, so they agreed that if I came back they would double my wage to eight pounds a week and that no one need apologise, that we could all just carry on as if nothing happened. So the following morning, I'm only with them two hours and realise how much I missed the constant laughing and how good it is to be back again with a regular wage. Pop is back from McMahons with one gallon of paint in each hand. He lays the paint on the floor and falls to his knees with the shoulders moving up and down and no sound, then holding his stomach and when he is able to tell us, he says he was walking back from McMahons and felt a ball of wind building up in his gut so he turned around to see if there was anybody behind before he left fly, and five foot behind him was the wife of one of their best customers. He said, 'good morning', crossed the road and when he got to the other side lifted his leg and exploded, looked around again to see if anybody else might have been behind him, and didn't the lady cross the road after him, and there she was with a big grin on her face, and Lar says aren't you an awful fupping eejit Harry. Then says, 'wait til I tell you what happened to m Last Friday, I came home from the Bedford and after drinking six fupping pints of porter on an empty stomach, walked up Thomas Street instead of fupping William Street, and a little fupper of a dog followed me barking his head off and by the time I got to the top of Thomas Street, I couldn't take anymore so I gave him a kick in the bollocks and the fupper bit me, so I lost the rag, grabbed him by the fupping throat and strangled the little fupper until he was well and truly fupping dead, and fupped him over the railing into one of the basements. I called into Mrs. Fitzpatrick in Thomas Street to do a tommer on Saturday morning and the poor woman was crying her eyes out, I asked her what was wrong. She said her dog was dead, that she found it in a cardboard box in the basement and wasn't it the same fupping dog I strangled the night before. Jesus, Harry between your farting into our customer's faces and me strangling their dogs we won't have a fupping job to go to'.

After three or four weeks back with Pop and Lar, more tommers are starting to come my way, most of them painting and decorating, so Saturdays are days to make money now, and that means no more 'is my arse too big for this, and tell me the truth' and if I get enough work over the spring and summer months I might be able to buy a car. So it's out to Pat Cooney over by Athlunkard Street to see what he might have. I'd love a mini but he won't take the money over a four or five month period. Elm Motors at the back of Stokes and McKiernan down by the Docks won't do it either. In fact, Tony O'Mara Motors, in Mulgrave Street, is the only one in the whole of Limerick that is prepared to take the money in fivers and tenners. He has a lovely red mini, the kind that has the starter button on the floor and I'm thinking of how great I'll look in it when I'm taking Mary out at the weekends, but he won't sell it because he says it's only fit for the scrap heap. He has other red minis but they're two and three hundred pounds, and I'd be working for two years to earn that much, but I'll pester him and he keeps saying no. I'll try other places in town and won't have any success. I'll be back again asking him to sell it to me. He'll keep saying no until eventually he gives in and says he'll take eighty pound for it and that I'm not to come back to him if anything is wrong with it. So I give him a tenner that I have in my pocket as a deposit. I can't stop looking at it, and sitting in it, and thinking about the time I'll take it home and touch it up with a bit of paint and polish the outside and put a nice bit of clean carpet into it and have it smelling nice and Paddy Taylor will be the only house in Claughaun Court with a car.

I have two shops up by the railway station to paint. I'll get fifteen pounds for the two. Five will buy the paint and all I'll need is sixty pounds to buy the red mini that has the registration FZA 166. But it's not going to be that easy as these two houses are three storeys high and I hate heights. I can just about manage being on a ladder when it's only two storeys high and I know I'll be bricking it when I start on Saturday. I have the ladder that Pop and Lar gave me hooked on to the handlebar and saddle of my bike with a bag of scrappers, sand paper, brushes and paint that I'll need for the preparation work. The first house has a newsagent shop on the ground floor with a constant flow of bodies in and out all the time. It's bad enough that I'll be rattling away above on the ladder but if I drop something and give someone a clout, I'll be in big trouble and I can say goodbye to the reg. number FZA 166. Any good painter worth his salt will start at the top of a building and work his way down. Not me. I'm going to work my way up so I can get acclimatised to the height and after five minutes, climb another step, otherwise I'll freeze at the top. That's if I get up there at all. It works and by twelve o'clock I'm down at McMahons for paint, having left the ladder against the wall and hope that no one will walk under it because of the seven years bad luck they think they'll get, and hoping as well that the ladder will still be there when I get back, because I'll need to get an undercoat on the entire front today, and if I do I'll only need the half of tomorrow, Sunday, to give it the second coat of gloss, and I can sit in the Savoy cinema on Sunday night with Mary,with the ten pound for Tony O'Meara in my pocket. The lady in the newsagent shop that asked me to paint her house says there's more people in the area that want some painting done, and has me earning another tenner by the following weekend, and all I need now is fifty pounds. I'll pass out O'Mara's everyday on my way back to work and walk around to have a look at my lovely mini that has dust, cobwebs and bird shit all over it but I don't mind. It'll be easy clean.

After another weekend I've another tenner and Mary says she misses me on the Saturday afternoons because she can't make up her mind when she's looking at clothes, and I'm thinking to myself that's news to me. Sure how the hell was I helping her to make up her mind. When I kept telling her to buy a dress or anything else and then watch her walk out of the shop and say she'd think about it. Work has dried up and I still owe Tony O'Mara forty pounds, and at the moment I haven't a clue where I'm going to get it. Pop and Lar have no overtime either so it's going to have to be two pound a week to Tony for the red mini until the next bit of work comes along, and when I call to give him the two pound, I'm looking for my mini and can't find it anywhere amongst the hundreds or so he has in his yard or parked on both sides of Mulgrave Street. I'm in an awful panic asking him where is my lovely red mini. He says 'it's down in his brother Pat's house at the bottom of St. Patrick's Road and out of the way,' I'm on my way down Garryowen after work at six o'clock on my bike, turning left at the bottom of the hill asking a neighbour where I might find Pat O'Mara's house. When he points it out to me the driveway is full of cars and so is the back yard. After five minutes of looking at the fifty that's there, there's my lovely red mini stuck in the corner and when I make my way over to it it's full of chickens. My heart sinks with the disappointment because my lovely red mini looks ready for the scrap heap and I'm thinking no amount of cleaning or scrubbing or even polishing will help this car look any different. I had to struggle to get enough room to open one of the doors and hunt the chickens out of it, and all the straw that's been put in it. I manage to close the two windows that got the chickens in there and hoped they wouldn't be back when I call again.

Mam has to go to Dublin for a small operation. It's the kind of operation she won't talk about so Jetta fills me in with information that Mam's womb needs support and Dublin is the only place it can be done. She won't have to stay there as it'll only take an hour. Mam says she's going to Clerys to buy some curtains for the downstairs windows while she's up there. Pop is going with her, and it's one of the few times I've ever seen them go anywhere together. I'm over at Mary's telling her about the ring Mam has to have fitted because Jetta says her womb is dropping,and that it's causing Mam a lot of discomfort and how the ring will give her womb the support it needs and stop the pain. I'm also telling Mary that I could have had another two siblings because Mam had two miscarriages, and ever since Harry was born Mam has had nothing but trouble with it since.

When Mam comes back from Dublin there seems to be new life in her face. It must be because the pain is gone. She's all excited about the curtains she brought back from Clerys. She has them out with Pop holding them against the wall over by the window. She's asking James, Mary and myself what we think of them. James says they're all right. Mary says they're gorgeous and I'm saying they're bloody awful and asking, 'are you really going to put them up on the wall'. She laughs because she thinks I'm joking but I'm dead serious, but I won't ruin the moment for her, and I've just realised how ill she has been because I haven't seen her so happy in a good few weeks. Sometimes Mary and myself will talk about the people we went out with before we met. She'll talk about the guy with the wet lips and bad breath when he asked her at the cinema would she like anything at the shop and how she asked for a bottle of fanta, a packet of crisps, a tub of ice cream, some toffee sweets and made the whole lot last until the film was over and not turn up for the next date. I'll tell her about her friend, Patsy O'Meara and myself and the time we had a great shift for about an hour down by the concrete wall by the canal and got a pain in the back of my neck because she's so small and Mary can't believe I went out with Patsy O'Meara from the Court on the other side of Garryowen and says she'll mention it to her tomorrow at work. Then she tells me about the fellow with the sweaty hands and the awful smell of body odour. How she thought he was nice until he asked her to dance and there they were, the two of them, dancing the slow dance and Mary thinking she was going to throw up. I'll tell her about the time I was dancing at the Hop in St. Patrick's Scout Hall and wearing a pair of shoes that were too sizes too big and didn't a girl put the heel of her shoe into the space between the heel of my shoe and my ankle and when I moved my leg doing the jive, I putt the girl flying all over the floor and the poor girl hadn't a bloody clue how it happened.

Mary says she is going to bake a rhubarb tart tomorrow night and that I'm to be sure to call over for a slice and asks me do I like rhubarb tart. I'm telling her as long as it's not like Mam's, all pastry with the odd lump of rhubarb or apple, and a slice is about as much as I can handle. I'll tell her about Christmas time in our house, how Mam will gather the ingredients for the Christmas cake a month before the twenty fifth, and will be shouting at whoever puts a key in the front door, back door, or any door, to close it gently, otherwise the cake will collapse in the middle while it's in the oven for the bones of three hours. She'll have whiskey or brandy in it, cherries and fruit that's like lumps of rock, that I have to spit out because there's no chewing in them, it will be as black as porter and will be left there for months after December because no one will eat it and Mary can't believe it, and says, 'sure your mother is a lovely baker'. She is I'm saying, 'but only with the spotted dick'. When the following evening comes I'm telling Mam about the rhubarb tart that I'm going over to eat it at Mary's house, that it's Mary's first time and that if I'm not in bed by one o'clock in the morning would she ring the guards because I might be poisoned. She'll laugh and say I'm not to be giving Mary a hard time but when an opportunity comes to tease Mary its difficult to let it go, so when I walk into No. 12 Cloughane Court, the smell is good and the entire O'Connell family is waiting for the tart in the oven to finish cooking and when it does, Mary takes it out with her father's good gloves that he'd uses in the winter time on his bike. Everybody says how good it looks, that it has a lovely rich light brown look about it and has the appropriate uneven lumps all round. Mrs. O' has the kettle on the boil and everyone has a plate with a fork ready for they're portion. Mary puts the bread knife into the middle of the tart and the whole thing sinks like air going out of a balloon, and everybody goes 'ahh'. Mary folds back some of the pastry and there swimming around in juice is several hard lumps of rhubarb. I think Mary is going to start crying and I'm saying can't you put the rhubarb into a pot and soften it up and give us all a slice of pastry with some juice and when the rhubarb is nice and soft so we can eat it.

Mary is over in our house the following night telling Mam about the rhubarb tart being a total disaster and asking Mam what she did wrong. I don't know what she's asking Mam for. With the stuff Mam does she'd be no help to her at all. It's three weeks now since I got a tommer and Pop comes to my rescue when he says Mr. Ferris is looking for me to do a bit of plumbing. I'm asking Pop and Lar for half an hour off work so I can go to see Mr. Ferris. Mr. Ferris says that ever since he opened the men's hairdressing salon he has a water shortage in the ladies. He says the Limerick Corporation has given him a two inch water supply down in the basement, but won't bring it up through the building to the roof to feed the four large storage tanks and that's where I come in. He wants me to bring a two inch black hydra plastic pipe from the basement up through all the floors to the attic to feed the storage tanks.

I don't even have to give Mr. Ferris a price. He says he'll give me fifteen pounds if I get the job done in three nights provided I don't run into any trouble. On the third night it's time to turn the water on. My heart is in my mouth as I turn the valve in the basement to give the tanks in the attic the extra water they need that will keep Mr. Ferris happy, and put fifteen pounds in my pocket. I'm rattling. And terrified as well and my heart is beating at an awful rate. What will I do if there is a leak? The place will be flooded in no time at all with the pressure from a two inch water pipe. I have fingers, legs and arms crossed as I hear the water making its way up through all the building and to my amazement there's not a single drop of water to be seen anywhere and it's another fifteen pounds for Tony O'Meara and only nineteen to go before I can take the red mini from the yard at Patrick's Road. It's Sunday night at the Savoy I'm asking Mary what would she like at the shop. It's the usual crisps, ice cream and orange but during the break Paddy is hungry, and is on his way down to the Savoia chipper for a large bag of chips. I have just about enough time to make it back for the main picture. I'm handing Mary her crisps and ice cream in the dark making sure she can't see the bag of chips. I put them under the seat and then she says 'oh there's a gorgeous smell of chips coming from somewhere, I'd love some' and then I produce the bag. She's giving out stink saying 'everyone in the place will be looking at us' and says she was wondering why I was so long at the shop. She's doing the giving out while she has both hands in the chips putting one into her mouth at a time and telling me I'm not to do it again, but I'll keep doing it every Sunday night when she'll tell me at the break with her finger under my nose not to go anywhere near the Savoia chip shop and devour most of the bag when I come back and still giving out to me all the time with a chip in her mouth.

It's three weeks now since I gave Tony O'Meara the fifteen pounds I got from Mr. Ferris. I haven't gone near him at all with the two pound a week because the only good pants I have that I wear every time I go out with Mary has a shine in the arse of it, and I have to give George Russell in bedford row the two pound every week for the suit that's costing fifteen, and still no sign of any work coming up in the near future until I call into the other Savoia café on Roches Street looking for a bag of chips during the week in my white overalls and the owner asks if I would paint the front of his premises. I'm outside looking up at the three storey house that is just like the others across the road from the railway station, and here we go again with another bloody job that I'll be rattling on the ladder because of the height. I'll be on top of it again trying not to look down in case I fall off and break my neck. I won't even have a concrete block at the bottom of the ladder in case it kicks or maybe somebody won't be watching where they're going and walk into it while I'm on top of it, and if Mam knew I was taking such risks there would be hell to pay. I'm telling the owner I'll need twenty five pounds but he says he'll only pay fifteen. I'll try to get more out of him but it's no use. He won't budge. I have to take it or Tony O'Mara might sell or scrap my lovely mini that's full of all kinds of animal shite in it and on it, down below in his brother's back yard on Patrick's Road.

I'm outside the chip shop in Roches Street on Saturday doing the usual, starting at the bottom and working my way up the ladder listening to the juke box in the café, blasting out Procol Harlem's great hit *A Whiter Shade of Pale* and others, all day. I won't have this job done until next Saturday and that will be another tenner for Tony O'Mara and another two Saturdays away from Mary, whose still worrying about how big her arse is in everything. Mary's friends Patsy and Margaret have boyfriends. Patsy is going out with Joe Buckley from Joseph Street. Joe's father was the man who shouted your name down at the dispensary and pounded the bottle on the shelf of the hatch, and gave you your free bottle, tablets, or cream. Margaret is going out with Gerry McMahon from Killely whose father works in the fire brigade. Sometimes the lot of us might go to the Jetland together, a birthday party, a trip to Galway or somewhere else. I'll tease Patsy about the pain in my neck I got from the one night stand, and the pain in my back that never went away from the rock I had to lift and bring to the wall for her to stand on. Margaret O'Brien is a sister of Tom who I sat next to in Christian Brothers School. The fellow whose left leg and hand went up and down together, whose mouth opened as wide as he could get it when Chuckser would administer the leather. It's coming up to Mary's seventeenth birthday. Tony O'Mara is still owed nine pound but the next few bob I'll earn has to go towards a good present for Mary. I've only three weeks before the seventeenth of June comes and no sign of any work coming. I hope I won't have to borrow off Mam or Pop. A few days later word comes to the Bedford that Sadlier's Fish Shop, and only two hundred yards down from the Savoy café in Roches Street, want the front of their shop painted because of the good job I did up the road. It's only worth eight pounds because the shop front is mostly glass and only takes a few nights to complete because I can't do it during the day. There's a small sweet shop next door and they want theirs done too once I've started the fish shop. I'm going to make ten pounds out of two jobs, enough to buy Mary a good present in two weeks time. Her birthday is on a Sunday which is great because we can make the birthday last the whole weekend. I'm only a couple of doors down from Eve's Smartwear on the weekend before Mary's birthday in Roches Street. I'm in the shop at twelve o'clock between coats of paint. I'm in my white overalls browsing around the ground floor. It's causing a bit of interest from the assistants and other customers. After fifteen minutes I'm putting two pounds on a dress and asking her to hold it until lunch time on Monday when I'll be able to pay the other two pounds. Now I'm down in Leavys Shoes at the corner of O'Connell Street and Shannon Street looking for a pair of shoes to match. I'm only there five minutes when I see what I like and leave a pound deposit and telling them, I'll be back Monday lunch time with the other pound. Now it's up to Little Catherine Street, there's a new jewellery shop there and I might get a good deal on a bit of jewellery. When I walk into the shop there's a tall man with a moustache and when he says good morning he's got an English accent. I'm telling him I'm looking for a present for my girlfriend, that I want something unusual

259

so he shows me a few trays of bracelets, rings and necklaces.
I'm not convinced so he shows me a new range of jewellery
only he says it's not gold and when he puts the tray down that's
it!, I'm saying, 'that's exactly what I'm looking for. Something
that I haven't seen before'. It's a lovely metal celtic chain with
a black metal medallion. There's a bracelet to match. I'm asking him how much. I'm also telling him if it's more than four
pounds I'll have to look for something else. He looks at the
price on both items, has a think about it, and says, 'go on then,
if you marry the girl you might come back to me for the engagement and wedding rings too'. So he wraps the two in lovely presentation boxes, then asks me would I give him a price to
paint the front of the shop and if the price is right I can start
whenever I like. I'll be wearing the white overalls more often
after this, but I have to tell him I can only give him a pound
until Monday lunch time, so we agree a price of ten pounds for
painting the front of the shop and things are looking good
again. I'm glad I've been able to buy the presents before two
o'clock because Mary will be in town doing her pilgrimage
around all the shops, and if I left it until afternoon and met her
in a shop, she'll be wanting to know what I'm doing there. So
roll on next weekend. When Monday evening comes I'm tearing home on the bike with the dres and shoes nicely wrapped.
I put them away under my bed til Wednesday night, and give
them to Mary just in case they need to be changed in time for
the weekend. It's hard waiting for Wednesday night and when
it comes Mary and Mam are doing their usual talking about
everything and nothing with the good delve out on the table. I
think the willow pattern is wearing away on the cups and saucers and everything else since Mary O'Connell started calling
every Monday and Wednesday nights for nearly a year now.
I'll come down the stairs with only the dress and shoes. I'll
leave the jewellery til Saturday night before the Jetland. I'll put
the two parcels on the table with the names Eve's Smartwear
and Leavys Shoes on the covers, and Mam wants to know
what's in the parcels and who are they for. 'Did you know that
Saturday is Mary's birthday Mam'. Mam looks surprised and

says, 'no'. 'Have you any idea what it's like going to town with a girl looking for something to wear' and Mam says, 'I'm to leave the girl alone, sure isn't she working hard enough and entitled to take as long as she likes until she's happy with what she buys'. 'But that's the point Mam. She's never happy even after she pays for it. So I bought her something to wear for Saturday night so it will save me having to put up with another four hours of wearing away the leather on the only good pair of shoes I have'. Mary looks shocked as I put the parcel in her hand, and when she takes out the dress she stands up, puts it under her chin like she always does every bloody Saturday. Mam says, 'oh that's gorgeous', and off goes Mary, 'really Mrs. Taylor, do you like it' and I'm telling Mam, 'Jesus Mam don't answer her because she won't believe you no matter what you say, or how many times you say it, and any minute now she'll ask you is her arse big in it' and Mam says, 'didn't I tell you to leave the girl alone, have you nothing to do'. I say, 'no'. 'Well get out and look for something so the two of us can decide whether we're going to keep these, things or tell you to bring them back and change them'. And there I am sitting on the wall of our garden again on my own smoking a fag and waiting for Pop to come, home and after two hours of smoking every fag I had, there's Pop getting off the bus after bingo. I'll follow him in the hall, and when I get into the room I'm dying to find out if I'll have to spend another four hours traipsing around the town next Saturday afternoon before we go out to the Jetland. Mam says, 'Mary loves the dress and the shoes, that they're a great fit' and there's Mary sitting on the chair with the knitting needles by the fire that never gets lit in the summer time except when someone wants a bath and is the only means of getting hot water. Mam takes the dress and shoes off Mary's lap, gives Pop a dig and says, 'look what your son got his girlfriend for her birthday next Sunday. There's no fear you'd go down town and buy me something like that'. Pop looks at me and asks, 'did you walk into a lady's dress shop on your own and buy a dress'. 'I did' I answer. Pop looks up to heaven, puts the sign of the cross on his forehead and says, 'Jesus, Mary and Holy

Saint Joseph what have I reared at all only an old Molly. I hope you didn't tell them your name'. I'm telling him that Johnny Canlon who works down at McMahons in the paint department, the fellow we buy paint from nearly every day, was standing outside Dunnes Stores on Saturday morning like he was waiting for someone and when he saw me, called me over and said, himself and the wife were hoping to go out that night, that she wasn't well at the moment, but if she felt better by seven o'clock she'd chance it, but that she needed a pair of nylons and that he was too shy to go in and ask, so he asked me, 'and what did you say' asked Pop. 'I went in and got them for him'. Pop looks up to heaven again, puts the sign of the cross on his forehead and says, 'Mother of Jesus,' I have reared an old Molly'. Mam is laughing and says, 'don't mind him Pa'. Mary is dumbfounded too 'and what did you say to the girl' asks Pop. I picked a pair of nylons off the counter, held them high in the air and said to the girl, 'could I have a pair of gipsy dreams and if you haven't got those, would you have a pair of French coffee'? Mary laughs and says, 'there the ones I buy. How did you know the names'? 'Johnny told me' and every time I'll go to Johnny at McMahon's, I'll ask him for a pair of gipsy dreams or French coffee and after another few weeks, I'll bet Johnny will wish to God he never asked me and say a I've a bloody holy show made of him.

We're our way over to Mary's house, she's telling me she'll kill me for going to so much expense, she keeps kissing and thanking me and when we arrive at No. 12 she's showing all the family the dress and shoes and the three women are all going, 'oh God, that's beautiful' and Mary is off with 'is it really, tell me the truth' and Mr. O'Connell is whistling away and diddly idle doing while all the women are fussing away and before I go home Mary wants to know will I come down town on Saturday evening because she won't be able to wear the new dress and shoes unless she has a handbag to match. I'm telling her I will, if she'll only go to two shops. She crosses her heart and promises she'll only go to three so I agree. What a gobshite.

It's Saturday at five o'clock. We've been to ten shops and there's still no sign of a bag being bought, and when five forty five,' arrives it's the usual rushing back to the first or second shop and making the purchase. We'll go home and while I'm having my tea, Mary is over home putting on all the paint before the dress goes on, then it's the shoes. She has the hair up and when I call over she knocks me over she's looking so good. She's saying goodbye to the family and before we go out the door I'm handing her the two small boxes with the ribbons in a bow, and saying to her'that's your real birthday present' I'm asking her to open the larger box first, and when she does her eyes that's already big and beautiful are bigger now with surprise and delight, she's saying 'you shouldn't have done this they're very unusual', and 'I've never seen anything like them before.' Then asks me to put it on then she has a look in the mirror to see how it looks and gives me a huge kiss, opens the other box and it's the same reaction, kissing me again but instead of giving out she is back in the kitchen showing the family, and off they go again, about how beautiful they are and how good and generous Paddy Taylor is, and Mr. O'Connell if off doing the diddley idle do again and the whistling because he doesn't want to be around when women are together nattering away about babies, flowers, clothes, jewellery and other feminine things, and if there's a film on the telly that has Auddie Murphy, John Wayne or Robert Mitchem in it. He'll be glued to it until one of them has his mouth around a woman's face. He'll come out of the trance his being in for ages, and start giving out saying, 'Jesus, Mary and Holy St. Joesph bloody women, they ruin a great film'. He'll get up and walk around looking out the window give a glance at the black and white T.V. and if they are still at it with the kissing he'll go out the front door whistling away saying 'isn't it a grand or miserable day depending on the weather', until he is back in again to the room where he'll get more agitated if they are still at the kissing.

Mary on the night I gave her the dress, necklace and bracelet

I'll look at this man and wonder how he ever managed to do the business under the sheets. I'm telling Mary we better go or we'll miss the bus. She says she has promised my mother she'll call in and let her see the dress, shoes and the new hairdo. And I know we'll be walking into town because there's no way the two of them when they get talking will be able to keep it to five minutes. And there's Mary turning left, right, and inside out for Mam so she can see every possible angle with the hairdo and the dress, and if I wasn't there sure she'd be showing Mam her new knickers and bra as well. Now Mary is showing Mam the jewellery and its 'oh that's beautiful, and oh my goodness, and more gasps and oh's', Pop is there too and not saying much because he is trying to listen to the news on the T.V. Mam has the sound turned down the minute we walked in the door. She gives Pop a thump on the shoulder saying 'do you hear me talking to you', 'What?' shouts Pop. 'Isn't Mary looking gorgeous tonight?' he looks at Mary, starting with the shoes first and then slowly taking his eyes up the legs taking in everything until he gets to the top. We all know he is not going to make a serious comment, like 'Mary O'Connell you're looking absolutely gorgeous tonight and I wish I was the one going out with you', but that wouldn't be Pop and out it comes, 'What time of the year is it?' his taking me completely by surprise I wasn't expecting a question. Mam asks him 'what do you want to know what time of the year it is?' well he says, 'Its June isn't it?', 'yes' says Mam. 'Oh thanks bit o God, Jesus for a minute there I thought it was Christmas and I was looking at a Christmas tree', were all laughing and Pop looks at Mary and gives her a wink of approval. Then there's another thump from Mam as she says, 'Is it too much trouble for you to say to the girl that she's looking lovely', But Pop wont stop there, he asks Mam 'Where did you put those Christmas decorations?, we can give Mary two of the crystal balls to hang out of her ears', and off go the shoulders up and down as we head out the door with Mam following us and laughing at the same time.

We'll walk down to catch a bus in Mulgrave Street that will take us to the Jetland and Mary will talk all the time about Pop and Mam and how she loves to go over to my house because there is so much laughter all the time. How Mam has become a second mother to her that she can talk to her about things that she couldn't talk to her own mother about. How Pop will look at her in the eye when he is talking, give her the odd wink and a hug and that's something her own father can't do, and it's hard for me to understand. I mean in our house we talk direct to one another, or even if we find a subject difficult, we joke about it. But as time goes on I'll understand more the huge difference between Mary's family and my own.

The good ole days at the Jetland

The good ole days at the Jetland

We're dancing the night away outside at the Jetland with Patsy and Joe, Margaret and Jerry who have come to celebrate Mary's seventeenth birthday and if Mary doesn't take it easy her hair that's ten inches above her head, that she spent the bones of thirty bob on is going to collapse and if that happens the bloody night will be ruined. We spend the last hour in the Savoia Café the six of us before we all head home. It has been a great success and Mary is purring away with appreciation. But there is a bomb shell coming my way tomorrow night and I never saw it coming. Mam wants to know how we got on the following morning at breakfast and I'm telling her every detail and Pop says will I ask Mary if she'd mind standing in the corner of the room when December comes, Mam tells him to shut up while she listens and looks for more information about the night before. Mary and myself are off to mass but Mam calls her in, and says 'would you come back for dinner'?, and when we do, Pop is inside the small room that has the hatch from the kitchen to take the mug of tea he'll get every half hour to keep his throat from going dry as he tries his best to sing along with Jose Boring for the next four hours.

I'm telling Mam, Mary has a terrible headache from the three story hairdo she had on her head most of yesterday and last night, and straight away Mam goes for Mrs. Cullens Powder that she hardly uses any more because Pop is still off the drink so long now. And after ten minutes Mary's head is back to normal and now all the talk is around headaches, how long they last, what they're like, and I think I want to be over in the green with the lads, thumping a ball around the place because when they finished talking about headaches they will be talking about other aches and pains and between Pop roaring his head off in the other room and Mam and Mary going on about another knitting pattern one of them got down town. Six o'clock will be here in no time at all and Mam will have the spotted dick out for the tea. Pop will be snoring his head off from exhaustion and we'll be on our way down to the Savoy after Mary has six slices of the spotted dick inside her. And at the interval find room for half a bag of chips while giving out to me at the same time for getting them. We'll walk up William Street and get to Tanyard Lane, when Mary drops the bombshell she says she has something to tell me, I am all ears, she says she wants to call it off. I am standing in the middle of the road in shock, then I smile and say 'your joking', ' no I'm not', she says, 'I have being thinking about it for awhile', and here I am, having feelings I have never had before, I'm panicking I never saw this coming. There was nothing to suggest this was on the way. Mary's mood has been the same over the last few days. I am getting very emotional. I put so much into this weekend I don't know whether I'm hurt or the awful dread I have that I might be losing the only girl I ever felt this way about before. So I burst into an explosion, a flood of tears I'm in a terrible state I can't believe this is happening to me. I've got my hands over my face trying to hide what I can't control, my emotions, and the visible evidence of tears flowing down my face like a burst pipe has Mary trying to pull my hands away. She's saying she's 'sorry', that she didn't mean it, that she's being a bit confused over the last few days, that it will be alright and I 'm thinking she's feeling sorry for me. And if she is I'll take it because I don't know what I'll do without her, so we'll walk while she'll try and explain what's going on in her mind, how confused she is. I'm telling her I don't want to be a dress or a pair of shoes that she can't make up her mind about. Now we have to go into Mam for the cup of tea and more spotted dick that I won't be able to eat at all. I wish we didn't have to because I need more assurance, and the hour I spent in my own house with my own mother is unbearable until I get away over to the outside of number twelve so Mary can convince me more, that everything is going to be o.k. and by one o'clock that morning I'm feeling more reassured and happy that Mary has done a good job telling me she never realised how much I felt about her. And I had to ask her was she stupid and not realise how much I enjoyed her company how I loved the way herself and Mam got on, how much Mam looks forward to Monday and Wednesday nights, Sunday nights too,and that she will be devastated if we weren't an item anymore. When the following weekend comes I'm down at J. W. Harrison jewellers on a ladder painting the front, and after Monday and Tuesday night I have a tener in my pocket for Tony O'Mara and another painting job across the road at the coffee shop. I have only another fifteen pounds to give Tony O'Mara and the lovely red mini FZA 166 that Tony never wanted to sell me, and warned me that it mightn't last, will be mine to have outside 36 Claughan Court, when I can clean all the chicken shite, straw and dust from it, and give it a good polishing on the outside. After the next weekend I have the coffee shop finished and after burrowing a fiver from Mam I'm up at Tony O'Mara with the last payment, he says he'll have the car ready for the Saturday coming and its hard to sleep thinking and dreaming about the days of walking will be gone soon, and when the winter nights come Mary and myself wont be frozen to death outside her front door, shifting the night away. Or I won't be giving out to her for putting our clasped hands into one of the pockets in my overcoat and making it ten times bigger than the other one. I'll ask her to go for a walk on Friday night and talk about nothing only the bloody car I'm collecting tomorrow. We'll take the usual route down through the middle of Garryowen and on over to Rhebouge to the canal, and we're only five minutes away from Mary's house and the fruits of my five months hard work every night is being towed up from Patrick's road.

I'm all excited when I see it and start shouting at Mary,' there it is, that's it, my lovely red mini', and as it drives past the two of us, the bloody boot door falls off right in front of the two of us. I'm running after the mini trying to get the attention of the driver in the car in front that's towing it, but its no use he's gone and there's the boot lying on the road and I don't know were to put my face, I am so embarrassed. I am trying to think of something to say to Mary, I've told her so much about this thing, she must have thought it was brand new.

We have to wait for the car to come back, surely they'll realise when they get to Mulgrave Street with my lovely red mini that it has no door in the boot and they will come looking for it. Mary is saying ' sure it will only be a matter of a couple of screws and that the boot door will be o.k' we're here thirty minutes waiting and there's a car coming, its the one that was towing my lovely red mini, I am waving at him and pointing at the boot door on the ground and when he stops he thinks I am a passer by, but when I tell him the car is mine his assuring me that the car will be fine once a mechanic gets his hands on it.

I am telling Mary that I didn't want her eyes to see it until it had being cleaned and ready to go, and no chicken shite on it either, because I never told her about the state of it. Mary says, 'she thought she saw a chicken behind the passenger seat' when it passed us on the way up the road and it starts the two of us into fits of laughter. I'm trying to tell her in between the laughing that the yard where the car was parked for the last five months is full of chickens and cats. She won't believe me, so when we pass Pat O'Mara's house near the end of Patrick's road, I'm taking her into the back yard that's full of cars with half of them full of chickens and Mary can't believe it. She wants to know when I will be able to use the mini and I'm telling her I can't until I have the money for the tax and insurance. That it will cost me twenty pounds in total and that I will have to get a licence too.

After I have worn Mary and myself out talking about the bloody car and where we can go with it. I'm talking to Mam and Pop about it too, Mam hands me a bottle of Lourdes water and says she wont have a minutes peace when myself and Mary are in it, and that I'm to be sure and spread plenty of it all over the car inside and out. I am asking her what good will that do 'you'll be safer', she says, 'with that in the car',

'Why Mam?.'

'It will protect you'.

'From what?.'

'A crash'.

And I'm saying 'Mam are you seriously saying that any car with a bottle of Lourdes water in side it, is not going to crash or that another car that doesn't have any would be less safer'.

'yes' she says.

I'm saying 'sure the Lourdes water can't be that good', and she says, 'will you put it into the car anyway'.

The following morning I have to wait until twelve o'clock before O'Mara's arrive with my lovely red mini and I have the rest of the day to clean it. I have buckets, cloths, brillo pads, smelly sackets and I am tearing into it. James has offered to give me a hand and when Mary comes over to go to town to do her usual pilgrimage, my lovely red mini is sparkling inside and outside. Mam, Pop, and Harry are outside on the road, having a look and some of the neighbours are over for a gawk as well, all commenting on how good it looks. And when Mary heads off into town Mam gives me a fiver and says I'm not to even think about giving it back, that it's for my birthday that's only two weeks away. When Pop sees her giving me the fiver and why, he does the same and now I have ten pounds towards the twenty I need for tax and insurance. I'm glad they didn't say anything about my birthday in front of Mary I don't want her going to expense because she has so little, after giving her mother half of what she earns every week. All I can do now is drive the mini a few feet forward then put it into reverse, with James longside me pestering me for a go and I am telling him to shut up that he is too young. He says he is sorry he washed the outside of the car and tells me what to do with it as he exits it and slams the door in anger.

I'll have the cup of tea after the dinner in it every day, and after the supper too the evening. I'll polish it again until it's dazzling. And wonder when the next job will come along and give me the tener I need to get it on the road. And when July the 22nd comes I still haven't the tax and insurance money. I really thought it would be on the road for my birthday. I told Mam, Pop, Jetta, James and Harry not to mention a word to Mary about my birthday. I want it to come, and go, like an ordinary day. It falls on a Friday so when Mary and I are on the bus out to the Jetland on Saturday night, Mary hands me a small box and says 'Happy Birthday', I am stuck to the seat and ask 'how did you know?' 'I asked your mother but I told her not to tell you',

'She told me you told her not to tell me but I had already asked her before that, are you going to open your present at all'?, it's a smashing gold square watch with a black face and gold numbers, I'm speechless. I am saying 'that's the watch I admired every week in John Harrison's jewellery shop', when we used to stop in front of his window every Sunday night on the way home from the Savoy. Mary says she has being putting two bob a week on it for the last five or six weeks and that she gave John Harrison the last pound this morning. I am asking her is she broke, she smiles and says, 'no' 'show me your purse',

'I won't' she answers smiling.

'Go on show it to me',

'No' she says.

'I'm letting no man look into my purse',

I know she's broke and I know she wont have being down town today on the pilgrimage looking for clothes or shoes or even putting more money on something she has put away. I'll give her a big long juicy kiss, she is trying to push me away because we're in the bus, it's full. I'll leave her go then pull her back, she's going 'will you stop every one is looking', I'm standing up in the bus looking around and telling everyone that my girlfriend is after giving me a lovely watch for my birthday.

She's telling me to sit down and shut up and says it's the last time she'll ever me you anything. She has a grin on her face but I need to let her know how pleased I am with my gold wrist watch.

I'm saying every few minutes, 'Janey, look at the time' now she is laying down the law about the new watch. 'I don't want to see any paint splatters or scratches on that, your to wear it only at the weekends, do you hear me?', I'm telling her she is spending too much time with my mother because she's beginning to sound just like her. She laughs and says 'I'm serious, your to keep the other watch for work' and I'm saying 'o.k. Mam, what ever you say Mam'. I'll keep drawing attention to the watch all night, and I'm telling Mary the time every few minutes. And when we're on the bus going home Mary says it was the longest night of her life, because the time went so slow. But had a great time none the less. Sunday night after the Savoy, Mary is reminding me not to wear the watch on Monday or any day that week. That if I do she'll brain me.

CHAPTER 12

One of the neighbours in Garryowen wants their house painted there's ten pounds in it, it will take a full weekend and when it's finished I'll have enough to get my lovely red mini on the road. Mary and myself are asking Jerry and Margaret to come to Killaloe on the Sunday afternoon, and I feel like a millionaire. What a feeling to own and drive your own car all earned with my own money. We'll stay in Killaloe on a lovely August Sunday afternoon and drive home, Mary says there's steam coming out of the bonnet on her side of the car and when I stop and get out, lift the bonnet,the radiator has steam flying out it and I haven't a bloody clue what to do, except walk down the road and look for a house that has a phone. And when I find one I'm asking my cousin Tom who lives with his mother Aunt Kathleen with the blue hair in Thomas Street, if he could come out and give us a tow back home. We have to wait a half an hour before he arrives in a grey mini that's much newer and better looking then mine. His working for Shiels garage outside in the Ennis Road, as a panel beater for the last year and half ever since he left Pop and Lar. And here I am again red faced from embarrassment. My lovely red mini has a rope on it again. I'm be back at Tony O'Mara's, in Mulgrave Street, on Monday morning telling him what happened and his telling me that he warned me about the car but I wouldn't t listen. And I'm asking him could he have a look at it and tell me what's wrong. He says the radiator will have to come out and if I bring it to a crowd called Abby Radiators they'll fix it for me for a fiver, but I have to take it out myself because I can't afford to pay someone else. When I bring it down to Abby Radiators off Catherine Street, their telling me its going to cost a fiver just like Tony O'Mara said it would. I'll have to find a fiver to cover the cost to put it right, so I leave the radiator with them. It's going to be another two weeks before I have a job got and finished so I can collect the radiator and put it back in the car and I'm on the road again, I'm driving up through town and the bloody steam is back flying out of the side of the car. Pop says, I should go to Joe Ryan around the corner he works at Stokes and McKiernans and knows a lot about cars, Joe says it's the pump that's leaking and not the radiator. And I can throw an egg into the radiator, that the egg will boil and the white part of the egg will fill the hole in the water pump and block it, and that it will keep me going for about twenty miles. He says a second hand pump should cost me five pounds at Peter Longs scrap yard near the Good Shepard Laundry. So there I am putting an egg into the mini everyday while trying to get another fiver together and listening to Mam giving out because I'm taking every egg that's in the house, it's the only way that I can get around in my mini. Mam hands me a fiver and says, it will be cheaper for her to give me the fiver to go and get the pump then to be constantly filling the press with eggs. And after I get the pump and have it fitted my lovely red mini is back on the road again.

The following morning I'm off to work passing the dispensary in Lower Griffin Street, Its great, the fella who works and earns just eight pounds a week and has a car, and the two fellas he works for only have bikes and a hand cart. It feels great and when I get to the junction of Lower Griffin Street where there's a bank on three of the four corners. I have to slow down because I'm driving too fast. I put my foot on the brake and nothing happens, my lovely red mini is heading straight through the junction. My foot is down to the floor on the brake pedal with my heart in my mouth and my head stuck into my shoulders trying to get the car to stop, and how I didn't hit another car coming up William Street is a mystery. I have to use the hand brake,which isn't very good, to bring the car to a stop by the kerb. I need a few minutes to compose myself and right now my head is boiling for Tony O'Mara and the heap of shit he is after selling me.

But I quickly realise how many times he told me that this would happen, but would I listen. I'm thinking of how hard I worked for the last five months working on top of a three part extension ladder inches away from ESB cables used to light up the street all night, and scared out of bloody mind because I hate heights and I hate electricity too. I'm thinking how the chickens down in his brother's yard made a shit house out of my car and all I got was a one way trip to Killaloe and a death wish up William Street. And, on top of that, had to spend money on a radiator that didn't need fixing when it was the bloody pump. And now I am asking Tony O'Mara can he give me another car, he says, 'didn't I tell you that this would happen but would you listen', he says 'I have another car that's not much good either, you can have your money back or you can have the car' 'I'll tried another car Tony' it's a blue Renault Dolphin and it feels like a good reliable car all ready to go. It's not as impressive as the mini, he says, its all he has for the kind of money I gave him. And that its not really company policy to be giving back money, so he asks me to make up my mind do I want my eighty pounds back or do I want the car, but if I take the car I am not to come back with it, and now I'm off down Mulgrave Street in a car that's much bigger than the mini, its more comfortable too except for the bloody gear stick. Tony O'Mara said it has a sincromash gear box whatever the hell that means. I never know when it's in gear or out. I mean, I can shove the gear handle all the way up to the dashboard and back down as far as the back seat or over by the door handle at the other side and still wont know if it's in gear or not. I'm tearing down Roches Street when the bloody thing congs out on me, and when I try to get it started again there isn't a tickle out of the thing because the battery is too low. I'll have to get out and push the thing, a Guard sees me in trouble, comes over, and tells me to get in and put the gear lever into second gear when the car is on a roll, then I'm to take my leg off the clutch while he is pushing it and off she goes first time. I'm bricking it because I never changed the insurance and it's not taxed either. I promised Mam I'll take her out to Cappamore to Nan's new cottage in the centre of the village because Nan hasn't been feeling well lately.

The drive is good all the way out. We stay for an hour or so, and on our way back home my brother Harry is in the back seat, he says he can smell something burning and when I turn on the inside light there's smoke coming up the back seat because that's where the engine is. When I go round to investigate the bloody car is on fire. I have to tell Mam and Harry to get out quick, and after another five minutes the bloody thing is burning out of control and all I want to do right now is fall down and cry. We're half way out the Ballysimon Road and have to walk to Garryowen and Mam is giving out about Tony O'Mara and the pile of shit he is after selling me. And, how it's a bloody disgrace and that she has a good mind to go up to him herself in the morning. She's ranting away saying, 'to think of all the weekends and week nights that you spent working to get that money together, Jesus, Mary and Holy St. Joseph, some nights you didn't come home until twelve o'clock'. I've never seen her walk so fast before. God help Tony O'Mara if she's like this in the morning.

I'm telling her that Tony O'Mara warned me about the first car and this one too, and I'm telling her it's not his fault, that I should have listened to him when he told me the first time. I'm asking her to promise me that she won't go near Tony O'Mara, that I'll go and speak to him myself. She's not listening I'll have to leave her cool off and when we get home Pop is there. She's laying into him like its all his fault, she's thumping him on the shoulder while he is sitting on the chair, 'are you listening to me', she shouts, 'I am' he answers, 'Jesus, I am', 'do you remember the state he came home in over the last five months, exhausted from standing on a ladder for hours, you know what that's like, don't you,? you complain about it often enough when you come home, when you have to do it, do you remember looking at him at the breakfast table in the mornings with his eyes hanging out of his head, do you' she shouts, giving Pop another thump and taking the living senses out of him. 'I do, I do,' he shouts 'Jesus I do',

'And what are you going to do about it?'

Pop is still in the sitting position and looking straight into Mams face, who is waiting for some kind of response, and so am I.

'What are you going to do about it?, she says.

'What do you want me to do about it?, he answers.

'I want you to go up to that so and so in the morning and get your sons eighty pounds back, that's what',

Pop goes silent, looks at me, turns back towards Mam and says' 'isn't he big enough to look after himself, I didn't have a mother or father to correct every mistake I made when I was his age'. This wasn't the answer Mam was expecting or looking for neither. it only makes her worse. 'Well he has a mother and a father too to keep an eye on him even though he's nineteen, I'll do it myself in the morning, don't bother your arse', and off she goes into the small kitchen banging everything she puts her hand to, and muttering away under her breath then shouting back into Pop with a twisted face and a voice that's trying to sound like Pop saying, 'I didn't have a mother and father to correct every mistake I made when I was his age'.

I'm sitting across the table from Pop who looks at me and gives me a wink and off go the shoulders then he gets out of control with the laughing and says, 'I better get out of the house', So I make my way out to the kitchen and in a soft voice say, 'Pop is right Mam, I have to learn from my own mistakes, let me deal with it tomorrow please', and in a soft low frustrated voice she says,..... 'I know, I know' then starts to cry, saying 'Jesus, Paddy you worked so hard to get that eighty pounds together to buy that heap of scrap and from that so and so above in Mulgrave Street'. I should have my arms around her consoling her, showing how much I appreciate the way she cares and feels about me and the hard work I did and what I have to show for it, but I can't, I just can't, and if I did, I don't know how she would handle it She wipes her nose puts her hands on my wrists and says 'you are not to let that man get away with anything, do you hear me now, or else I'll go up there myself tomorrow'. I promise her that Tony O'Mara is a good decent man and he will look after me when he sees my plight tomorrow, and the following morning I'm telling Pop I am going to be late for work because of the car.

Tony O' Mara and myself at his showrooms at the Tipperary Road

I'm there in Mulgrave Street at nine o'clock and when Tony sees me he has a look on his face that matches the words that's coming out of his mouth after I tell him about the car, how it went on fire and he says, 'look, I told you that you wouldn't get your money back so I am going to give you sixty pounds, tell me where the car is so we can go and get it', and he says 'you are not to come back here again unless you want to buy a good decent car'.

I'm back with Pop and Lar showing them the money I got back from Tony O'Mara. I'll hang on to it for another month or two maybe I can even add to it after I earn another few pounds from more tommers and buy a better one. Lar is asking me 'what the fupp do you want a car for, between tax and insurance, petrol, tyres and repairs you'll never have a fupping penny in your pocket'. he says 'my brother has a fupping car and never has a fupping penny in his pocket, his arse is hanging out of his pants all the time', and when I go home for the dinner at

1 o'clock Mam is crying again saying 'is there's any God there at all'. But the days and months will roll on, I've forgotten all about the mini.

Christmas is on the way and St. Michaels boy scouts in Pery's Square will have their annual rag day parade all around town. Mature scouts from all over the city will gather at the hall across from the Mechanics Institute, and get the big float that will have all kinds of cardboard monsters on top of it. Others will dress up in costumes, so will I, but I'll want to get a laugh, I'll go to with the can that has a slot on top to take the few bob I'll get.

Nan has brought me in one of her old bras from Cappamore. She has breasts like large heads of cabbage and I should have great crack when I walk around town wearing it and the pelmet of a mini shirt Jetta made for me. I'll get a big chunky polo jumper to keep me warm, I'm with Tommy Deegan, his wearing his wife's beetle boots with the high heels. He's walking around like he is scuttered out of his mind and I think he's going to break the heels the way he is walking, and if he does he's wife Mary will be telling him to go down to Levy's shoe shop in O'Connell Street, and get her a new pair. He's got two round sponges tucked under a black jumper that he'll keep adjusting all the time, because they won't stay in the one place. He's wearing a mask over his face because he says he doesn't want half the workers at Ranks Flour Mills on the Dock road to recognise him. I'm telling him he's wasting his time because every five minutes there is a shout of a male voice when its passes us and says 'Good man, Tommy Deegan that's a grand pair of legs you have', We'll go into every pub in town and I'll charge two pounds for a feel of one of the cups of my grandmothers bra and make a small fortune.

There's a drunk in every pub and I'll stand longside them, like I did in the Brazen Head in O'Connell's Street, he looked at me and the blonde wig I was wearing that I borrowed from one of the girls in Richards hairdressing salon. He'll run his eyes up and down my big chest put his hand under the mini I'm wearing, grab my jewels which causes me to jump with the fright.

He'll look at me and say 'Jasus what kind of a woman are you at all? It will happen again and again till my jewels can't take any more, and neither can the tin can because its full of money and I have to hold the thing with both hands because it is so heavy. Mary is down town doing the tour of all the shops looking for the usual, while looking around every corner nervously because I told her if I get a glimpse of her she'd better run because I'll make a holy show of her. When the collecting comes to an end and the counting of the contents of each tin. I'm told I have collected a record amount, hardly any copper coins, mostly silver and a few ten bob notes. 22 pounds seven shillings and six pence in total and Taylor is the toast of St. Michaels scouts.

When Christmas night comes Mary and myself are back in Billy Madigan's house until four o'clock in the morning with my guitar and a voice that's hoarse from roaring out all the songs we've sang. It's been another dry Christmas for Pop and it's hard to remember the days in Carey's Road when he would come home looking for an argument and getting one too. When January comes we're off to Killaloe again for more painting. Pop and Lar will be at it again with Pop on the celebration beer that will have him doing more strange things. I'll make more money because I'll have nothing to do. We'll head off out the Dublin Road, the three of us, with a gallon of white emulsion in each hand, keeping a distance of a hundred yards apart while thumbing away, leaving one tin on the ground while putting the hand out with the thumb sticking up, along with the confident smile. I'll get a lift and arrive first on the job and wait for one of them to show up and tell me what to do. Work until nine or ten o'clock and wait for the other two to start. Mary will wait at the new public phone box fitted only weeks before that now has two for the whole of Garryowen and is only a hundred feet from her own house. She'll wait at one o'clock every day for me to ring from the phone booth in the hotel. And we'll talk for fifteen minutes before she has to go back to work.

Pop has a problem with his back and has to wear a red flannel cloth that covers his backside that he wears inside his long johns. The doctor says it will keep his back warm all the time and that he has to wear it in bed and that he is never to take it off except to wash it, and tonight half the female staff in the hotel are going to get a good look at it. We're not in the staff quarters this time, but instead are accommodated in luxury with red carpets everywhere, central heating and other comforts. Its eleven o'clock, I'm on my own in the room that has three beds, and after thirty minutes I'm on fire, I can hardly breath, its all because of the bloody radiator that's under the window that I can't touch, its so hot. I have the bottom part of the sliding sash window open as high as I can get it. I'll put my head out into the cold frosty night air trying to get it into my lungs and give me back the sense of normality I'm used to at Garryowen. When we pushed the table against the wall and sat around the fire with our knees and faces red hot and our backs frozen while listening to the wind howling in through the gaps in the two steel windows, its no use, I cant get enough cold air into the room. Now I'm pushing the bed against the wall and under the window. Ten minutes later I have every stitch of clothing on the floor and eventually go to sleep. Hours later I'm waking again because Pop is fupping and blinding in his sleep. I'm sitting up in the bed with the cold damp air freezing the right side of my naked body and looking over at Pop throwing punches in the air at somebody he thinks is there. Lar is across in the other corner with his hands over his mouth snorting and hissing doing his best not to let Pop hear him laughing. Pop is sitting up in his bed pointing his fore finger at the wall fupping the person he thinks is there and telling him what he'll do to him if he doesn't shut up, sit down and play the game of cards properly.

I'm thinking any minute now he'll go back to sleep and Lar and myself can get with ours, but that was wishful thinking, he's getting out of the bed still giving out and trying to get on his feet, his on his hands and knees and doing everything he can to stand in an upright position but keeps falling back into the bed. I'm in hysterics holding my stomach that's going to get very sore. Lar has the bed clothes over his head trying to camouflage his loud snorting and heavy intakes of breath, along with the muffled laughter, because if Pop hears him laughing there will be fists flying in all directions. After several attempts, Pop gets on his feet, with the red flannel and nothing else hanging over his arse. He turns around,stumbles a bit like he is looking for something, and there with his back to me is geromo full of fire water and ready to go on the war path. He turns around again and walks in a hurried stumble straight into a wardrobe, bounces back three or four steps, looking dazed and confused. He should be on the floor unconscious, his still standing there trying to figure out what a wardrobe is doing in his way. Lar has rolled out of his bed onto the floor, still covering his mouth with both hands, and I'm out of control laughing so much. I think I'm going to die because I cant get any air into my lungs. 'Who put that fupping thing out in the middle of the road?' says Pop, looking at the wardrobe, my laugh has gone into silence and if I don't get some air into my lungs fast I'll die. Pops now making his way over to me when he does the edge of my bed stops him, he puts both hands out on my chest which brings my laughter to a quick stop. He throws one leg over me and the bed and there, about four inches over my nose, is the place were I started my journey to Bedford Row over twenty years ago, and it's not a pleasant sight. I'm thinking in a panic of the stories himself and Lar have told me about the drunks and what they did to their wives when they came home drunk out of their minds, and any second now he is going to fire right into my face and I won't be laughing anymore. But wait, he's reaching over to the window sill while raising one of his legs to go out the window. We're two stories up, he'll fall out and break his bloody neck. I'm saying 'no Pop, no the sink is over there,'

'Fupp off', he says.

I am on my feet trying my damnest to pull him back, I am roaring over at Lar to help me but he's scuttered too and can't stop laughing. If anyone coming in or out of the hotel looks up at the window and sees two naked men trying to get out of a window the Guards will be called. After what seems like hours I have him redirected over to the sink, he's muttering away something like 'Oh, you must be very proud of your fupping father,' He's there by the sink emptying the gallons of celebration beer into the sink in the corner that he must have drank over the last six hours down at the hotel bar and I don't think I've ever seen a pee to last so long. When he's finished he turns around walks over to were he thinks the bed is and bounces back off the same wardrobe while fupping the thing out of it. And, the laughing is back again only worse then ever. I don't know where Lar is. I think he is under the bed because he can't disguise the laughing any more and I think if there are any guests in the hotel at this time of the year they'll be banging on the door any minute giving us a mouthful or worse still down at the reception complaining about the drunken residents in room no. 131.

The following morning Pop is complaining about a very sore nose, bruised knees and chest. He's scratching his head trying to figure out how he got them. I'm asking him has he seen the state of the wardrobe in our bedroom that has its door off the hinges. He looks at me puzzled and I'm telling him he gave the wardrobe an awful hiding last night and Hector Newenham will be looking for compensation when he sees it. He gives me a sarcastic look and says 'very, funny'.

The following night I'm back in bed at ten o'clock having done another three hours over time. At this rate I'll have twelve hours extra work done. I might be able to buy myself something to wear. Mam will have an extra few bob too, but I can't go to sleep worrying about Geromo and his wanderings while he is under the influence of the fire water. I mean what will I do if I wake up and find his hydraulics hanging over my face again. But exhaustion from all the extra hours I am working takes over and sends me into a pleasant sleep, that I am woken out of later in the night. It's Pop on his feet again completely naked except of course for the red flannel around his waist. He is a bit steadier on his feet than he was last night, he is not making much of a racket either, he is starting to walk, not in my direction but straight over to the sink in the corner by the door and I'm saying thanks be to God, he wont be trying to go out the window again, but just as I am relaxing instead of firing into the sink like we all do when we are down here, he opens the door walks out into the hallway turns left and heads down the corridor, I'm up and out of my bed with my head stuck out the door calling him back in a loud whisper. I can't follow him either because I'm starkers too. I'm over at Lar's bed shaking him violently, his drunk too, 'Lar, Lar will you get up please Lar', Lar opens one eye, looks up at me and says, 'Whats wrong?' I am telling him Pop is wondering all over the hotel in the nip, that he is sleep walking, 'fupp off', he says, 'don't be winding me up look over at his bed Lar, his gone', Lar sits up looks over at Pops bed, Lar is like the rest of us, naked as the day he was born, then starts laughing uncontrollably and that starts me off too.

I have a picture in my mind of the things that could happen, and the people that might see him. Lar manages to say 'any minute now we'll hear a fupping scream, if a young one sees your father in the fupping dark' and I just can,t take any more of this laughing. I think I have done myself an injury. An hour later Lar and I can't laugh anymore because we're worried. Lar says 'where the fupp could he be at all', now he has me really worried because he says he could be below in the fupping lake and dead for the last half an hour.

I'm putting on my clothes when the door opens and in walks Pop, says nothing, throws himself into the bed and goes into a deep coma. Lar looks over at Pop and then looks at me and says 'where the fupp has he being for the last fupping hour', and we're off again killing ourselves laughing. Next morning we're down in the kitchen sitting at the big table for all the staff. Pop looks terrible, his sniffing and coughing giving out that say-ing, 'that fupping central heating has him fupping killed', Lar looks at me. I look at him then two waitresses enter the kitchen one has the arm around the other, she seems to comforting her saying 'look I am sure you are mistaken it had to be a dream', and the two girls sit on the long timber bench at the other side of the table. Pop opens his mouth and says 'what's the matter girls'. The girl that has her hand around the other that's crying, says, 'she's convinced a naked man wearing a red cloth was in her room last night', There's a sudden burst of a timber bench being dragged across the floor because Lar and myself have to get out of here fast. The two of us are out in the back howling with Lar making the matter worse by repeating the words the girl said 'she thinks she saw a fupping naked man in her room last night', now Pop has joined us with a look on his face saying, 'was that me?', and that sends Lar and myself out of control we have to run away but he's following us laughing saying 'for fupps sake, will you tell me was that me?'. We can't answer him but he knows it was, now he is out of control and when we can't laugh anymore we're back at the table again.

The two girls have gone back to work Pop is in shock because he's saying 'what would he do if he was caught?', Lar finishes his words saying you can be sure Hector Newenham would have us out on our ear, word would go round the whole of Limerick and we wouldn't have a fupping customer left, and adds, you had better stay off that fupping stuff tonight Har, Pop nods his head in agreement and says 'you can chalk it down'.

Lakeside Hotel, Killaloe and the room upstairs that Pop wanted to climb out the window from

It's a pity because Author Guinness makes Pop cranky but the celebration makes him crazy and there will be no more laughing in the early hours of the morning with Pop and his antics. I'll be telling Mary on the phone every day about Pop, and she'll say I'm making it up. I'll tell her about the half an hour I spent every lunch time out in the lake in a boat that I get to use from Jimmy who works in the boat house. And it will never dawn on me how dangerous it is to be out in a boat with no life jacket. And I don't even have a bloody clue how to swim. J.W. Harrison, the jeweller, wants the entire inside of his shop remodelled, shelves and counters made, new wood, different ceilings, and a moss green straw like paper on the walls. He says he'll buy all the materials if I just give him a price for the labour. That I can work at night, all day Sunday too. It's my first ever biggest challenge I'll get one hundred and fifty pounds for whole lot, he'll even let me make suggestions that he and his wife Geraldine will listen to and take on board.

I don't want to take any money until I am finished and I'm back thinking about a car again. I still have the sixty pounds Tony O'Mara gave me I can add it to the hundred and fifty and at long last will be able to buy myself a decent car. I'll be here four weeks of nights and weekends, no standing on ladders three storeys off the ground either. I won't have to worry about the weather, so its all systems go. And after three weeks John says I need to speed the work up a bit and that I can spend Friday and Saturday night through to the following morning in the shop on my own. And that I should be able to finish the job in time. I'll be there from six o'clock in the evening until nine o'clock the following morning, locked in like a prisoner behind a door with four locks in it and a protective barrier at the front of the shop, working away, listening to radio Luxemburg, taking a tea break every hour and a smoke as well. And when eight o'clock arrives I'll have to have all the saw dust off the carpet and have the place clean for nine o'clock when John wants to open. After three weeks of working every night I'm getting large boils all over my body. Mam says I need a tonic because I am running myself down from all the late nights and weekends too, but I'm nearly finished and looking forward to getting the most money I've ever had into my hand. But I should have been happy with two hundred and ten pounds; I could have bought a good car for that.

But the coffee shop across the road have seen the work I've done for John Harrison, and want me to make ten new tables and a large counter. I am looking for two hundred and forty pounds including the materials and if I get it, I'll invest two hundred and thirty pounds along with what I get for this job into a good decent nearly new car with enough money for tax and insurance as well and have some left over, and my mind has me gone again with the dream. There will be no radiators leaking, the brakes will work too and Mr. Stackwill, who ownes the coffee shop, says I am to go ahead with the job. I'm asking Mam if I can store the tables at home when they are made because I have to give every one of them a couple of coats of varnish, and the house that Mam loves to clean has tables everywhere with a strong smell of varnish with Pop, Harry and James complaining that its too hard to go to sleep. Mam hasn't an ounce of comfort trying to keep the house clean or polish anything. She won't say a word of complaint and supports me in every request I make. She'll give me advice like, 'Pa, will you please make sure you get somebody who knows about cars this time and not have the same thing happen to you. 'I'm promising her that I will. That I am not going to make the same mistake again,' and when the day comes to bring the ten tables, three at a time, down to the coffee shop in Little Catherine Street, on Pop and Lar's handcart, I'm weak with excitement. I have butterflies in my stomach, in another couple of hours I'll be above in Tony O'Mara's with the bones of three hundred pounds in my pocket that I can hand over for a good car. A car that looks and sounds like a new one. I have my second load of three tables delivered and Mr. Stackwill wants to see me. He says I am to take the tables back that they are no good because people are putting the hot kettles on the surface and they're are sticking to the varnish, that there's nearly been a couple of accidents. He said he thought the tables would have a hard formica tops on them like the last ones. He says he's sorry, that he knows I spent a lot of money on materials but the simple fact is that I haven't given him what he asked for. I see his lips moving and for some reason I can't hear the sound, especially after his words that I am to

288

take the other tables back. I'm gone into shock with tears in my eyes. I must be asleep, this has to be a nightmare, any minute I'll wake up and collect the two hundred and forty pounds and go and buy my car. Only it's not a dream. I'm standing outside his shop in Little Catherine Street, leaning against the handcart trying to figure out how I'm going explain this to Mam and Pop who have being so good to me letting me turn the house into a workshop. What will Mary think of me. Its bad enough making a mistake once but a second time is just stupid, and where am I going to bring all these ten tables and the big counter with all the glass in it. So its down to the back of the Grand Central cinema making three return trips to Garryowen and Mam asking me every time, 'Is Mr. Stackwill happy?' I'm telling her he's delighted but that I have changed my mind about the car, she wants to know why, I'm telling her what Lar told me, that I'll never have a penny in my pocket if I own a car. She puts the sign of the cross on her forehead and says, 'Thanks bit to God', that she'll be able to sleep at night.

John Harrison's shop far left and coffee shop across the road

John Harrison

I'm walking back down to the Grand Central cinema with the large counter that was supposed to hold a variety of cakes and buns. I'm in a terrible state of depression, I don't like telling Mam lies, sure she's happy now because I won't be in a car seven days a week, worrying if Mary and myself will be killed. I couldn't bear to think what she would say or do if I told her the truth. I'm thinking too of all the bloody hours I spent making a hundred and fifty pounds in John Harrison's shop across the road and it's making me sick that all I have left to show for it is sixty pounds.

Pop wants to know what all the tables I made at home are doing at the back of the Grand Central cinema. I have to tell him what happened and I'm asking him not to tell Mam. He says he won't and adds that I am an awful fupping eejit, why the hell didn't I put the formica on the tops of the tables, and I'm saying because it was too dear, 'too dear', he says 'look at what its after costing you now, you had better get rid of these things fast, because the owners of the Grand Central cinema will want to know who put them there and how long they are going to be there for?'. Tom King owns a restaurant on O'Connell, Street he is a builder also. He says he'll give me twenty pound for the lot and I have to tell Mary we will still be walking to the Savoy every weekend and getting the bus the Jetland every Saturday night and I think I don't ever want to do a tom job again. A week later Mary and I are gone off one another we have called it off. She's still coming over to Mam every Monday and Wednesday night and I am over in her house, Tuesday, Thursday and Friday nights. Mam isn't saying anything but I know she is disappointed, it will last ten weeks until Mary accepts an invitation from a guy on the other side of the green in Garryowen to go out with him. I know him well and can't figure out how a good looking girl like Mary would go out with a fella who has no neck, its just like his head is resting on his shoulders, he can't wear a tie with his shirt because he has nothing to put the tie around. It never dawns on me she might be doing it to make me jealous, I'm not, if he was good looking I would be. Mary says that Sam the foreman said that if it was off between herself and myself longer then ten weeks that we would never get back together again. And that frightens the living daylights out of me, so it's on again.

We'll be down in the hall of her house kissing and grunting, I'll be saying, 'Oh Moll,' and she'll be saying, 'Oh, Pa', and we'll be both 'Oh Mollying' and 'Oh Paaing' for ages. And Mr. O'Connell will knock on the floor and shout down, 'Oh, Pa will you go home' I'll go home in an awful state and think about Mary all night.

Mam will be in great form again until Pop gets an invitation to cousin Tom's wedding who is marrying a girl from the Bedford Bar and Mrs. Dennehy is sitting in a rocking chair below in the basement giving out to Pop saying, 'Urawarher Harry Taylor, I can't keep a girl with ye Taylor's' it seems that every girl who comes to work at the Bedford Bar will marry a Taylor, just like Pop did with Mam and Pop's brothers too. Pops long spell of behaving himself and giving Mam the peace of mind and happiness she deserves is coming to an end. Maybe it's the three weeks we spend in Killaloe every year that causes it. I don't know. But Mrs. Cullen's headache powder will be well in stock at 36 Claughan Court from now on, as will power seems to have emigrated somewhere and will show no sign of coming back

Cousin Tom's wedding will have Pop on the tear again, a tension will come back to number 36 and bring with it the old childhood memories. Its there a week before the wedding, and finds good reason to be there, when Pop comes home in an awful state with that awful stale porter smell, and the watery drop. Mam will give him hell but I'm not a child anymore I don't have to run to a bed in fright. I can stay to make sure he doesn't get out of hand.

I'm older now so is Mam and she can dish out the words to Pop in a way that might cause him to retaliate ,so I will stay put to make sure she'll be ok, but Pop won't stay for his breakfast on Sunday morning because he won't be able to eat. Maureen Fay will let him into the bar around eleven o'clock. He'll be there all day and all night too, and come home in the early

hours of the morning, an hour or two after Mary and myself
have gone. With Mary worrying about the awful atmosphere
in the house and Mam rubbing her head all the time, yawn-
ing too, because she's not getting as much sleep as she needs. I
have to tell Mary on the way over to number twelve that Pop is
back on the drink, how bad he is when he's on it, and not like
her dad Mr. O' who is drunk every weekend after only three
pints and wouldn't say boo to anyone.

It's hard to go to sleep waiting for the key to turn in the door
that will start him off trying to wake everybody up, especially
Mam. With comments like, 'I suppose it would be too much
trouble to expect a dinner', if there is a dinner on the table
with another plate on top of it to keep the flies off it, he's out
in the hall shouting up to Mam saying,' do you expect me to
eat, that fupping stuff, it's frozen', all the time needling her to
get her out of the bed and down the stairs to give him a mouth
full. She won't! On Monday nights Mary is over with the knitting needles sitting by the fire with Mam doing her best to be
cheerful. I'm out on the wall smoking, like I do every Monday
and Wednesday night, looking for someone to talk to. Pop's
getting off the bus with the help of the conductor. He's too
early,Mam wont be expecting him and in he goes with the
watery drip hanging all over the place while trying to get his
key in the door. I'm behind him hoping he'll head up the stairs
to bed, but that would be too much to hope for, he's on his
way into the living room for his fix of trying to upset Mam or
anybody else. When he walks into the room he's surprised to
see Mary ,does his usual with the fore finger under the chin
trying to genuflect, stumbles, makes a remark, 'Oh, her highness from around the corner is here', he'll sit on the chair and
demand his dinner. Mam brings it in and bangs it under his
nose with the plate the same size over it and says, 'I hope it
chokes you'; he lifts the plate off and says, 'What's this?' Mam
shouts, 'your dinner, and if you don't like it, don't eat it'.

Pop at Cousin Tom's wedding, with Pop well on it

I'm looking at Mary not knowing what to say or do. I want to get her away but I don't want to leave Mam on her own with Pop either. 'I am not eating that stuff', he shouts, Mam stands up grabs the plate and says, 'right you don't have to,' walks into the kitchen opens the back door and throws the lot plate and all into the bin. Comes back, looks him in the eye and shouts, 'you can bloody well starve'. Pop looks at Mary and says, 'Oh, it will be all over Garryowen in the morning', Mam is off her feet again longside Pop with her fore finger under his nose. She's shouting into his face, 'are you suggesting for one moment that, that girl is going to spread all over Garryowen what's going on in this house,?'

'I never said she would'.

'No but you bloody well suggested it, how dare you speak about that lovely girl like that, apologise, do you hear apologise'!

Pop looks over at Mary puts the fore finger under his chin, mutters out a muffled apology. stands up, turns to the door opens it and says, 'it looks like I am not wanted around here', goes out the hall and up the stairs muttering away, his voice getting louder as he climbs every step. Mam is rubbing her head again apologising to Mary and Mary says, 'sure, it's alright Mrs. Taylor, sure my own father takes the few drinks and says things he shouldn't'. Mam starts crying but quickly wipes her nose and eyes, saying,' 'that bloody man, when he gets that stuff into him he's impossible to live with'. Mary says, 'good night', I'll walk her home and tell her about the early years again in Upper Carey's road, how we dreaded Christmas time or a wedding in the family and waited around the table for him to come home, before he would eventually stop and give the family a bit of normality. He'll be at it again all next week and Mary will be gone before the bus comes with Pop in it, on Monday and Wednesday nights before he cops himself on and waits another week for Mam to talk to him once she's sure he is going to stay away from it for another year. The laughter and good humour that Mary looks forward to and loves, is back again and it's like nothing happened at all. It's coming up to my twentieth birthday, I am going out with Mary over two years. She's my best pal so is Mam. I'm at the table having my supper before I go over to Mary's. Pop is watching the news and Mam is asking me will I do something for her before I go over to Mary's. I am not in the best of form for some reason, I don't know why. I'll always do what ever it is Mam asks, except paint the back of the house before I'll do the front. I'm telling her I can't that I'll be late for Mary. She asks, 'are you going out somewhere', 'no' I answer. She smiles and says, 'so you are not going to do a small thing for your mother that's looked after you all your life and put your girlfriend first', I snap at her real cross and say without thinking, 'Oh, for goodness sake will you cop yourself on', I have taken her completely by surprise, the smile is gone, her bottom lip is quivering and straight away I'm feeling terrible. Mam has her handchief out wiping her eyes saying that she was only joking, 'sure I am mad about that girl', Pop looks at me and says, 'now look at what you have done', I'm gutted and don't know what to say, I have my head in my chest saying, 'I'm sorry Mam', I should go over and put my arms around her and reassure her with a hug. I have no problem doing it with Mary when I put my foot in it, but I am awkward with Mam and when it comes to expressing and showing emotion I'm useless. As a family we'll do things for one another, its how we show love, I'll tell Mam I'm sorry again while she puts her handchief under the sleeve of her cardigan, I'll tell her I'm sorry again and again. She says it ok. I'll go over to Mary and tell her what happened and how bad I feel over hurting Mam, how awkward I felt about not being able to give her a hug. Mary says it's the same in her family, that her parents wouldn't be able to cope with giving or receiving affection, especially her father. I'll tell Mam again the following morning at breakfast that I didn't mean to snap at her the way I did. She says it's, ok, that we all have our moments and the lovely smile is back. My brother James is seventeen now and has brought three American tourists a couple of years older then himself, home. They're all over Mam and Mam is all over them because they want their photograph taken with her.

She has the spotted dick out and the three of them are shoving it down their throats telling her they have never tasted anything like it, they want to know if they can bring a cake back to America at the end of the week. Mam is delighted and says, 'of course,' and when I come for my supper the bloody spotted dick is gone and another two days to go before Mam makes another. She says I'm not to worry that she will make another three tonight, because the boys from America will be back for more tomorrow, and will want a whole cake to take back to the States with them. The following night they're back again with a massive bunch of flowers for Mam, thanking her for her lovely Irish hospitality. Mam is cooing, genuflecting, and floating around the kitchen, dancing attention to the three American tourists and shoving more spotted dick down their throats and putting the flowers into two containers of water and putting each one on the two windowsills so all the neighbours can see them. The following night she is out the back talking to Mrs. Moloney over the fence about the three American boys James brought home and how they're eating her out of house and home. Then she'll run into the house and bring out the two containers of flowers to show her, with James inside bricking it because Mam doesn't know where the flowers came from. She thinks the three boys went to the florist shop just like Mrs. O' Connors at the bottom of Henry Street, and between the three of them bought the large bunch of flowers out of appreciation. Well that's what they wanted her to think even though there was no evidence of fancy paper, or a coloured bow or even a card. James is still bricking it because the flowers came from a house in Rossa Avenue from a garden filled with every kind of a flower you could find from the man who owed the house, the garden and the flowers too and spent every hour of his time looking after it and wouldn't cut one for himself or any of his family either. He just wants to have it there in its natural environment and there's Mam out the back showing the lovely flowers to Mrs. Moloney and Mrs. Moloney says they are gorgeous and tells Mam they are just like the ones that were stolen from her fathers house up the road in Rossa Avenue and isn't it terrible that a retired man can't leave his garden for a minute and someone steals his lovely flowers.

Mary is making an extra two pound a week and, added to the four she's already getting she's able to get herself something extra every week but has to work all the hours God sends from six o'clock in the morning to ten o'clock that night. She'll come home at five thirty prepare and cook a meal for her father, two sisters and one brother, for the hours break. She'll do it seven nights a week because her mother will be down in the Savoy at the 'Talk of the Town Restaurant', on her feet from five o'clock til midnight every night of the week. Mrs. O'Connell is going through the change of life, I haven't a bloody clue what that is. I won't know or understand it until I'm thirty. Mrs. O'Connell will come home giving out to Mary about the state of the house. Mr. O'Connell will ask her to be quite and she'll tell him to shut up and mind his own business. I'll be sitting there listening to it night after night until I can't take anymore and explode in temper. I am telling Mrs. O'Connell shouting out the word 'Jesus, will you leave her alone, she's here every night looking after your children for you, cleaning the house, giving them their dinner and working fourteen hours a day in the factory. You're only working seven hours a night and you expect her to be doing her job and yours too, looking after your house and your children as well.' Mrs. O'Connell rises to her feet and says, 'how dare you speak to me like that', and that I am to get out of her house this minute. She's shoving me out the door, Mary is crying. Mr. O'Connell is above in bed sleeping his head off and I'm on my way around the corner worrying about Mary and not regretting a word I said. Everyone is in bed when I get home; I can't sleep a wink all night, and when five thirty comes the following morning I am over at the wall outside Mary's house waiting for her to come out so I can walk her up to work and find out if the girl is still going out with me.

It's five forty five and, Mary's door opens she's surprised to see me then smiles which tells me straight away I still have a girlfriend. As she walks down the long foot path with a smile of appreciation that I stood up for her last night. She gives me a kiss and then a hug, I'll ask her how she got on last night, she says she just went to bed and not another word was spoken, that she hardly slept a wink all night. And thanked me for my support. I'm telling her I am not one bit sorry I would do it all again and how hard it is to sit down and listen to her being wronged. And the nights of playing the guitar with several cups of tea in Mary's house will be a thing of the past for the next foreseeable future, after walking Mary to the shoe factory and getting a good bye kiss. I'm back at home in bed again and able to sleep because my girl isn't cross with me. I'll be able to relax now and get a couple of hours under the blanket. When eight thirty comes I'm at the table having my breakfast asking Pop for a hour off he says its 'ok', but I have to make sure it's only an hour and not three or four. I'm on my way over to St. Camillius Hospital out the Ennis Road to see Mr. O'Connell. He works in the small house at the entrance to the Hospital, he looks after the switch board all day for the last few years ever since the Doctors, nurses and staff took a liking to him during the six years on the flat of his back with T.B.

I want to see him and apologise for my behaviour even though I would do it all again. When I knock at the door he opens it and apologises to me, 'isn't she an awful woman, Paddy upsetting the whole house like that, I'm very sorry, you're welcome in my house anytime you like', I'm asking him what's he apologising to me for, sure I am the one that needs to apologise to him, he says 'not at all, I'm delighted you stood up for Mary, I don't know what's wrong with that woman these days she has the whole house upset, giving out to everyone all the time', But its only a matter of months before I'm back in 12 Claughan Court again singing away on the guitar, and all in the house singing out of tune because Mary and I have announced that we are getting engaged next month and Mrs. O'Connell can't have her future son-in-law that's able to decorate the house every couple of years and add on an extension, making built in wardrobes from the money she'll borrow every two years from St. John's Credit Union and Mary will be giving out to me because I'll tell our friends that she tricked me into getting engaged. I'm turning out just like Pop winding everybody up belonging to me mostly Mary, just to see them getting upset. Mary will give me a thump on the shoulder just like Mam gives Pop, stick her finger under my nose and tell me with a smile on her face to apologise. I will after telling her 'sure you did trick me', she'll laugh and say how the hell did 'I trick you', and I'll say, we were out in Muroe Valley right,

'right', she says.

'We went out on our bikes for a picnic, right.'

'Right' she says.

'There was no talk from any of us about a marriage or getting engaged, right'

'Right' she says.

So there we were lying out on the grass having a great ole shift, saying how we felt about each other, no talk about, 'I love you', or 'you love me, right',

'Right', she says.

And then out of the blue you sit up and say 'will we get engaged'? not will we get married right.

'Right' she says.

I looked at you and said 'you're joking' and you said. 'What do you think, right'?

'Right' she says.

Then I said 'ok, lets get engaged'.

And you laughed and said 'will we really, right?'

'Right', she says.

So then you said 'When will we get engaged'? and I said 'When do you want to get engaged?' 'Right'.

.' 'Right' she says.

'So you said next June' and I said 'ok'Right

'Right' she says.

And all the way back home on our bikes, off you go with the Saturday afternoon routine, like 'I don't know', 'what do you think, do you think we should , tell me the truth now I wont mind are we doing the right thing?'

'Are you sure?'

'sure the whole thing was your idea you started it and then talked me into it'

She's really cross with me walking away out in front with her nose stuck up in the air, I'll tease her more and ask or 'did your mother put you up to it?' she'll turn around with a sour look on her face telling me that her mother did the right thing when she turned me out of the house and should have kept me out. I'll walk up behind her, put my arms around her nuzzle her in the neck and tell her I was only joking. She'll tell me to get away talking out through her teeth just like Mam used to do. I'll keep at her nuzzling away until the cross face goes and the laughter comes back. We're holding hands again she'll put the finger under my nose and warn me never to say that to anyone again, but I will because I love her being mad at me and the challenge of winning her over is just too hard to resist.

Mam is thrilled about the engagement but tells Mary how worried she is about her getting married so young and having babies, and, the responsibility of trying to find some place to live, is very hard these days' and Pop is asking every one of our customers to know would they try and talk a bit of sense into me, but they'll just laugh and say would they have listened to anyone in their day trying to talk them out of getting married, and Pop won't say anything. But the man outside in Ballina-curra Gardens that Pop and myself are working for during the evenings to give me the chance to earn some money for the ring we've picked at John Harrison's jewellers in Little Catherine Street. A small cluster of diamonds for sixty pounds and will take me the bones of four months to get the money together for the ring that we'll look at in his window every Sunday night on the way back from the Savoy, before we go into 36 Claughan Court for one cup of tea and four or five slices of spotted dick. The man says that if he had a second chance, he would marry at my age. Pop wants to know why and I'm all ears, he says he got married at 45 that he has three girls. 'I'm 55 now and if I'm alive when they're growing up I'll be lucky and if I'm alive when they have grown up I'll be even luckier but I'll be too old for them, I'm nearly too old for them now. They'll want me to play with them but I'll get too tired so it's a big regret for me not marrying younger. I'll never forget that man and what he said, and think how I'll be able to grow with my children and when they're twenty I'll be only forty. And still young enough to have the same interests as them.

June is coming fast and so are the arrangements for the party outside in the Parkway Hotel. I'll collect the cluster ring from John Harrison after giving him the last of many teners and fiv-ers over the last two months of working late nights with Pop and sometimes on my own. I'll give the ring to Mary on Satur-day morning and tell her I love her and its one Saturday I don't mind following Mary around the town. Mam and Pop won't be coming to the party at the Parkway Hotel because he's off the drink and won't want to be tempted, but they'll come over to 12 Claughan Court later in the night for a singsong. We'll met Mam down town in Bedford Row, she wants to see the ring and when we met her she's all excited, she gives Mary a big hug, congratulates her. I'm asking Mam 'aren't you going to con-gratulate your own son at all?' and here it comes a short quick hug and a peck on the cheek, we're kind of awkward about it.

I must have been five or six years old the last time Mam done that. Now Mam is running all over the place calling one or two people she knows on the street, then complete strangers telling them her son has just got engaged pulling Mary over, and getting them to have a look at her hand while she holds it out. Mam's gone all giggly like she's drunk, or carrying on like a thirteen year old. I'm saying 'Mam will you calm down for goodness sake, you'll do yourself an injury' but its no good she'll just carry on. Mary is looking at me in amazement but delighted at the same time, Nan is over is Southampton with her daughter Nelly and husband she's being there for the last three months and she's probably sticking her nose into everyone's business while she's there. She'll write home to Mam giving out about letting me get engaged so young and Mam,will write back and say, 'wait until you met the girl his going to marry you'll change your mind', The Parkway Hotel bar is full of friends and relatives wishing us well and drinking to our future. I'm breaking my promise to Mam, the promise I made the last time Pop walked in the door mouldy drunk looking for an argument and getting one too, mostly from Mam because I can't stand the sight of anyone drunk, stumbling around with the heavy breathing and the watery drip that allways turns into a long snot. I'll stay quite for a while and won't be able to control my temper because of the way he is upsetting Mam. He'll go to bed muttering away how the whole family is against him, Mam has her head in her hands crying away and asking me to promise that I'll never put a drop of alcohol to my mouth. I'll promise and mean it too, sure why would I want to bring this kind of unhappiness on Mary and on any children we might have. And here I am putting a glass of Vodka to my mouth because I can't stand the awful taste of porter, beer, or lager. I don't like this stuff either but it's the best of a bad lot, I'll throw the whole glass down in one go and cringe. I'll have four in all, because I just want to celebrate and now I'm starting to laugh, in another ten minutes I won't be able to stop and at eleven o'clock I can't stand up. I have to be escorted to a car and driven home laughing at everyone, asking Mary 'what am I laughing at?', and that makes me laugh even more, until I have a pain in my stomach. I can see and hear everything, understand it too, so I couldn't be drunk, could I? I mean when you're drunk you're not supposed to be able to understand what you're saying. They're taking me out of the car outside number 12 Claughan Court my brother Harry who is coming up to his ninth birthday is playing on the road, sees me and the state I'm in, runs in home shouting, 'Paddy is drunk, Paddy is drunk'. Mam is shocked, she can't believe it, she says to Pop how could Paddy be drunk? Pop shrugs his shoulders and says 'the only time I ever saw me drink was the time in Richards when I was trying to fart', Harry is still shouting, 'his drunk, sure he can hardly stand up, two people had to carry him into Mary's house. Mary has me carried up to her bedroom and says I'm to lie down for an hour it doesn't take long for me to nod off and by eleven o'clock I'm back on my feet like nothing ever happened. And I'm wondering how I can remember every thing I said, and did, and asking myself why I'm not laughing anymore and can walk down the stairs like I've never had a drink. I'm only down the stairs and into the room when Mrs. O'Connell puts the guitar into my hand and asks me to play 'The Blackboard of my Heart', and before I can put the strap around my neck she's off with only half the words, 'my tears have washed I love you from the 'Blackboard of my Heart, la la al'. and then goes completely out of key before I bring her back to the right one. Mam has a face like the one Nan has when she's giving you the awful stare as she walks into the room with Pop following behind her.

She looks over at me sees me playing the guitar and not a sign of drunkenness to be seen in my voice or demeanour. She smiles a smile of relief, sits down with Pop while Mary fusses and fusters over the two of them. Pop is as quite as a mouse drinking a cup of tea from one hand and a fag in the other, if he was drinking he'd have being here hours ago singing his heart out and be the life and soul of the party, they'll only stay an hour because it would be too much of a temptation for Pop with all the drink that's floating around. With Mr. and Mrs. O'Connell well on their way to a good night and beyond understanding that Pop has a problem with the drink and will want to see him with one in his hand just to be sociable.

In the weeks to come Mary and I will set a wedding date for September twelve months to give us a chance to get some money together and find a place to live, we'll treat ourselves to the Jetland one Saturday in every month because of the money we'll save, but keep the Savoy and the walk home every Sunday night. I'll be working most nights and Saturdays too, and I'll open a account at the Munster and Leinster Bank, in William Street. James will finish school in August and will want a job some place and one is coming soon only none of us know where it will be. The fall outs and arguments that Pop and Lar had down through the years are going to reach a climax any day now.

A great partnership will come to an end and I'll have to take sides, it won't be easy. Its starts with the usual one of them saying something and the other taking offence and I suppose because Pop has his son nearly finished his time, he tells Lar he is splitting the partnership, and taking me with him. Pop says because I'll be getting married soon and his going to make me a partner, that I'll be earning more money and will have a say in what's going on. Its very exciting, there's loads of work and Maureen Faye at the Bedford is having to take messages for Lar, Pop and myself, but I want to run a business properly and wont wan't to be pushing a iron handcart around Limerick City, I want proper transportation like all the other contract company's in Limerick who got rid of their handcarts a couple of years ago, and bought proper transportation like a truck ,or a van. Pop isn't keen on the idea but I insist and after a week I'm up to Mr. Howard at the Munster and Leinster Bank, looking for money to buy a van and because I have such a good savings record he says, 'I can have up to two hundred and fifty pounds and can pay it back over 3 years'. So I'm over at the National garage in Thomas Street, right next to the Standard garage looking at one of three small mini vans green and white with the R.T.V rental sign on each one, they want two hundred and twenty five pounds and if I'm going to buy one I have to promise to blacken out the R.T.V.

sign on both sides of the van after I take it away. I'll pay the two hundred and twenty five pounds and there's just enough in the twenty five pounds to pay the tax and insurance, and there I am sitting in a car that's only two years old and I don't know myself, I'm driving around anywhere and everywhere, taking Mary for a spin and her having to sit on a cushion because the only seat in the bloody thing is the one I'm sitting on.

I'm taking Harry and James too, Mam as well and there's no sign of the brakes not working or a smell of smoke or even steam finding its way into the car and when next Sunday morning comes I want to give Mam a lift to mass with Mary.

Mary has me going to mass ever since we started getting serious and I think that's one of the reasons that Mam loves her, but I have a problem, who is going to sit on the cushion in the front and who is going to sit in the back on top of the spare wheel that has a blanket over it, its an awful dilemma for me but Mary comes to the rescue and offers to go in the back, and there she is God love her, sitting on top of the wheel and not enough room for the three story hair do. She's in her Sunday best tight skirt, she's watching her nylons, finger nails, shoes and hairdo as she crouches up in ball on top of the wheel until we reach the top of Garryowen and then down to the Cathedral. My promise to the National garage in Thomas Street is gone out the window because of the woman at the top of Garryowen who ran out in front of my van waving me down wanting to know was I coming in to fix her rented T.V. Pop is with me in the van we tell her we're going to the pub for a few drinks and we'll be back tomorrow or the day after.

She says if we don't come in and fix her T.V. that's full of white spots and can hardly see a thing, she'll go over to the public phone box and complain us to R.T.V rentals that we should be ashamed of ourselves. We'll drive off and leave her there killing ourselves laughing, it will happen again tomorrow. This time we will go into the house stand in front of the T.V. slap it on both sides a couple of times then on the top. Pop will give it a kick and say out loud he hasn't a bloody clue what's wrong with it, with the shoulders going up and down and the woman will say, 'should you not be taking the back off and look inside to see what's wrong?' and Pop will say 'sure, we know nothing about TV's'. The women will ask then what the hell are ye doing driving around in an R.T.V. rental van. We'll tell her we're advertising and the woman will look at us in amazement and say,' is that what you're doing all day driving around Limerick in that van advertising', 'that's right Misses', we'll walk out the door listening to her giving out stink about what she is going to say to that bloody R.T.V rental crowd below in O'Connell Street.

It will keep happening every day until we are blue in the face and paint over the sign because it's interfering too much with our work. We have so much work now we're able to take on James but James wont get the same training that I got from the master himself, and he hasn't spent the weekends or school holidays working for Pop like I did, but James has it in him, and it will be only be a matter of time before its brought to the surface over the next few months. Mary and I will carry on with the savings, Mam says that we can have a new bedroom suite or any other kind of furniture that the choice is ours, but I'm worried about the extra expense it's going to put on her. I know the suite or whatever it is we'll choose, will be paid on the weekly from Cavendish's in O'Connell Street, and she's going to be minus the five pounds I give her every week. I'll make several attempts to talk to her about it but she won't go into it. She says her first son is not going to the altar without a good present from his parents. Pop won't be asked about it only told what's happening. They'll get lots of thanks from Mary when she's told about it on one of the Monday or Wednesday nights, and if it wasn't for Mam we wouldn't be getting anything at all. Mr. O'Connell is the same he'll just bring home the money give Mrs. O' her share and Mrs. O'Connell can do what she likes with it as long as there's food on the table he won't mind. Mrs. O'Connell is just like Mam great with the money pays all her bills on time, would worry herself sick, if she fell behind with anyone. And just like Mam seems to get two pounds out of every one, she has her purse. Mam gets a job down at the Savoy looking after the ladies toilets standing outside the door making sure everything is ship shape in her new nylon smock with the Savoy badge over the top pocket. She's a different woman since she started, rushing out the door every morning at ten o'clock after filling the mouths of her four useless males who are just about able to put their hands up to their faces, she'll have the dinner prepared and ready for the oven when she comes home at six o'clock. She'll get the bus home from Patrick's Street at 1 o'clock rush around the home giving us our lunch at one thirty while the four of us sit on our arses looking at her, and never give her a thought, we should get off the chair and offer her a hand and when everything we need is on the table she'll have five minutes to throw the few slices of brown bread with a rasher into her stomach. Clear off the table that we've just walked away from, moaning that we have to wait until six o'clock every day to have the dinner we are suppose to have when we come at lunch time, like we've being having ever since I can remember. But Pop isn't a bit happy about his wife working, because it makes him feel he's not the breadwinner anymore, he'll make the odd comment to me at work that no matter how bad or hard things were before, his wife never had to go outside the door and bring money into the house. And worse still she is only working across the road from the Bedford bar were Lar will be sure to see her in her blue smock and might think he's not able to make the money he used to make when they were together.

Now his brain is gone haywire, because he says all his customers will find out that Harry Taylor's wife is working below in the Savoy cleaning out the toilets because Harry Taylor isn't able to bring home the money he used to. I'm trying to tell him the difference it's making to Mam's life, how she's singing most the time. When she gets home doing the polishing and cleaning after seven o'clock every evening, the cleaning she used to do in the afternoons before. She's meeting people now, is out and about every day and can he not see how happy she is, but its no good, he cant get his head around the fact that his wife is bringing home as much money as he gives her every week. He'll ask her to give it up saying he'll give her extra money, but Mam is trying to reason with him that she has too much time on her hands at home with only Harry going to school. Harry is big enough now to be left at home doing his exercise for the hour and a half until she arrives home.

And the whole thing winds up being an excuse for Pop to indulge himself with Author Guinness again, and the awful bloody atmosphere is back at 36 Claughan Court. It will last for three weeks, Pop will leave me running things on my own with James, the two of us trying to earn a wage for three and also trying to keep the customers happy. They'll want to know were Pop is, because he wont be seen any day of the three weeks because he's gulping all the time in the Bedford Bar day and night. I wont be able to save a penny because the money James and myself will earn that has to be split three ways and Mam will do what she feels is the right thing and that's give her notice to the Savoy management and Pop will go back on the wagon after a week of Mam not talking to him. And the atmosphere that causes the laughter to return is back again at 36 Claughan Court. Mam isn't singing anymore our dinners and suppers are back to there usual slots and the four males in number 36 are happy again, but Mam has had a taste of independence and is on the look out for something that will give it to her, something that will keep her man and young men happy and it wont be long before she finds it.

Christmas 1968 has come and gone, its been a good one,with Pop happy and still on the dry work is plentiful with Mary and myself managing to save ninety five pounds at the Munster and Leinster Bank in William's Street, Limerick. We're trying to do a costing on how much we'll need for the big day, like dresses for bridesmaids, wedding rings, flowers, a wedding dress for Mary, suits that will have to be hired for Pop, myself, and the best man and the cost of the honeymoon and God knows what else. Mrs. O'Connell says the first wedding in her family is going to be a good one. One that we are not to worry about, that she is going to look after the hotel expenses and we can invite as many guests as we like. We reckon we'll need the bones of a hundred and fifty pounds and are well on our way to meeting it. It's not too long before the months are heading towards September. Its April and Mam has found another job at Shannon Industrial Estate, doing what she loves best, cleaning; it's after six o'clock too. She feels it's a good decision because she will be out of sight of Pop and his customers and that he won't have to worry about anyone seeing her, she'll be home for the dinner every day and back to singing all the time, but Pop isn't happy he's wife isn't at home every evening at six o'clock. She wont be home until one o'clock in the morning after he's been out three nights of the week at bingo and will come back to an empty house. Mary wont be over on the Monday's or Wednesday evenings anymore and its only a matter of time before Author Guinness is in his hand again looking for a mouth and Pop will oblige, but Mam is digging her heels in this time and wont budge. And why should she sure, she's spent all her life pleasing others, I'm telling Pop he should cop himself on, and so is Jetta but its falling on deaf ears. He can come home drunk every night where there is no one to fight with. It's the month of May, Jetta and her husband have put a deposit on a new house that will be ready in six months. There's talk that Mary and myself might be able to get their flat above in Catherine Street. Mam says we can stay at number 36 Claughan Court after we're married until Jetta's new house is ready, and can enter the flat at the top of Catherine Street. Mary says she cant wait to be living in a house were there is so much laughter all the time except for the odd occasion that Pop decides to go on the tear, but he's at it two weeks now, and no sign of him stopping either, because Mam is into her third week at Shannon, and showing no signs of giving Pop his way. Jetta tells me quietly that Mam's old problem is back, that she's bleeding heavily all the time and said to Mam 'for goodness sake Mam why don't you get rid of that thing once and for all'.

So Mam is above at Doctor Holmes' surgery in Glentworth Street and calls over to Jetta's flat after forty minutes telling her an appointment has been made in St. John's Hospital to have the operation the following Friday the 29th., The singing has stopped because Mam is worried and the husband that's only home when he's drunk is no bloody use to her at all. The poor woman doesn't have a husband to lean on and get a bit of support. I don't even know if he knows that she is going in to have the operation and all the three men in the house are worried about is will their bellies be looked after. Harry won't know the difference because he is only nine so the only one giving Mam the bit of support is Jetta. It's Thursday morning Mam and myself are in the mini van on our way up the hill in Garryowen heading towards the hospital and Mam has a face, God love her, that an idiot like myself knows she's worried sick. We're heading towards the hospital gates and have to wait for a funeral cortège that's heading from the hospital mortuary over to St. John's Cathedral, and, as it passes, Mam's worried face has all the blood gone out of it. She sighs and says, 'that's the way I'll be coming out of this place' and I'm saying, 'for goodness sake Mam will you don't be saying things like that you'll be fine', but these words will haunt me for the rest of my life, I'll bring her to the front entrance of the hospital, say goodbye. She doesn't answer because she's in an awful state. I'm rushing away because I have three people's wages to earn, and I'm landed with the responsibility of looking after his customers. If I was older and wiser I'd stay longside Mam and make sure she was looked after before I went away. She could do with Pop being here and I don't even know if the eejit knows she's going into hospital. I leave her there, waiting to be taken to her ward, and never forget her face and the anxiety that was written all over it. And here I am now standing longside my cousin Harold listening to his voice telling me they are looking for me below at Mam's ward when I get there, there's no sign of Pop or Jett, James is there with all the others who have come since word got around about Mam. After five minutes the door opens Pop comes out first, puts his huge hand on top of my head and says, 'she's gone, Pa', I'm stuck to the floor, Jett is out next, she's crying and says, 'She's gone to heaven Pa,' The nun with the thick glasses and the funny walk asks me if I'd like to see my mother. I nod my head in response; I'm expecting to see Mam lying peacefully with her head on a pillow, her hands clasped maybe a rosary bead wrapped around them looking relaxed and at peace.

Mary holds my hand tight as we walk into the ward. The nurse on my other side holding my other hand, she pulls back the curtain that has being hiding Mam's last moments and there before my eyes is a sight I'll take to my grave. Mam's head is hanging out over one side of the bed with her mouth wide open and her eyes staring over at the wall. I can't believe it my two legs bend at the knees in shock. My mouth opens as wide as I can get it, I'm roaring in silence. I'm not making a sound, but the screams in my head are deafening. Harold was right. The fight has gone out of Mam. She wasn't strong enough. We'll find out days later that she should never have had the operation in the first place because she just hadn't the strength. The house of laughter will be a thing of the past now, because life at 36 Claughan Court for the Taylor's will never be the same again, the glue that kept the lot of us together is gone and God help us, but like I said before that's another story for another book. I'll be talking to you.

Letter my mother sent to her sister Tess, five days before she died.

The handwritten letter follows here and the details can be found on page 314.

2 Clapham Road,
Garryowen.
Sunday 25th May.
(.....)

Dearest darling ever loving sister husband
and two Sons.

Sorry for not answering your letter
before now. Sorry to hear that you
were all sick and Don. You had
better look after that pain as it could
be the same as Mam had a few
years back. She was here last Sat
she was telling me that you are
better also Don and back at work. I
was so glad to hear it. I think Mam
told you I got a job in Shannon from
5 to 12. Cleaning the Offices of one of the
Factorys. Its not very hard and it
gets me out of the house. I have only
1 week done. There are 2 of us there
we have no one over us and no
body to tell us the next one that
its not being done properly. The fore-
-man told me what to do and said
it was up to myself to get it done
how and when I liked. But Jess I'm
a Magpie. I have my visitor for the
past 8 weeks and its beginning to get
me down. Its pretty bad for the past
3 days. I should have gone to my
Dr to his clinic last Wed but I
was trying to get so much done on
account of having to go to Shannon

311

2

I did go up to his house yesterday
while Mum was here and want for
it he was away since last wed
and would not be back until late
so I am to see him tomorrow at
2.30, I will let you know what he
says before I mail this. You see
less I am in the change. I've missed
2 months since Xmas and it was
only gone about 2 weeks when it came
again and is there since and I am
on the Iron capsuls for the past 3
months as my blood was gone very
low again. I do hope that he will
put me into hosp and yank this
thing out altogether and I would be
finished with it for good, what
do I want it for anyway at my
age. I am not talking to Henry
or sleeping with him. He went
to a wedding and had been at
it since so I couldn't be bothered
squaring with him. I have more
peace when I am out with him.
and he is hopping mad that
I am working in Shannon. He
was waiting up one night when
I got home at 10 to 10. He says
to me (you give up the job and
I'll give up the drink I said to
him I have no intention of doing
so and I did not ask you to give
up anything. So if I have to go to
hosp. and should I loose the job

3

I think that when Harry gets his
holidays I will go over to ye for
a few weeks. Would I be able to
get a job. Jetta would look after
the boys and her Dad if he
behaved himself of course! I'd
frighten the sugar in him.
Well I think I have told you all
my troubles for now. Oh yes Noel
and Jetta will be going into there
new house in Oct. D.V. they are
having it built as its the only
way that they could get one. When
they leave the Flat Paddy and Mary
will get the Flat at least they hope
too as they cannott get a place
either. I was glad to hear that you
got the blue paper I suppose
you used it for toilet paper to save
money. I will send you the postage
some other time and a piece of
twine. Mary said to tell you she
asking for you also Jetta and Noel
and all the Taylors send
their love to all the Wards
at Jetta's   x x x x

I have just come back from the
Dr and he is going to take my
womb out I'm glad. I have to call
to the hospital on my way home to
find out if they have a bed for me
Mam will write and let you know
Bye for now God Bless Biddy x x x

36 Claughan Court,
Garryowen,

Sunday 25ᵗʰ May

Dearest Darling ever loving sister, husband and two sons.

Sorry for not answering your letter before now. Sorry to hear that you were so sick and down. You had better look after that pain as it could be the same as Mam had a few years back. She was here last Sat. she was telling me that you are better also Don and back at work. I was so glad to hear it. I think Mam told you I got a job in Shannon from 5 to 12 cleaning the offices of one of the factories. It's not very hard and it gets me out of the house, I have only 1 week done. There are 2 of us there, we have no one over us and no body to tell us the next eve. that its not being done properly. The foreman told me what to do and said it was up to myself to get it done how and when I liked. But Tess I am a magpie. I have my visitor for the past 3 weeks and its beginning to get me down. Its pretty bad for the past 3 days. I should have gone to my Dr. to his clinic last Wed but I was trying to get so much done on account of having to go to Shannon.

I did go up to his house yesterday while Mam was here and wait he was away since last Wed and would not be back until late so I am to see him tomorrow at 2.30. I will let you know what he says before I mail this. You see Tess I am in the change, I've missed 2 months since Xmas and it was only gone about 2 weeks when it came again and is there since and I am on the iron capsules for the past 3 months as my blood was gone low again. I do hope that he will put me into Hosp and yank this thing out altogether and I would be finished with it for good. What do I want it for anyway at my age. I am not talking to Harry or sleeping with him. He went to a wedding and has been at it since so I couldn't be bothered arguing with him. I have more peace when I am out with him and he is hopping mad that I am working in Shannon. He was waiting up one night when I got home at 10 to 1 o'clock. He says to me (you give up the and job and I'll give up the drink. I said to him I have no intention of doing so and I did not ask you to give up anything, so if I have to go to Hosp and should I loose the job

I think that when Harry gets his holidays I will go over to ye for a few weeks. Would I be able to get a job. Jetta would look after the boys and her Dad if he behaved himself of course. I'd frighten the sugar in him.

Will I think I have told you all my troubles for now, oh yes, Noel and Jetta will be going into there new house in Oct, D.V. they are having it built as it's the only way that they could get one. When they leave the flat Paddy and Mary will get the flat at least they hope too as they cannot get a place either. I was glad to hear that you got the brown paper I suppose you used it for toilet paper to save money. I will send you the postage some other time and a piece of twine. Mary said to tell you she is asking for you also Jetta and Noel and all the Taylor's send their love to all the Wards

I have just come back from the Dr. and he is going to take my womb out. I'm glad. I have to call to the Hospital on my way home to find out if they have a bed for me. Mam will write and let you know.

Bye for now, God Bless

Brid XXX

This is the cover of my next book entitled

MAM DOESN'T LIVE HERE ANYMORE

for more information and downloads go to

www.pjtaylorsite.com